Deregulation and Development
in Indonesia

Deregulation and Development in Indonesia

Edited by Farrukh Iqbal and *William E. James*

Westport, Connecticut
London

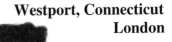

Library of Congress Cataloging-in-Publication Data

Deregulation and development in Indonesia / edited by Farrukh Iqbal and William E. James.
    p. cm.
   Includes bibliographical references and index.
   ISBN 0–275–97407–3 (alk. paper)
    1. Deregulation—Indonesia—Congresses. 2. Trade regulation—Indonesia—Congresses.
3. Industrial policy—Indonesia—Congresses. 4. Investments—Government
policy—Indonesia—Congresses. 5. Indonesia—Economic policy—Congresses. I. Iqbal,
Farrukh. II. James, William E.
HD3616.I53 D44   2002
338.9598—dc21   2001036317

British Library Cataloguing in Publication Data is available.

Library of Congress Catalog Card Number: 2001036317
ISBN: 0–275–97407–3

First published in 2002

Praeger Publishers, 88 Post Road West, Westport, CT 06881
An imprint of Greenwood Publishing Group, Inc.
www.praeger.com

Printed in the United States of America

The paper used in this book complies with the
Permanent Paper Standard issued by the National
Information Standards Organization (Z39.48-1984).

10 9 8 7 6 5 4 3 2 1

Contents

CHAPTER 1

Deregulation and Development in Indonesia: An Introductory Overview

Farrukh Iqbal *and* Faham Rashid

INTRODUCTION

Until the mid-1980s, Indonesia lagged behind its East Asian neighbors in liberalizing trade and investment policy. The resource cushion provided by primary sector (mostly oil) revenues during the 1970s induced a complacency about the need for opening up the economy to domestic and foreign competition. Betting on a continuing stream of such revenues, policy-makers gave less importance to productivity and efficiency considerations and paid more attention to objectives such as national self-sufficiency. This is not to say that the economy was poorly managed. To the contrary, macroeconomic management was typically good and an environment featuring low inflation and a competitive exchange rate was maintained for the most part. While several other oil-rich countries experienced Dutch Disease-style crises during this period, Indonesia avoided the same through timely devaluations accompanied by credible sterilization policies.[1] At the same time, much progress was made in general economic development as buoyant oil revenues were used to fund infrastructure, agriculture and human resource development projects across the country. Nevertheless, there was a sense in which overall economic policies were not in harmony and not pulling together towards the same goals. While macro-economic policies were consistent with overall economic efficiency considerations, microeconomic policies were not. Many sectors remained protected behind high tariff walls or outright prohibitions against imports or foreign investment. As a result, high levels of inefficiency existed in several sectors and overall employment and productivity growth remained below potential.

The mid-1980s mark a watershed in Indonesia's modern economic history. By that time it had become obvious that the oil sector was in secular decline and could no longer be expected to contribute substantially to the country's growth momentum. It had also become clear that some of the policies introduced in the heydays of the "oil economy," namely policies that supported import substitution, public sector expansion and resource-based growth, could not be counted on to deliver sustained high growth into the 1990s. As the realization grew that a new engine of growth was needed, the policy pendulum swung in favor of export expansion and nonresource-based, private-sector-led growth. During the latter half of the 1980s, Indonesia undertook substantial reforms in its trade, investment and financial regimes. These reforms dramatically changed the thrust of its overall development strategy. Tariffs were cut, non-tariff barriers were reduced, a duty-drawback system was introduced for export activities, a complex investment licensing system was replaced by a much simpler and relatively short "negative list," foreign investment regulations were significantly eased, credit ceilings and interest rate controls were abolished, and entry into the banking system was made substantially easier. These wide-ranging reforms give the period since 1985 its characteristic flavor of "deregulation." (The term "deregulation" is typically used in the literature to denote reforms pertaining to regulated sectors such as utilities whereas "liberalization" is more commonly used to denote reforms pertaining to trade and investment. In the Indonesian case, however, government preferred the former term to the latter perhaps because of unease with the political implications of the translation of the word "liberalization" into Bahasa Indonesia. We use the two terms interchangeably in this book.)

Some information on the key aspects of liberalization during 1985–1995 is provided below while details can be found in Chapters 2 and 3. In trade, nominal tariffs were slashed from an average of 27 percent to 20 percent (see Table 1); the coverage of non-tariff barriers was reduced from 41 percent of gross production to 22 percent (see Table 2); and duty exemption and drawback facilities were expanded for exporters. In investment, a long and complex positive list featuring over 7,000 sub-sectors was replaced by a short negative list; the number of specific requirements for investment approval was reduced from 24 to 10; the validity of the investment license was increased from 5 years to the life of the project; and regulations pertaining to direct foreign investment (in terms of permitted sectors, minimum amounts, minimum domestic ownership) were progressively relaxed.

These reforms by themselves produced a major change in the incentive structure governing the choice between investment and consumption in general and, within investment, between import substitution and export orientation. This effect was bolstered by a macroeconomic stance that featured a large devaluation in 1986 (following one in 1983), tight expenditure policies (public investment was reduced by 30 percent in real terms during 1984–1986), a comprehensive tax reform (introduction of VAT, reduction in number of income and corporate tax bands, reduction in marginal tax rates); and monetary and fiscal policies geared to a low inflation target, low overall fiscal deficits, and a competitive real exchange rate.

TABLE 1
NOMINAL TARIFF RATES, 1985–1994 (PERCENT)

	1985	1987	1989	1991	1992	1993	1994
Unweighted Average Tariff	27	24	27	20	20	20	20
Weighted Average Tariff							
-by import value	13	15	12	11	11	12	12
-by domestic production	19	18	19	15	13	11	10

Source: World Bank staff estimates.

The main objective of this chapter is to provide an overview of selected issues in the deregulation experience of Indonesia and their treatment in various chapters in this book. The main issues reviewed relate to the impact of deregulation on productivity, exports, the manufacturing sector, the labor market, and regional income distribution. Some sector-specific microeconomic issues are also covered, especially those relating to the sugar, soymeal, cocoa, and cement sectors.

TABLE 2
PRODUCTION COVERAGE OF RESTRICTIVE IMPORT LICENSING, 1986–1994 (PERCENT OF 1987 PRODUCTION)

Sector	1986	1987	1988	1990	1991	1992	1993	1994
Agriculture	54	53	41	39	35.5	35.5	35.5	35.5
Manufacturing (excl. oil and gas)	68	58	45	33	31.6	31.1	31.2	30.6
Total	41	38	29	25	22.3	22.1	22.1	21.9

Note: Production coverage estimates for 1986 are based on 1985 production weights.

Source: World Bank staff estimates.

While financial sector reform was central to the post-1985 deregulation experience, few in-depth analyses of this are available.[2] The lack of good empirical work on the impact of financial liberalization in Indonesia is a matter of concern because weaknesses in the financial sector, exacerbated in part by liberalization, contributed significantly to the crisis of 1997. The crisis itself is another major watershed of modern Indonesian economic history and deserves careful empirical documentation and analysis. The main features and implications of the crisis are reviewed in the concluding chapter. A detailed analysis is, however, not attempted here.

The rest of this chapter is organized as follows: Part I provides a brief discussion of some characteristic features of the reform process in Indonesia. Part II focuses on the impact of deregulation on various aspects of economic efficiency and welfare in Indonesia. Part III discusses some sector-specific policy issues and reforms. Part IV concludes.

PART I: FEATURES OF LIBERALIZATION PROCESS IN INDONESIA

Political Economy Considerations

Since the 1970s, Indonesian trade and industrial policies have evolved through several stages. These stages have been influenced by external conditions, the status of the oil sector, and political economy considerations.[3] In the early years of the Suharto or New Order government, emphasis was placed on sound macroeconomic management and attracting capital from abroad since the domestic economy had just gone through a period of hyperinflation and little domestic investment was forthcoming. Key macroeconomic reforms included the passage of a balanced budget law and the lifting of controls on capital movements in and out of the country. Some restrictions on foreign trade and investment were also relaxed. During the oil boom years of the 1970s, however, a more self-reliant policy approach came into effect. High-technology, resource-based industries received priority for investments within a progressively closed regime as the need for foreign resources and policy approval was no longer felt so keenly. When oil prices dropped in the early-1980s, policy-makers went through a period of ambivalence. Facing mounting debt problems,[4] government was forced to undertake austerity measures to cut expenditure, but the external situation was not unfavorable enough for wide-ranging, politically-risky liberalization measures. There was even hope among some groups of policy-makers that oil prices would start rising dramatically and provide the country with renewed economic buoyancy.

Despite this optimism, the external situation worsened between 1982 and 1985. Finally, when the oil prices fell to $10 per barrel in 1986, the political climate became ripe for several reforms to be undertaken (Pangestu 1991). Subsequently, the Indonesian economic outlook was fundamentally transformed through gradual reform packages aimed at reducing distortions in the incentive regime. The goal of the reform process was to open the economy up to foreign competition and provide domestic manufacturing firms with larger markets, more diversified sources of funding, and advanced technology.

Among the factors responsible for the shift in strategy, and successful implementation of the new strategy thereafter, was the availability of a group of senior policy makers in the economics ministries who were not only well trained and cohesive but enjoyed, as well, the trust of President Suharto. Indonesian policy experts of the time fell into two broad categories: the "technocrats" and the "technologists." The technocrats were mostly academic economists affiliated with universities and academic research centers, while the technologists were a mixed group of technically oriented professionals, politicians, former military officers, nationalists, and economists with a "structuralist" philosophy. The technocrats argued for an open economy and export-led growth while the technologists argued for self-reliance and indigenous industry-led development. A synopsis of their spheres of influence and responsibilities is presented in Table 3. In the early 1980s, the technologists sought to battle the economic emergency through higher trade barriers and subsidies to selected industries. For example, despite the austerity measures of the early 1980s, some high-technology industries continued to receive subsidies and priority for investment.

The crisis that arose when oil prices dropped sharply in the early 1980s was a precipitating event which brought the technocrats and their liberalization agenda once again to the center of policy discussion. Since that time and till the fall of the Suharto government following the financial crisis of 1997–1998, economic management in Indonesia was dominated by the technocrats and featured increasing (though not complete) convergence between the objectives of macroeconomic and microeconomic policy and a more consistent strategy designed to move the economy away from resource-dependence towards competitive export-led development.

Gradualism

An important aspect of the Indonesian reform process was the fact that, typically, reforms in the trade and investment policy area were doled out in gradual, incremental steps which cumulatively made the economy more open and less restrictive over a period of 10 years or so. Such gradualism was in contrast to deregulation in other parts of the economy, especially the tax sector where major deregulatory components were developed and approved simultaneously (Lewis 1994). It was also in contrast to patterns seen later among the transition economies of the former Soviet Union and Eastern Europe. The lack of political will to press for widespread reforms all at the same time and the need for public support and trust may have made gradualism the preferred policy alternative. Of these, the issue of trust and credibility appears to have been a bigger concern. Gradualism allowed public trust to be built up steadily as sudden or large adverse changes in employment or output were avoided. Also, gradualism was combined with regularity. Every year after 1985 a number of deregulatory packages were announced, keeping momentum behind the program and providing a sense of continuity and coherence. Such continuity strengthened the credibility of the program. Finally, gradualism did not necessarily imply minimalism. At times, when the nature of the problem required bold action, some fairly drastic measures were undertaken. An example of this is the complete replacement of the customs services by a Swiss private firm at an early stage of the reform process.

TABLE 3
INDONESIAN TRADE AND INDUSTRIAL POLICY MAKING
STRUCTURE (1985–1997)

Ministry	Composition	Responsibility
Finance	Technocrats	Set and administer government expenditures and tax policy
Coordinating Ministry of All Economic Affairs (EKUIN)	Technocrats	Provide general guidance and coordination
National Planning Body (BAPPENAS)	Technocrats	Participation in trade and industrial policy
Industry	Technologists	Promote industrial development and help set trade and industrial policy
Trade	Technologists	Control trade regulations and issue licenses
Capital Investment Coordinating Board (BKPM)	Technologists	Issue investment licenses and administer incentives; close and open sectors to investment

Source: Rodgers (1994).

On the whole, observers have regarded the gradualist feature of the Indonesian experience with favor. For example, Lewis (1994) notes that although removing one set of distortionary measures while keeping others untouched could theoretically worsen welfare, the Indonesian experience clearly generated high benefits and steady improvements in welfare.

Unorthodox Sequencing

Viewed across the decades of the 1970s and 1980s together, Indonesia followed an unorthodox reform sequence in that it opened the capital account much before it started to open the current account and it undertook financial sector liberalization more or less simultaneously with real sector liberalization. The orthodox sequence favored by most economists is one in which trade liberalization occurs first, followed by financial sector reform and then by capital account opening. A discussion of the reasons why the orthodox sequence has been preferred by development practitioners is provided by James and Stephenson in Chapter 2. They also consider various reasons why Indonesia's unorthodox reform sequence was successful or, at least, did not falter seriously until the crisis of 1997. Among these reasons was sound macroeconomic management, a characteristic feature of Indonesian economic policy since the advent of the New Order government, reflecting the continued steady influence of the technocrats in macroeconomic matters at least. The timing of the mid-1980s reforms may also have been instrumental. Indonesia started opening up to foreign investment just as many of its East Asian neighbors were looking for outlets for their growing capital surpluses.

Did Indonesia's unorthodox reform sequence contribute to the crisis of 1997? It is hard to answer this question. On the one hand, the fact that the capital account was open allowed for significant capital flight at a point in the crisis when financial collapse and ethnic conflict was widely expected. At the same time, Malaysia was able to limit the fall-out from its crisis by quickly slapping on capital controls. On the other hand, it is widely recognized that capital controls would not have prevented capital flight in an environment characterized by high corruption and poor supervisory capabilities. To the extent also that capital flight in 1997/1998 was a response to underlying problems of a political and social nature, it would seem unnecessary to point to openness as a major contributor. And, finally, it may be argued that the surge of direct foreign investment into Indonesia in the early 1990s may have been stimulated in part by the open capital account. At that time, foreign investor confidence in the Indonesian economy was probably bolstered by the fact that no restrictions were placed on currency conversion and capital withdrawals.

A somewhat different issue is posed by the sequencing of financial liberalization. As noted, this was undertaken simultaneously with real sector liberalization in the late 1980s. It clearly exposed the deficiencies of the Indonesian banking system and may well have exacerbated the crisis. In retrospect, greater regulatory and supervisory control over the financial system might have prevented the crisis from becoming as severe as it did.

PART II: THE IMPACT OF REFORM

The relationship between long-term economic development and liberal trade and financial regimes has been a matter of considerable debate in academic circles. In the early post-war years, when a large number of former colonies became independent developing countries, the consensus on trade policy was that they ought to pursue import-substitution type regimes featuring high tariffs, non-tariff barriers and subsidies to "infant" domestic sectors. This consensus was based on several related assumptions, the most prominent among which was that, without production capacity for manufactured goods, developing countries would specialize only in primary products and would remain condemned, as it were, to underdeveloped status for a prolonged period. The way to break out of this trap was to overlook contemporary comparative advantage considerations and leap into manufacturing with the help of a protective trade and investment policy regime. Initial endorsement for import-substitution also included GATT exemptions for developing country trade protection. As a result, many large countries, including Brazil, India, and Turkey established protectionist regimes.[5]

Import-substitution regimes failed to produce sustainable results. The 1950s and 1960s were characterized on the one hand by growing trade volumes in developed (and relatively open) countries, and by rising real exchange rates, budget rationing and periodic financial crises in developing countries on the other. Numerous IMF stabilization programs were launched during this period, and economic emergency and development followed each other in a cyclical manner in protectionist regimes (Krueger 1997). In contrast, during the same period, relatively open developing economies like Korea, Taiwan, Singapore, and Hong Kong were able to achieve and maintain high growth rates and better standards of living. By the early-1980s, oil price shocks had crippled many debt-burdened economies, but these East Asian economies were able to service their debt and resume growth. This "miracle" experience and a growing strand of cross-country literature, including Little et al. (1970), Bhagwati (1978), and Krueger (1978), led to a reconsideration of the desirability of import-substitution policies. A new consensus emerged among development economists, and subsequently among practitioners in many developing countries, on the importance of liberalizing trade and investment regimes and on following a (manufacturing) export-led path to development.

Under the "miracle" scenario, greater openness to trade and investment was observed to bring in its wake high growth, falling poverty, rising industrial employment and wages, and growing diversification in exports and increases in total factor productivity. To what extent did Indonesia share this experience? The next few sections examine the actual experience of Indonesia to assess the contemporaneous impact of the burst of deregulatory policies introduced over the period 1985–1995. The discussion is based both on empirical work produced for this book and elaborated in the chapters contained herein as well as on secondary literature. For some aspects of deregulation, such as its effect on regional inequality, we rely largely on secondary literature.

Effect of Deregulation on Income and Productivity Growth

It is generally assumed that the gains from trade translate both into higher incomes and greater productivity for the trading countries. Greater trade and foreign investment can increase productivity through both supply and demand factors. Supply-side factors include firms' ability to import better technology, management skills, and more diversified financial resources to support their domestic operations. On the demand side, firms in a newly open economy find themselves competing with a greater number of rivals, and therefore have to improve their productivity and level of specialization to survive profitably (Urata 1994). Researchers have pointed out several other supply and demand factors, which include economies of scale from greater production, absorption and spillover of better technology into other sectors (especially agriculture), greater "X-efficiency," efficient resource allocation, and increased research and development (Kawai 1994).

There have been many attempts to empirically model the links between greater openness and both income per capita growth and total factor productivity change. For example, Frankel et al. (1996) finds that for a world sample (between 100 and 123 countries) between 1960–1985, every 1 percentage point increase in the trade share of GDP was accompanied by a per capita income increase of 0.34

percent. The predicted effect of going from a closed economy to one in which trade is 200 percent of GDP is a boost in the per capita income of 68 percent. Ghani et al. (1995) divided countries based on the "intensity" of their reforms. They find that annual income growth rates for intensive reformers went from 3.8 percent per annum in 1972–1982 to 4.7 percent per annum in 1986–1989, and that intensive reformers benefited more than moderate reformers. In an earlier study, Dollar (1992) found outward-oriented Asian economies to have indeed grown more rapidly. He estimated that the potential gains of shifting to Asia's level of "outward-orientation" and real exchange rate stability were increases of 1.5 percentage points in Latin America's per capita growth rates and 2.1 percentage points in Africa's per capita growth rates.

The empirical results for the link between liberalization and productivity growth are less robust. Kawai (1994) finds, for a cross-section of Asian, Latin American, and OECD economies, that trade deregulation generally led to higher total factor productivity (TFP) growth. Due to data limitations, his empirical modeling of the relation between foreign direct investment (FDI) and TFP growth was limited to Taiwan and Malaysia, but for both economies he finds that FDI reforms led to higher TFP growth. However, Levine et al. (1992) fail to find a consistent effect of greater openness on long-run growth even after utilizing a variety of openness measures. Reflecting on a number of such studies, Harrison et al. (1995) argue that our knowledge of the determinants of productivity change is far from definitive.[6]

For Indonesia, Dasgupta, Hanson, and Hulu (see Chapter 4) confirm that TFP growth did indeed increase between 1985 and 1992—about 31 percent of the 3.8 percent annual growth in GDP per worker during this period is attributed by them to higher productivity growth. They note that estimates of TFP growth are sensitive to many assumptions and choices made by researchers. For example, if TFP growth is estimated over the longer period, 1978–1992, it shows a stagnant trend. This is because of the averaging of an earlier period of stagnant or declining TFP growth before the mid-1980s with the latter period of rising TFP growth in the early 1990s. They conclude that it is very likely that TFP growth rose in response to the raft of reforms introduced in the mid-1980s.

Reforms and Growth in Manufactured Exports

The ability of such economies as Korea, Taiwan, Hong Kong, and Singapore to grow rapidly on the basis of the production and export of light manufactured goods during the 1970s and 1980s showed that developing countries were not necessarily trapped by their low wage and low skill endowments. These endowments could be converted into sources of advantage provided impediments to labor-intensive exports were removed. Among the key impediments identified in the literature are high tariffs and non-tariff barriers, overvalued exchange rates, and obstacles to foreign investment. These impediments tend to bias production towards *domestic* rather than *export* markets.

Indeed, the link between trade and investment liberalization and manufactured export growth holds true not just for the original Asian "tiger" economies but for a broader set of countries. The World Bank's well-known "Miracle" study (1993) showed this relationship to hold for eight high performance economies in East Asia. A more recent publication by the Asian Development Bank entitled *Emerging Asia* (1997) comes to a similar conclusion based on its analysis of 117 low- and middle-income countries over the period 1970–1990.[7]

Two chapters in the present volume investigate related aspects of the link between deregulation and developments in the manufacturing sector in Indonesia in the period since 1985. Dasgupta, Hulu, and Das Gupta (see Chapter 5) report that Indonesian non-oil exports grew from $5.9 billion in 1985 to about $26.6 billion in 1993—a five-fold increase over eight years, and the share of non-oil exports went from 30 percent to over 70 percent. Garments, textiles, and plywood grew more rapidly than other exports, and by 1993 the value of such exports had increased to about $11.3 billion or 43 percent of total exports. Also, diverse and new manufactured products such as footwear, handicrafts, and processed food became prominent in the export table. By 1993, the share of these types of products was about one-third of non-oil exports. From their econometric analysis of these developments, the authors conclude that the lowering of trade barriers and sustained increases in world income were more crucial to Indonesia's manufactured export performance than other factors. This indicates that deregulation was indeed effective in orienting the Indonesian economy toward manufacturing.

Iqbal (Chapter 6) examines structural changes that took place in the manufacturing sector after 1985. He finds that the sector's share in total output increased from 16 percent to 20 percent within a few years. At the same time the manufacturing sector became more export-focused. Structural shifts within manufacturing were more substantial and rapid than changes experienced by other sectors over the same period. The rise of manufacturing had repercussions for labor and value-added growth. Employment in manufacturing rose more than one and half times during 1986–1991 compared to 1980–1985, while most manufacturing sub-sectors also experienced rapid growth of value-added during the latter half of the 1980s.

Perhaps the most significant result in Iqbal's analysis is the relation between market structure and performance in the manufacturing sector. He conducts simple regression analysis to show that there is a significant *negative* relationship between concentration and export shares. In other words, sectors featuring higher concentration (e.g., sectors dominated by cartels, price controls, exclusive licensing, government agencies, or other distortionary elements) have been less competitive and have experienced lower export shares.[8] Iqbal also finds that the overall concentration declined from 50 in 1985 to 47 in 1991, which reflects a decline in concentration for 15 out of 28 sub-sectors at the 3-digit level. He concludes that deregulation has had a competition enhancing effect on the manufacturing sector.

Liberalization and Labor
Market Performance

Three aspects of the link between trade and investment liberalization and labor market performance are important. First, does liberalization lead to an increase in employment and wages? Second, is the inter-personal distribution of income adversely affected? Third, are there any prominent regional or gender patterns to the effects of liberalization on labor flows and earnings? The first issue is clearly important for developing countries with large pools of low skilled labor often earning very low wages and often underemployed. If liberalization leads to a decline in employment and wages for this group, the welfare and political consequences could be quite disruptive. Political consequences may also flow from changes in the distribution of income across individuals, gender and regions that may be brought about by liberalization. Economic theory allows for some generalizations to be made with respect to the expected impact on the level and pattern of wage and employment effects but the qualifications that arise when moving to actual cases are such that empirical studies are often a much better guide in this area.

Since the early 1980s, various cross-country studies have been conducted to evaluate the effects of deregulation on wages and employment. Some of the prominent ones are Balassa (1982) and Krueger (1983). More recently, the World Bank (1996, 1995), Wood (1994) and Wood et al. (1994) have also produced comprehensive studies on the effect of trade policy on labor market performance. The general empirical finding of Krueger (1983) is that, given reasonably open international markets, export-oriented strategies promise to be more effective than import-substitution in expanding employment in developing countries. The country cases on which this conclusion is based include Brazil, Chile, Colombia, Indonesia, Cote d'Ivoire, Pakistan, South Korea, Thailand, and Tunisia. It was found that that labor employed per unit of domestic value-added was greater in exportables than in import-substitution industries in all countries except for Chile. For Brazil, Thailand, and Indonesia, the ratio of labor inputs in exportables to import-substitution industries was more than 2:1. Also, export-oriented industries were generally found to use more unskilled labor than import-substitution industries.

The World Bank's *World Development Report* (WDR 1995) takes a careful look at various developing country labor markets in the context of growing integration among world economies. Using data from 1970–1990 for a sample of sixty-nine countries, Bank staff find that in countries where export-orientation increased, wages rose an average of 3 percent a year, while in those where export-orientation decreased, wage growth was negative. In a follow-up study, World Bank staff have shown that liberalization under the Uruguay Round would greatly benefit East Asia's workers (World Bank 1996).[9] Their findings for the textiles and garments sector are presented in Table 4.

TABLE 4
URUGUAY ROUND EFFECTS ON WAGES AND EMPLOYMENT
(TEXTILES AND GARMENTS)

	Unadjusted Wages	Consumer Prices	Wages Adjusted for price changes	Employment in textiles & garments
Newly Industrialized Economies	-0.1	-1.3	1.2	decrease
ASEAN	5.0	1.1	3.8	increase
China	5.6	2.8	2.9	increase

Source: World Bank (1996)

Studies of the effect of FDI on the labor market are relatively rare. The World Bank study noted earlier (WDR 1995) reports that foreign direct investment accounts for as much as 30 percent of capital flows to low- and middle-income economies, and is responsible for creating "many" additional job opportunities. Sixty percent of the worldwide growth in MNC employment has occurred in developing countries. Therefore, *ceteris paribus*, FDI liberalization is expected to increase employment and wages.[10]

The evidence on income distribution effects is also sparse. One recent study by Edwards (1997) finds that there is *no* evidence of a systematic link, that is, neither reformer nor non-reformer countries can be shown to have experienced reductions in income inequality between the 1970s and 1980s. The results are robust across different openness measures. Edwards does find that, other things being equal, countries that had improved their educational system during the 1960s and the 1980s experienced a reduction in inequality. This result confirms the importance of human capital long-run benefits to labor.

To sum up then, under certain conditions favoring the expansion of labor-intensive production, deregulation of trade and investment has the potential to raise wages and employment in developing countries. Most, though not all, country studies of labor market performance following episodes of deregulation show rising wages and employment both over the short and long runs. The impact on inter-personal income distribution is not clear.

Similar results are found in the case of Indonesia. For example, Fujita et al. (1997) look at employment created by light manufacturing industries (garments, footwear, etc.) between 1980 and 1990. They find that employment increased dramatically in these industries and far exceeded the employment created by primary exports. Total employment in Indonesia grew by 2.9 percent per annum between 1980 and 1990, adding about 18 million new workers. Employment created by manufactured exports increased at a rate of 21 percent per annum during the same period, and accounted for over 23 percent of the total increment in employment, of which light manufacturing exports constitute about 64.2 percent. The authors also argue that since the growth rate of employment in non-manufacturing sectors decreased over the last decade, the effect of the large employment growth in manufacturing was even more important for the welfare of the domestic economy.

In this volume, Agrawal (Chapter 7) reflects on various aspects of Indonesian labor market performance after 1985. She shows that both levels of employment and wages typically rose in the period under consideration, especially in the manufacturing sector. Indonesian wage employment grew at an average rate of 4.5 percent per annum over 1986–1990, and was prominent in manufacturing, agriculture, and domestic retail trade. These trends indicate both the growing internationalism and dynamism of the economy. Agrawal also examines gender patterns in wage and employment behavior and reports that employment gains were larger for female workers. She shows that the rate of job creation for female workers in the manufacturing sector increased substantially in the post-reform period: during 1982–1986 the number of manufacturing sector jobs for women increased by 13 percent, whereas during the following four years, the number of jobs increased by 53 percent. As a result, while the share of female workers in the manufacturing workforce remained unchanged at 32 percent between 1982–1986, during the next four years it grew to 35 percent.

Reforms and Regional Inequality

The extent to which inter-regional inequality within a country is exacerbated or attenuated by trade and investment policy liberalization depends on many factors including the comparative regional distribution of factors of production (skilled labor, unskilled labor, land) and the scope for internal migration. None of the chapters in this volume deal explicitly with regional inequality. However, there are some useful references in the literature that shed light on the relevant issues.

The typical argument regarding regional inequality in Indonesia goes as follows: Prior to the mid-1980 reforms, government invested oil revenues from Sumatra and Kalimantan into human resource and infrastructure development projects throughout the country. Consequently, income inequality across the country declined and was, in any case, lower than would have been the case without such inter-regional transfers. After 1985, however, export-oriented manufacturing became the leading growth sector. Since most manufacturing industries were based in the densely populated islands of Java and Bali, it might reasonably be expected that incremental earnings from the manufacturing sector would have accrued largely to residents of these islands, thereby exacerbating regional inequality. However, a recent paper by Manning (1997) suggests that this has not necessarily been the case. Spillover effects from the development of Java and Bali have also contributed to increasing incomes in the outer islands, especially Sumatra and the Eastern Islands, while resource-based growth and fiscal transfers have continued apace.[11]

Some complexities of inter-regional analysis are worth noting in this regard. First, not all regions are entirely dependent on one sector, be it manufacturing or agriculture. Indeed, Java is an important manufacturing *and* agricultural region. Therefore, changes in the balance of manufacturing employment and earnings in Java have a complex and not easily predictable effect on its position relative to other regions. Second, while the manufacturing sector has grown rapidly (at 12 percent on average per annum) after 1985, other sectors have also experienced acceleration, at different rates in different regions.[12] And finally, developments on Java have prompted dynamics in other islands, leading to tightening labor markets and rising agricultural wages in neighboring areas such as southern Sumatra and Lampung that are providing labor to the manufacturing industries.

PART III: SECTOR-SPECIFIC REGULATORY POLICY ISSUES

The preceding section has discussed the impact of trade and investment liberalization on economy-wide variables such as employment, incomes and productivity. Additional insights can be gleaned from sector-specific experiences. Four such experiences are documented in this book covering the cocoa, soymeal, sugar, and cement sectors. These sectors were chosen for review because they illustrate different aspects of the costs and benefits of regulations.

Cocoa: Effects of a Hands-Off Policy Regime

Nishio and Akiyama (Chapter 8) analyze the performance of the cocoa sector since the early 1980s. They note that cocoa production in Indonesia is dominated by small holders based largely on the island of Sulawesi and grew substantially during 1980–1995 so much so that Indonesia became the third largest cocoa exporter in the world by 1995. They investigate the causes of dynamism in the sector and conclude that the following factors were most important: availability of suitable land, low production costs, a highly competitive marketing system resulting from a "hands-off" policy resulting in very limited government interventions, relatively good transport infrastructure, favorable macroeconomic policies, and the entrepreneurship of the small holders. Focusing on the lack of government intervention they show how the sector is different from other agricultural sectors in Indonesia in that production and distribution have been left free of government or privately organized cartels, monopolies and monopsonies as well as of production quotas and domestic or international trade restrictions. The resulting fierce competition in the marketing system has led to two benefits. First, the distribution margin is one of the lowest among Indonesia's major export commodities, a feature that has undoubtedly aided its competitiveness in export markets. Second, the returns to cocoa farmers are very attractive. Farmers' shares of export prices for cocoa are the highest among all export commodities in Indonesia.

While the *absence* of government intervention in production and marketing arrangements has undoubtedly been good for the cocoa sector, Nishio and

Akiyama also note where the *presence* of government intervention has helped. This is in the matter of providing adequate infrastructure. Road and port investments made by the government in Sulawesi have helped open up more areas to cocoa planting and reduced the costs of transport to markets.

Soymeal: The Costs of Supporting a Monopolist

The soymeal sector provides a dramatic contrast to the cocoa sector. In this case, government introduced a set of regulations in the late 1980s that were designed to create and sustain a domestic monopolist in the conversion of soybeans to soymeal. These regulations initially banned soymeal imports and restricted domestic production to only one producer with close links to the family of President Suharto. While domestic criticism and the inability of the monopolist producer to meet full local demand led to the relaxation of some of these restrictions, first in 1991 and then again in 1993 and 1994, the overall regulatory environment and its implementation by the concerned government agencies, remained geared to the financial viability of the domestic monopolist. Pomeroy (Chapter 9) provides details of the evolution of regulatory arrangements in the soymeal sector between 1988 and 1995 and conducts an empirical analysis of the costs and benefits to different groups (consumers, producer, government) from these arrangements. Her analysis supports three main conclusions: (a) Government was spending $21 million (in 1991 prices) of Indonesia's scarce resources to sustain the operation of a plant that was worth only about twice that amount, (b) The net cost to the economy of the jobs "created" by preventing unrestricted imports of soymeal was in the order of $60,000 per worker employed, and (c) The loss to consumers from prevailing policies in 1991 was of the order of $33 million. In contrast to these "costs" the only benefit that accrued was to the domestic monopolist.

Cement: The Case for Modified Regulations

Plunkett and Pasinringi (Chapter 10) analyze the cement sector, a strategically important sector (especially for construction growth), which is characterized by seasonal shortages and high prices. Because of the geographic dispersion of markets, relative importance of transport costs, marked economies of scale, and high costs of entry and exit, the cement sector has a natural tendency to become a geographically concentrated oligopoly. Experience from other countries, especially the United States, indicates that the complete deregulation of the industry would *not* necessarily lead to more competitive behavior among producers. Strong legislation (and enforcement) aimed at maintaining competition within the sector is required to underpin deregulation efforts. In the Indonesian case, existing regulations involve the use of guiding prices for retail sales and geographic distribution quotas for cement producers. These arrangements keep in place relatively high domestic prices for cement and a small cartel of cement producers including several state-owned firms and have not been successful in raising production capacity to cope with periodic shortages. These regulatory arrangements could be modified through the use of production licensing which could be used to control the number of production facilities and ex-factory prices while freeing up the transport and distribution system. One advantage of such a modification would be a reduction in the transaction costs associated with the current system that involves regular negotiations between government and producers on the geographic allocation of cement supplies, both domestically and for exports. However, as already noted, such a modification should be backed by legislation to maintain competition in the sector.

Sugar: Efficiency and Distributional Aspects

Until recently, the sugar sector in Indonesia was governed by regulations that affected both production and marketing aspects. A government agency (BULOG) had the sole authority to import sugar and to buy it from domestic mills as well as to appoint distributors to deliver the sugar to retail outlets while farmers (in certain areas) were required to meet "area quotas" for sugarcane planting. Not all of the interventions were in the nature of implicit taxes, however. Farmers were provided subsidies of various kinds to plant sugarcane, mills were given prices that covered their costs, and consumers were provided sugar at subsidized prices. Panggabean analyzes this welter of interventions in Chapter 11 and compares the efficiency and distributional consequences of possible reforms. His main conclusions are: (a) consumers are the main losers from the regulations described above since, even with subsidized retail prices, they end up paying more than what sugar could be imported for; (b) while consumers would be the main winners from import liberalization, other groups such as sugar farmers and millers would lose unless they continued to be subsidized by the government; and (c) partial reforms, in which only one of the array of regulations is lifted, would not be enough to meet various efficiency, self-reliance and distributional objectives; for this to happen, a comprehensive set of reforms would need to be implemented but such a move would carry the risk of significant disruption to the sugarcane and sugar production and marketing system unless properly sequenced.

PART IV: SOME CONCLUSIONS

The foregoing has shown that, for the period under review, deregulation proved to be an effective means of meeting several important development objectives in Indonesia. Its main initial impact was on exports: it helped diversify the export base into new manufactures while generating a huge increase in volume. The export boost was instrumental in meeting growth, employment, and balance of payments objectives. Rapid export expansion helped achieve high economic growth in a period that would otherwise have been characterized by relative stagnation. This growth was achieved without serious balance of payments pressures despite the fact that Indonesia's principal source of foreign exchange earnings, oil and oil-related products, suffered from prolonged price weakness during most of the 1980s.

Export expansion was associated with a large and rapid increase in employment in manufacturing. In a labor-abundant context, employment expansion is of critical importance to raising the incomes of the poor and the near poor, especially in urban areas. Indeed, in employment-intensive manufactured exports Indonesia may well have found a new and powerful tool to combat poverty. There are two ways in which this tool works. First, it helps the poor directly through increasing wage-labor incomes. Second, it provides a new source of revenue for government to use for poverty-oriented programs; this is all the more important in view of the decline of oil as a source of revenue. While definitive empirical evidence on this connection between employment expansion and poverty reduction has not been presented in this volume, the circumstantial evidence points strongly in this direction.

In view of the largely successful experience so far it would seem obvious for Indonesia to continue to use deregulation as a principal element in its development strategy. There are three other reasons as well to persevere with deregulation. One is the need to increase productivity growth in order to maintain high overall economic growth in the future. A second is the rising degree of competition in external markets. The third is an opportunity to take advantage of a rising tide of liberalization in international trade and investment arrangements, exemplified by the passage of the Uruguay Round Agreement in 1994 and the increasing momentum behind regional initiatives under the aegis of APEC and AFTA.

Need for Productivity Growth

Long term growth is determined by the processes of factor augmentation (i.e., an increase in the stock of labor, capital and natural resources, differentiated by quality) and productivity change (i.e., obtaining more output from a given stock of factor inputs). Until the mid-1980s, Indonesia's growth was determined largely by factor accumulation, based largely on the exploitation of its ample natural resource base, but also to a considerable extent on growth in its stock of educated/skilled labor. Productivity change, aside from rice-based agriculture, played a negligible role. In the future, productivity change must play a more substantial role if past levels of growth are to be maintained. This is because the rate of growth of the stocks of two key factors of production for Indonesia, namely, labor and natural resources, may be expected to decelerate. Indonesia's population growth rate has been declining steadily, and while the (formal sector) labor force is being boosted by increasing participation rates (especially for women), this may not be enough to increase the overall labor force growth rate. Similarly, natural resource stocks (especially petroleum and timber) are on a stagnant or depleting trajectory. Thus, future growth must come primarily from increasing the stock of physical capital, from further improving labor force quality, and through productivity change.

The Future Competitive Challenge

Developments in the international context also make it important for Indonesia to improve the functioning of its private markets. Indonesia faces increasing competition from other developing countries, and especially from China and India, in world markets. While it has performed impressively in recent years to build a more diversified base of exports and gain a foothold in many overseas markets, the challenge of improving its position will be stiffer in the future. Some evidence of this may be found in the rising share of China in two of Indonesia's main markets, the United States, and Japan. During the 1990s, China increased its share of these two markets at a faster rate than Indonesia. And while the 1997 crisis-related depreciation of the Indonesian Rupiah has conferred a competitive advantage to Indonesia in the short run, the long-run competitive challenge from China remains.

Opportunities in Multilateral Trade Liberalization

The passage of the Uruguay Round Agreement on trade liberalization in 1994 and subsequent discussions on global trade arrangements suggest that world trade and integration is likely to be a dominant influence on national economies over the next quarter century. Indonesia stands to benefit from participation in such arrangements. Lewis and Robinson (Chapter 12) show that Indonesia will clearly be a net gainer from full implementation of the Uruguay Round Agreement: its exports are likely to increase by an incremental 3 percent and its GDP growth rate by 1.6 percent per annum (i.e., compared to the base case of 1992). However, the extent to which Indonesia gains from the opportunities offered by multilateral liberalization depends critically on its relative competitiveness in external markets. Further deregulation is the best guarantee of enhancing such competitiveness.

NOTES

1.   Indonesia's agricultural recovery from virtual stagnancy in the late-1970s was remarkable. To avoid an extreme case of "Dutch Disease" and to create a favorable price environment for sustained agricultural growth, the government undertook a significant devaluation of the Rupiah in 1978 (Timmer 1994). In addition, while maintaining a balanced budget in principle, the government recorded budget surpluses from the oil-boom as "deposits" (Usui 1996). This type of demand management policy helped to ensure that the effects of devaluation were sustained. The result of these policies is highlighted by the dramatic success of the rice sector. From being a net importer in the 1970s, Indonesia became self-sufficient in rice production by 1985, and has been able to maintain that status since then.

2.   For a recent review, see Montgomery (1997).

3.   Rodgers (1998, 1996, 1994), Hill (1995), Lewis (1994) and Pangestu (1991) provide useful surveys of policy evolution in Indonesia.

4.   The deficit on the current account of the balance of payments increased to $5 billion in 1982 and $6 billion in 1983. These were by far the largest deficits recorded ever (Radelet 1995). At the same time, however, the government was able to keep the debt-export and the debt-GDP ratios relatively lower than those of other

large debtors like Mexico and the Philippines through prudent macroeconomic management (see Rodgers 1996). Austerity measures include devaluations, adaptation of a flexible exchange rate system in 1983, and a freeze on all public salaries was instituted in 1985, and kept in effect until 1987.

5. This survey of the debate on trade policy is based on Krueger (1997). Krueger pays particular attention to the learning process that contributed to the transformation of the consensus on trade policy from import-substitution to export-promotion. Edwards (1993) and Baldwin (1992) have also authored broad-ranging reviews of trade and development policy in developing countries.

6. There has been an active debate on total factor productivity issues in East Asia. One might start with the World Bank's *East Asian Miracle* (World Bank 1993) report that argued that in high performing Asian economies the contribution of TFP growth to per capita income growth was as high as 33 percent. However, Young (1995, 1994, 1992) and Krugman (1994) have argued that overall economic growth in East Asia has rested mostly on factor augmentation (growth of inputs) and *not* high TFP growth. In a much discussed paper, Young (1995) shows that between 1970 and 1990 the annual TFP growth in the Singapore manufacturing sector was actually negative (-0.10 percent). It is generally accepted that the results of empirical studies on TFP growth depend critically on the researcher's priors, especially those regarding the form of the production function and the scope for factor substitution.

7. Only twelve countries out of the entire sample demonstrated an average growth of manufactured exports of more than 1 percent per annum (while eleven recorded per capita GDP growth of 3 percent or more per annum). Of those twelve, seven were in Asia.

8. Evidence shows that for Korea and Thailand lower concentration has led to higher TFP growth (Urata 1994). In both economies sectors which experienced a reduction in concentration tended to achieve higher growth rates.

9. Revenga (1995) presents contrasting results from the Mexican labor market. She finds that reductions in quota coverage and in tariff levels were associated with moderate *reductions* in firm-level employment. In particular, a 10 point reduction in tariffs is associated with a 2 percent-3 percent decline in employment. Further, changes in quota coverage did not seem to have any discernible effect on wages.

10. This impact is conditional on the country's skill level. If the average skill level of the workers rise, only then would gains in employment and wages be sustainable over the longer term. In addition, researchers have found that the initial gains from FDI may not advantage workers (especially unskilled workers) at all. For example, Feenstra et al. (1994) looks at FDI and relative (skilled/unskilled) wages among Mexico's Maquiladoras. They find that FDI is positively correlated with the relative demand for *skilled* labor. In regions where FDI was most concentrated, FDI growth could account for over 90 percent of the increase in the share of skilled labor in total wages after Mexico's deregulation. This finding is consistent with the authors' argument that FDI (or "outsourcing by MNCs") would raise worldwide demand for skilled labor. This argument stems from the following assumptions: (a) outsourcing would dominate sectors that utilize "unskilled" labor from the developed country perspective, and (b) since average skill-levels in developing

countries are low, these sectors would actually be regarded as "skilled" sectors from the developing country perspective. Therefore, most outsourcing to low-income economies would tend to benefit relatively skilled workers.

11.   Manning's paper also shows that land-abundant islands have experienced less favorable growth. This finding echoes Bourguignon et al.'s (1990) macro result that countries comparatively well-endowed with mineral resources, land or climate tend to be less egalitarian than others.

12.   Both agriculture and government grew more rapidly outside Java than on Java. In addition, outside Java and Bali employment and wage growth has been less even. The absolute decline in agricultural labor in Java and the continued absorption of labor into agriculture in other islands remains a striking counterpoint to the overall employment pattern.

REFERENCES

Asian Development Bank, ADB (1997) *Emerging Asia: Changes and Challenges,* (Manila, The Philippines: The Asian Development Bank).

Balassa, Bela (1982) *Development Strategies in Semi-industrialized Countries,* (London and New York, NY: Oxford University Press).

Baldwin, Robert E. (1995) "The Effect of Trade and Foreign Direct Investment on Employment and Relative Wages," *National Bureau of Economic Research Working Paper No. 5037.*

Baldwin, Robert E. (1992) "Are Economists' Traditional Trade Policy Views Still Valid?" *Journal of Economic Literature,* 30 (June), pp. 804–829.

Bhagwati, Jagdish (1978) Foreign Trade Regimes and Economic Development: Anatomy and Consequences of Exchange Control Regimes, (Cambridge, MA: Ballinger for NBER).

Booth, Anne (ed.) (1992) The Oil Boom And After: Indonesian Economic Policy and Performance in the Soeharto Era, (Singapore: Oxford University Press).

Bourguignon, F. and C. Morrison (1990) "Income Distribution, Development and Foreign Trade: A Cross-sectional Analysis," *European Economic Review,* 34, pp. 1113–1132.

Dollar, David (1992) "Outward-oriented Developing Economies Do Grow More Rapidly: Evidence from 95 LDCs, 1976–1985," *Economic Development and Cultural Change,* 40, pp. 523–544.

Edwards, Sebastian (1993) "Openness, Trade Liberalization, and Growth in Developing Countries," *Journal of Economic Literature,* 31 (September), pp. 1358–1393.

Edwards, Sebastian (1997) "Trade Policy, Growth, and Income Distribution," *American Economic Review: Papers and Proceedings,* 87 (2), pp. 205–210.

Feenstra, Robert C. and Gordon Hanson (1995) "Foreign Investment, Outsourcing and Relative Wages," in Robert Feenstra, Gene G. Grossman and Douglas A. Irwin (eds.) *Political Economy of Trade Policy: Essays in Honor of Jagdish Bhagwati,* (Cambridge, MA: MIT Press).

Frankel, Jeffrey A., David Romer and Teresa Cyrus (1996) "Trade and Growth in East Asian Countries: Cause and Effect?" *National Bureau of Economic Research Working Paper No. 5732.*

Fujita, Natsuki and William James (1997) "Employment Creation and Manufactured Exports in Indonesia, 1980-1990," *Bulletin of Indonesian Economic Studies,* 33 (1), pp. 103–115.

Ghani, Ejaz and Carl Jayarajah (1995) "Trade Reform, Efficiency, and Growth," *World Bank Policy Research Working Paper No. 1438.*

Harrison, Ann and Ana Revenga (1995) "The Effects of Trade Policy Reform: What Do We Really Know?" *National Bureau of Economic Research Working Paper No. 5225.*

Hill, Hal (1995) *The Indonesian Economy Since 1966: Southeast Asia's Emerging Giant,* (Cambridge, England: Cambridge University Press).

Kawai, Hiroki (1994) "International Comparative Analysis of Economic Growth: Trade Liberalization and Growth," *The Developing Economies,* 32 (4), pp. 373–397.

Krueger, Anne O. (1978) Foreign Trade Regimes and Economic Development: Liberalization Attempts and Consequences, (Cambridge, MA: Ballinger for NBER).

Krueger, Anne O. (1990) *Perspectives on Trade and Development,* (Chicago, IL: University of Chicago Press).

Krueger, Anne O. (1983) *Trade and Employment in Developing Countries, Vol. 3: Synthesis and Conclusions,* (Chicago, IL: NBER and University of Chicago Press).

Krueger, Anne O. (1997) "Trade Policy and Economic Development: How We Learn," *American Economic Review,* 87 (1), March 1997.

Krugman, Paul (1994) "The Myth of Asia's Miracle," *Foreign Affairs,* 73 (6), pp. 62–78.

Levine, Ross and David Renelt (1992) "A Sensitivity Analysis of Cross-country Growth Regressions," *American Economic Review,* 82 (September), pp. 942–963.

Lewis, Jeffrey D. (1994) "Indonesia's Industrial and Trade Policy," *Harvard Institute of International Development Discussion Paper No. 491.*

Little, Ian, Tibor Scitovsky and Maurice Scott (1970) *Industry and Trade in Some Developing Countries,* (London and New York, NY: Oxford University Press for OECD).

Manning, Chris (1997) "Regional Labor Markets during Deregulation in Indonesia: Have the Outer Islands been Left Behind?" *World Bank Policy Research Working Paper No. 1728.*

Montgomery, John (1997) "Indonesian Financial System: Its Contribution to Economic Performance and Key Policy Issues," in John Hickling, David Robinson and Anoop Singh (eds.) *Macroeconomic Issues Facing ASEAN Countries,* (Washington, DC: The International Monetary Fund).

Osada, Hiroshi (1994) "Trade Liberalization and FDI Incentives in Indonesia: The Impact on Industrial Productivity," *The Developing Economies,* 32 (4), pp. 479–491.

Pangestu, Mari (1991) "Managing Economic Policy Reforms in Indonesia," in Sylvia Ostry (ed.) *Authority and Academic Scribblers,* (San Francisco, CA: The ICS Press).

Radelet, Steven (1995) "Indonesian Foreign Debt: Headed for a Crisis or Financing Sustainable Growth," *Bulletin of Indonesian Economic Studies,* 31 (3), pp. 39–72.

Revenga, Ana (1995) "Employment and Wage Effects of Trade Liberalization: The Case of Mexican Manufacturing," *World Bank Policy Research Working Paper No. 1524.*

Riedel, James (1988) "Trade as an Engine of Growth: Theory and Evidence," in David Greenaway (ed.) *Economic Development and International Trade,* (London, England: Macmillan Education).

Rodgers, Yana van der Meulen (1998) "Empirical Investigation of One OPEC Country's Successful Non-Oil Export Performance," in *Journal of Development Economics.*

Rodgers, Yana van der Meulen (1996) "Indonesia's Macroeconomic and Trade Performance," *The Journal of Developing Areas,* 30 (January), pp. 149–166.

Rodgers, Yana van der Meulen (1994) "Indonesia's Policy Reform: An Overview," Southeast Asian Chung-Hua Institution for Economic Research Economic Studies Series No. 9402.

Timmer, C. Peter (1994) "Dutch Disease and Agriculture in Indonesia: The Policy Approach," paper prepared for a conference on lessons from Indonesia for Colombia on managing sudden increases in petroleum revenues, Bogota, Colombia, March 24–25, 1994.

Urata, Shujiro (1994) "Trade Liberalization and Productivity Growth in Asia: Introduction and Major Findings," *The Developing Economies,* 32 (4), pp. 363–372.

Usui, Norio (1996) "Policy Adjustments to the Oil Boom and Their Evaluation: The Dutch Disease in Indonesia," *World Development,* 24 (5), pp. 887–900.

Williamson, Jeffrey G. (1997) "Globalization and Inequality: Past and Present," *The World Bank Research Observer,* 12 (2), pp. 117–135.

Woo, Wing Thye, Bruce Glassburner and Anwar Nasution (1994) *Macroeconomic Policies, Crises, and Long-term Growth in Indonesia, 1965–90,* (Washington, DC: The World Bank).

Wood, Adrian (1994) "Trade and Employment Creation: Possibilities and Limitations," in J. Edward Taylor (ed.) *Development Strategy, Employment and Migration: Insights From Models,* (Paris, Washington, DC: The OECD).

Wood, Adrian and Kersti Berge (1994) "Exporting Manufactures: Trade Policy or Human Resources?" *Institute of Development Studies Working Paper No. 4.*

World Bank (1993) *The East Asian Miracle: Economic Growth and Public Policy,* (New York, NY: Oxford University Press for the World Bank).

World Bank (1996) Perspectives on World Development Report: Involving Workers in East Asia's Growth, (Washington, DC: The World Bank).

World Bank (WDR 1995) *World Development Report 1995: Workers in and Integrating World,* (New York, NY: Oxford University Press for the World Bank).

Young, Alwyn (1994) "Lessons from the East Asian NIEs: A Contrarian View," *European Economic Review,* 38 (April), pp. 964–973.

Young, Alwyn (1992) "Tale of Two Cities: Factor Accumulation and Technical Change in Hong Kong and Singapore," *NBER Macroeconomics Annual 1992,* Cambridge, MA: MIT Press).

Young, Alwyn (1995) "The Tyranny of Numbers: Confronting The Statistical Realities of the East Asian Growth Experience," *Quarterly Journal of Economics,* 110 (August), pp. 641–680.

CHAPTER 2

The Evolution of Economic Policy Reform: Determinants, Sequencing and Reasons for Success

William E. James *and* Sherry M. Stephenson

CONVENTIONAL WISDOM ON THE CONTENT AND SEQUENCING OF REFORMS

The economic policy reform process is typically viewed as comprising two parts, stabilization and structural adjustment. The *stabilization* part works towards the correction of imbalances in foreign payments, government budgets and the money supply, with the aim of controlling inflation and reducing macroeconomic instability. The *structural adjustment* part typically covers measures aimed at changing the structure of production (towards tradable goods) and increasing the efficiency and flexibility of the economy.

It is generally argued that stabilization should be a *precondition* of longer-term structural adjustment policies on the assumption that such policies can succeed only if carried out in a stable macroeconomic framework. This is because reform packages depend on attaining and maintaining relative prices that reflect economic scarcities. This is true for domestic relative prices (between factors of production), for the cost of borrowing and for the ratio between domestic and foreign prices. An inflationary environment weakens the competitiveness of a country's industries to the extent the difference in inflation between the domestic and foreign markets exceeds the depreciation of the exchange rate. Exchange rates tend to become overvalued, with consequent balance-of-payments problems. Moreover, inflation distorts incentives and leads people to focus on protecting their relative income through political influence. Controls on selected prices (e.g., interest rates, urban public transportation, fuel and electricity) are typically resorted to in a bid to lessen the erosion of living standards. However, these lead to shortages and discourage investment in these sectors.

Rapid inflation erodes confidence since it deprives a currency of its function as a store of value and lessens its convenience as a medium of exchange. In order to avoid conflict and to institutionalize adjustment of salaries so that nominal incomes are protected, "indexation" is sometimes resorted to. However, indexation of incomes to prices only accelerates the inflation because it undercuts the motivation for discipline in fiscal and monetary policy. Real interest rates are typically low and negative so that lenders concentrate on short-term finance. As a result, the supply of long-term investment is reduced and entrepreneurs concentrate on hedging against inflation rather than on increasing productivity.

Once an effective stabilization program is in place, the next objective of policy makers is to undertake reforms to restructure the economy for renewed economic growth. There is broad agreement on what kinds of components should form part of a structural adjustment package. These components include, among others: liberalizing and deregulating markets so that prices are freely determined and can adjust to true scarcity values, shifting resources from government into private hands, and reforming institutions. The agenda for the first component of a structural adjustment reform program—letting markets work to get the prices right—has been affirmed in many reviews published in the 1970s and 1980s (Bhagwati 1978; Balassa 1982; Michalopoulos 1987).

In practice, it is difficult to distinguish stabilization measures from structural adjustment measures. Many policy elements are common between the two groups of measures: exchange rate devaluation, interest rate increases, etc. Also, although stabilization should be a prerequisite for the implementation and success of structural adjustment policies, in practice governments rarely allow a large amount of time between implementation of these two aspects of reform. Therefore, when the two are considered together, the question of sequencing of reforms becomes crucial. Economists have realized that the speed with which economic reforms are enacted and the order in which they are implemented may have just as much to do with their success as the actual content of a reform package.

Neoclassical economic theory imparts little guidance on the optimal reform sequence. This is partly because the theoretical analysis of economic reform has traditionally been conducted in a comparative static framework, while deregulation remains an inherently iterative, dynamic process. From theory we know that a deregulated economy is more efficient than an economy subject to controls, but not much more. We lack a dynamic framework with which to analyze the optimal pathway from a distorted regime to a neutral one. Certainly a learning process is at work as economic agents respond to changed incentives, and this leads back to the officials overseeing and implementing the reform program.

In an ideal world, all sectors should be deregulated simultaneously and all policies for promotion of deregulation adopted and implemented in tandem. However, theory does not take into account the rigidities and market imperfections present in the real world, which makes such simultaneous implementation impractical. The problem is further complicated because the theory of the "second best" reminds us that implementation of *partial* reforms, through the adjustment of only some prices or the removal of only some controls, does not necessarily bring about greater efficiency or welfare gains. This means that the *way* in which reforms are implemented is all-important and can make a crucial difference in the outcome. The question of sequencing is not only difficult and technical, but it is also critical because it can have a great deal of influence on welfare and income distribution.

In the absence of substantial guidance from theory, policy makers have to rely on the accumulation of case studies of actual experiences with alternative paths of economic reforms. The countries most studied have been in Latin America since interest in reform was stimulated by the experience of the Southern Cone countries (Chile, Argentina, Uruguay) in the 1970s. Based on this experience it is generally agreed that domestic financial market reform should precede the deregulation of capital controls, and the deregulation of the real sector (trade barriers, etc.) should precede the relaxation of capital controls (Edwards 1984, 1990). This means that in terms of order and priority, reforms should be implemented first through the deregulation of the trade sector, second through the deregulation of the financial sector and third through the deregulation of capital markets. The reasons for this sequence are examined below.

Relaxation of Capital Controls After Financial Market Reforms

With reference to the relaxation of capital controls, economists argue that if capital controls are deregulated when domestic financial markets are still regulated and interest rates are fixed at arbitrarily low levels (even at negative levels, as is often the case), then capital will flee abroad, thereby reducing the domestic supply of investment funds. Thus the domestic financial sector should be strengthened and deregulated before capital controls are fully eliminated.[1] This means domestic interest rates should be raised to internationally competitive levels reflective of positive real rates of return.

Argentina is a case where the domestic capital market was deregulated in the late 1970s and early 1980s without a reduced fiscal deficit. Reform proved unsustainable as the foreign debt increased to make up for the reduced tax base, and the sequencing of reforms was subsequently reversed (Edwards 1990).

Trade Reform Before the Lifting of Capital Controls

McKinnon (1991) argued that capital controls should only be relaxed after domestic financial reform is accomplished and after the real sector has been deregulated. This is because substantial inflows of capital are likely to follow the relaxation of capital controls, and these capital inflows serve to push up or appreciate the real exchange rate and reduce the competitiveness of the tradable goods sector. The resulting appreciation can also frustrate attempts to liberalize the trade sector through the reduction of tariffs and elimination of non-tariff barriers. Therefore, deregulation usually requires an exchange rate depreciation to help encourage production of exportables. McKinnon further argues that a structural reform of the trade accounts should deliberately avoid an unusual or extraordinary injection of foreign capital.[2]

Williamson (1991) has also argued in favor of this pattern of reform sequencing for the following reasons. First, capital account deregulation causes an appreciation of the currency through capital inflows that bring export growth to a standstill and threaten the country with renewed financial crisis. Second, importing capital before fiscal discipline has been established simply allows the maintenance of unsustainable budget deficits for a time. However, this supposes that macroeconomic stabilization has not already been completed, which is not one of our assumptions. Third, capital inflows which occur before the real sector has been reformed and deregulated will flow into the wrong industries and thus cause a misallocation of resources which is welfare-reducing in both the short and the long runs. Finally, capital that flows in before the financial system has been deregulated may be inefficiently allocated. For example, state enterprises or private conglomerates may have "first call" on credit that is rationed under a repressed financial system even though such credit might have higher returns if it was allocated to more efficient and competitive firms.

Williamson goes further to refine the above argument and to state that not only should this order of sequencing be applied to capital inflows, but to capital outflows as well, although the latter should be subject to a different set of preconditions. These conditions would be even more stringent than those for the deregulation of capital inflows, and would mean that deregulation of capital outflows would come at the very end in a reform process. However, in order to attract inward capital flows, investors should be notified that it is the government's intention to remove all controls on outward flows once certain conditions have been achieved. The actual deregulation of outward capital flows can be done in stages and should occur only when the new policy regime in place is regarded by investors as permanent, and when arrangements have been made to limit the erosion of the tax base even in adverse circumstances.

Frenkel (1983) has emphasized the differential response in terms of timing of the real sector and the capital sector, arguing that while asset markets clear almost instantaneously, the restructuring and attainment of equilibrium in the goods markets usually takes much longer. Therefore, a synchronization of the structural reform process will require that the trade sector or the goods market be deregulated before financial markets and before the lifting of capital controls.[3] He supports this recommendation through a comparison of the costs of distortions.

As to the question of sectors and markets outside the goods and capital markets, not a great deal has been written. The few economists who have treated this subject have argued in favor of labor market reforms in the overall economic restructuring and for the need to place this policy at an early stage of the reform program so as not to reduce overall efficiency gains from adjustment and to lower the ultimate costs in terms of unemployment and political resistance (Edwards 1989).

Maintenance of a Realistic Exchange Rate

Discussion in this section would not be complete without mentioning the importance of government policy towards the exchange rate. The importance of the exchange rate cannot be overemphasized. Depreciation of the exchange rate is assumed under the stabilization components above, but in fact a realistic exchange rate policy must be followed at every stage of the reform process. Countries need a unified exchange rate set and maintained at a level sufficiently competitive to induce a rapid growth of non-traditional exports.

Sachs (1987) discusses in some detail the linkages between exchange rate policy, budget policy, and debt relief in carrying out reform programs. He emphasizes that exchange rate policy cannot be divorced from budget policies and issues of income distribution. However, he points out that an exchange rate policy that attempts to stimulate exports at all costs through aggressive depreciations can often undermine stabilization and reform programs through inflation and capital flight. One of the main reasons cited to explain the success of Japan, Singapore, Korea, and Taiwan, China with adjustment programs is their maintenance of nominal exchange rates at fairly stable levels with low inflation so as not to jeopardize export profitability.

The Speed of Economic Reforms

There is less consensus on the speed of economic reforms than on the question of sequencing. Opinions and country experiences have differed and continue to differ widely. Discussion of the issue is linked to that of the role and the burden of adjustment costs generated by the reform program.

On the one hand, an early study by Little, Scitovsky, and Scott (1970) advocated a gradual approach to reform implementation. The authors felt that a faster pace would mean larger short-term adjustment costs that would create opposing interests to the reforms, thereby rendering them less likely to succeed. Michaely (1991) has also argued that a gradual implementation of reforms in the trade area would minimize political opposition and better enable the reform process to be sustained over time.

On the other hand there are economists who favor faster rather than slower implementation of economic reforms, arguing that the latter carries with it the costs of prolonged uncertainty and probably a longer period of poor economic performance. Summarizing some earlier studies and opinions, Michalopoulos (1987) favors faster reform implementation on the grounds that, "experience suggests that a lot can be accomplished within two to four years," and that an unduly slow pace of reforms could delay the development of export activities. The required reallocation of resources will not occur unless the signals given to relative prices are strong and convincing enough for factors to be redeployed. Moreover, a protracted reform period could allow interest groups opposed to reform efforts to strengthen their position and influence.

However, it is clear that the speed of any reform package must be partially determined by the extent of the original distortions and the pace at which adjustment to reforms could be expected to take place in a given society. Initial conditions in each country determine the speed at which the redeployment of resources can take place. Further, technical solutions for optimal transition cannot be designed without taking account existing political constraints.

Importance of Credibility

Even a well-structured reform program will not succeed if reforms are not considered to be credible by the public at large: *credibility* is critical if a reform attempt is to survive over time. Many economists believe that the central factor determining the success of a stabilization and/or structural adjustment reform program is in its *impact* on the public's expectations. This is because if economic agents do not believe in government's attempts to deregulate the economy (as has been the case during many reform attempts in Latin America), then they will actually take steps that undermine the effectiveness of the reform program.

It has been recognized that one of the main factors determining the credibility of a reform effort is *leadership*. The government must be clear and strong in expressing its support for economic reform. In this context, Williamson (1994a) emphasizes the importance of the "technopols" in the implementation of reform programs and of economic policy makers who assume positions of political responsibility for the purpose of improving economic performance. Technopols should constitute a team with similar policy views, allowing for cohesiveness in the design and implementation of policy reform. Further, the continuity of leadership, backed by strong executive authority, is the best combination for a reform program to maintain its credibility as a consistent government effort.

ECONOMIC POLICY REFORMS IN INDONESIA: CONTENT AND SEQUENCING

Economic policy reforms in Indonesia prior to the crisis of 1997–1998 can be conveniently organized in three periods: the early years of the Suharto New Order government from 1965–1972, the oil price boom years of 1973–1982, and the deregulation period since 1985.

Early Period Reforms: Deregulation of the Capital Account

Hyperinflation and political chaos created an emergency situation in the mid-1960s to which the New Order government responded with a major stabilization and reform program from 1966 to 1971. Inflation was reduced from over 500 percent to under 20 percent by 1969. The macroeconomic stabilization process also involved the adoption of a "balanced budget" policy because it was recognized that monetization of government debt was a key source of inflationary pressures. By law, the government was prevented from borrowing domestically to finance budget deficits; however, external finance for development projects was not covered in the categories that defined the "balanced budget."

Following this, in 1972, the country took the highly unusual and innovative step of liberalizing all capital account transactions, including both inward and outward flows. This step was preceded by unification of the exchange rate. From that point on, movements of capital into or out of the country could be freely undertaken. Deregulation of capital flows followed the decision taken in 1966 to welcome and encourage foreign direct investment in Indonesia. Foreign and domestic investors responded positively to the capital account deregulation, and net private capital inflows increased from an estimated $108 million in 1967 to $956 million in 1972. The bulk of the net private inflow of funds in 1967 was accounted for by the repatriation of capital that had been withdrawn from the country during the crisis. Thereafter, however, inflows of funds were largely to finance new investments by foreign and domestic firms (Pitt 1986).[4] Realized foreign direct investment inflows jumped from a cumulative $83 million in 1967–1969 to $271 million in 1972, providing evidence that the open capital account policy was effective in stimulating investment inflows from abroad.[5] The open capital account has been consistently maintained since 1972.

Interim in Reform in the Oil Boom Years

The oil boom that took place in 1973 obviated the need for systematic deregulation of the real sector for some years. As oil prices stayed buoyant during 1973–1978, windfall revenues accrued to the Indonesian government, permitting expansion of development expenditures and enhancing Indonesia's ability to borrow abroad. The period of the first oil boom (1973–1978), however, was not without moments of near crisis. In 1975 the state oil company, Pertamina, suffered a financial crisis that threatened to mar Indonesia's international credit standing. Swift action was taken by the government to meet the financial obligations of the company and to adopt stricter oversight of state enterprises' financial affairs.

Inflation during the period of the oil boom accelerated and threatened macroeconomic stability. Credit controls were adopted in the mid-1970s to restrain inflation. Financial repression was quite serious with negative real interest rates and government-directed allocation of credit resulting in further distortions. Increasingly inward-looking trade policies were also adopted. Together with the fixed nominal exchange rate, inflation and proliferation of non-tariff barriers were discouraging development of non-oil and gas exports, stifling the growth of efficient manufacturing industries. In order to partially correct this a sharp devaluation of the Rupiah was undertaken in 1978. This served to give a boost to the most efficient manufacturers' exports. A "mini-boom" led by exports occurred in manufacturing sectors such as textiles and wearing apparel (Arndt and Sundrum 1984). However, the devaluation-induced rise in manufactured exports was short-lived, as the second oil shock and increased inflation wiped out the real depreciation of the Rupiah by 1982.

Trade policies became increasingly inward-oriented with greater emphasis on import substitution and "technology-based" industries, including heavy transportation equipment like aircraft and ship building (World Bank 1987). For this reason, the World Bank classified Indonesia as "moderately inward-oriented" during 1973–1985. The adoption of non-tariff measures such as quotas, import bans, import licensing, import surcharges, special "deletion" programs and other restrictions increased effective rates of protection in the early 1980s compared with previous years. Imports were controlled by licensing. For example, the government issued licenses to "approved importers" for nine categories of goods. Under this scheme, a few importers or a single importer was licensed to import certain raw materials and agricultural products or a sole agent was selected to import certain brand name products. At the same time export restrictions were being tightened in some sectors and applied in other sectors and this represented a regression from the relaxation of export taxes that had taken place in the late 1970s. Imports and exports of selected commodities—sugar, wheat and flour, soybeans and soy flour, cotton, cloves, milk and milk products, and rice—were placed under direct government control through the Bureau of Logistics (BULOG). BULOG or an authorized private licensee remained the sole importer of these items into the late 1990s.

In addition, export controls or bans were introduced to protect *downstream* processing industries, especially plywood. A progressively restrictive ban on export of raw logs and sawn timber was introduced in 1979 that fully restricted log exports by 1985.[6] A similar ban was imposed on raw rattan exports. Export taxes were also imposed on leather hides, animal skins, and some other primary products.

The overall effect of the increase in trade restrictions and regulation of industry was to create a "high-cost" economy that grew ever more dependent on petroleum and gas.[7] Industry outside of petrochemicals had a small share of GDP, and manufactures made-up only 10 percent of exports in 1983. In 1981 industry, including petroleum, mining, utilities, construction and manufacturing, provided only 12 percent of total employment, much lower than in other ASEAN countries.

Despite this failure to advance much in the areas of Indonesia's manufacturing comparative advantage, progress was made in other areas of the economy, particularly agriculture, during 1973 to 1985. Indonesia went from being a net importer of rice in the mid-1970s to becoming self-sufficient in rice by the mid-1980s. Moreover, this was largely accomplished through higher productivity and investment in infrastructure and farmer education, though efforts to compensate rice farmers for the higher cost of inputs were made by subsidizing fertilizer and pesticides and maintaining floor prices at or above international prices (Piggot et al. 1993, Timmer and Falcon 1975; Timmer et al. 1983).

Investments were also made to boost output and productivity in exportable agricultural products like palm oil and rubber. The successes in agriculture and the development of infrastructure also helped to boost growth in services.

Taken together, these areas of domestic growth provided much needed employment and income growth to relatively poor people during much of the 1970s and early 1980s and helped to offset the adverse consequences of the protectionist policies in the industrial sector.

Reforms from the Mid-1980s

The inward-looking phase of policy-making in Indonesia was reversed in the mid-1980s and a far-reaching program of deregulation of trade, investment and financial sector policies was launched. Such programs are rarely, if ever, enacted because governments suddenly become convinced of the correctness of economic logic. More often than not they are carried out as a response to some crisis. In the case of Indonesia, the reforms of the mid-1980s came in response to the cris's unleashed by the rapid decline in world prices of petroleum. Petroleum and gas accounted for nearly 80 percent of exports and 70 percent of government receipts in 1981. After 1982, oil prices began to weaken somewhat and continued to do so until 1985. However, no one foresaw that prices would suddenly collapse from $27 per barrel in 1985 to less than $10 in 1986. Indonesia's merchandise exports, which averaged $22 billion per year from 1980 to 1984, collapsed to $17 billion per year from 1985 to 1987. Debt service payments as a percentage of exports rose from about 13 percent in 1980 to nearly 40 percent in 1986.

The practical necessity of increasing non-oil exports in order to service debt, maintain growth and sustain Indonesia's international credit standing lent *urgency* and *legitimacy* to proposals for deregulation of trade and investment. However, it is important to note that some reforms complementary to the major deregulation packages enacted between 1986 and 1989 had already been underway since 1983. These reforms were being implemented in response to structural problems that had been recognized previously. During the recession of 1982, these problems became more obvious, particularly the rising public debt and the over-dependence on oil as the key source of government revenue. Tax reforms were instituted in 1984 in order to expand the revenue base. A value-added tax (VAT) was introduced and coverage of the income tax was extended with improved tax administration. Another important prior action was the decision to hire the Swiss firm Societe Generale du Surveillance (SGS) to manage customs in replacement of the somewhat notorious Customs Service. This step had important psychological effects in demonstrating the government's determination to take resolute action.

A good early discussion of the reforms undertaken in the mid-1980s is available in Azis (1994) who provides also a very handy timeline of the key measures. The following steps to open the economy were taken in 1986: the implementation of the duty drawback scheme for exporters, the relaxation of investment regulations including a one-year tax exemption on imported equipment, relaxation of visa requirements, enhancement of access to domestic markets for foreign and export-oriented firms and allowing 95 percent foreign equity in export-oriented investments (May); a massive (31 percent) devaluation of the Rupiah (September); and reduced import licensing, shift from NTBs to tariffs and cuts in tariff levels (October).

Throughout the year efforts were also made to improve government implementation of development projects, including infrastructure vital to export-oriented firms.

In 1987 the pace of reform continued to be rapid: there were further reductions in import licensing (January and July); efforts to improve the system of textile quota allocation (July); deregulation of investment and capacity licensing (July); and capital market deregulation to permit foreigners to purchase stocks (December).

Reform efforts were concentrated in the final quarter of 1988: financial deregulation was accelerated by reduced reserve requirements, issuance of new licenses to domestic and joint-venture banks, stimulation for competition between private commercial and state banks, and easing of regulations for existing banks (October); further financial reforms, which included currency market reform (November) and deregulation of insurance and other financial services (December); important trade reforms, including the removal of import monopolies in steel and plastic and the deregulation of both inter-island and international shipping (November).

In 1989 the reform process focused on investment: a negative list replaced the "priority" list (May); plans for increasing efficiency of state enterprises through managerial reforms or privatization were announced (June); portfolio investment by foreign interests was deregulated allowing up to 49 percent equity in publicly listed non-bank companies; and specific steps to increase efficiency or move towards privatization were undertaken affecting almost 90 percent of state enterprises (November). In 1990 reforms again deregulated trade: non-tariff barriers were reduced and were replaced by tariffs, the number of import surcharges was reduced; pharmaceuticals and animal husbandry imports were deregulated (May); and privatization was given new momentum by the sale of up to 30 percent of the shares of three state cement firms.

The reform process entered a period of consolidation after 1990. This was in part because the response of the economy was so phenomenal in terms of growth that overheating and inflation re-emerged as principal concerns. That year prudential regulation of the banking system received priority attention. Efforts to build up the capital adequacy ratio to meet standards set by the Bank of International Settlements (BIS) accompanied tight monetary policy. There was continued implementation of cuts or elimination of some import surcharges. Controls on imports of soybeans and soy flour were loosened and a tariff and import surcharge instituted.

In 1992 further reductions in the incidence of NTBs were announced (July). Efforts continued to push banks to increase capital adequacy towards BIS standards. The negative investment list was shortened to 51 sectors. In 1993 deregulation packages were announced in June and October. In the June package NTBs were again reduced and replaced by tariffs and other indirect taxes. In particular, outright bans on imports of completely built-up (CBU) vehicles were replaced with tariffs, an import surcharge and a luxury tax. The negative investment list was further reduced from 51 to 34 sectors. The 35 percent import surcharge on soybean meal was eliminated and imports of wheat and wheat flour were also partially deregulated.

The October package sought to encourage investment by reducing tariff and import surcharges on six major categories of imported parts and machinery including steel products. Divestiture requirements for foreign investors were modestly reformed as well.

In direct response to the reforms, economic growth surged after 1987 and averaged 6.4 percent between 1986–1990. Average real GDP growth remained above 6 percent between 1990 and 1993. Another indicator of economic success was the response of exports to the reforms. Non-oil and gas exports grew on average by over 25 percent between 1986–1992. Manufactured exports grew by more than 30 percent per annum during this period. Investors also responded well to the reforms. The investment share of GDP averaged 25 percent from 1973–1985, while the average for 1986–1992 was 33 percent. Whether the efficiency of investment improved through greater private and foreign shares, as opposed to government shares, is an important question. The pattern of allocation of investment is one rough indicator of this. In manufacturing, investment increased most sharply in textiles and apparel, paper products and chemicals. The investments in textiles and apparel were associated with the boom in exports of these relatively labor-intensive products.

The remarkable performance of the Indonesian economy as a result of the implementation of the subsequent reforms makes a study of their content and sequencing particularly interesting. It is important to remind ourselves here that the bold moves to reform trade and investment policies were made nearly 15 years *after* macroeconomic stabilization had been achieved and maintained. During the period following 1982, the government had carried out spending cuts that included cancellation of large-scale capital projects, and had made efforts to enhance revenues through new income and value-added taxes. Low inflation and fiscal prudence (albeit with slower growth) made it that much easier to phase-in measures to promote investment in areas of strong potential for export expansion in manufacturing.[8]

DETERMINANTS OF REFORM PATTERNS AND SUCCESS

Certain historical and institutional factors were essential in determining the pattern and sequence of reforms in Indonesia since the mid-1960s. One such factor was a sense of "economic nationalism" that has been expressed in varying and increasingly sophisticated forms in the period since independence (Thee 1993). The presence of abundant natural resources, particularly petroleum, also had a strong influence on the pattern and sequence of reforms. The disastrous experience with hyperinflation, capital flight and social unrest in the mid-1960s is still another element that shaped the reform process. The hardship of the poor and low-income groups during this period is difficult to imagine now. Indeed, the notion that the government's legitimacy is derived largely from its ability to physically and economically "protect" the weaker elements of society was widespread.[9] Reducing the incidence of poverty and ensuring that the farmers, rural and urban laborers, and the middle classes receive a "fair" dividend from economic growth has been a key political economy issue confronting political leaders and bureaucrats.

The role of external, as opposed to internal or domestic, forces or interests in pushing forward reforms has been an intensely debated issue. In our view, there have been alternating periods in which external influences and events have outweighed domestic concerns, and vice versa. The major deregulations during the early years of the New Order government can be characterized as externally-driven reforms because of the focus of the policy-making process on external credit, investment and exports. The very success of stabilization and resumption of economic growth during that period required access to foreign goods and assistance. Further, successful direct appeals to donors and foreign investors was also paramount for restoring equilibrium in balance of payments.[10]

It has been suggested that the need for Indonesia to reestablish its international credit standing, particularly in conjunction with its renewed membership in the IMF, was a major stimulus behind the government's decision to completely open the capital account in 1972. This major step towards reform was thus aimed at allowing Indonesia to resume its place within global institutions and the world economy.

In contrast, in the period following the first oil boom, attention of policy-makers shifted from external concerns to domestic ones. Hence, reforms became concentrated on building-up the agriculture sector and, in particular, on the goal of attaining self-sufficiency in rice through enhanced farm productivity. Note that the bad experience BULOG had in trying to procure rice during the early and mid-1970s harvest shortfalls (partly due to external events, but also due to miscalculations at BULOG) only reinforced the reorientation of policy-making to domestic concerns (Piggot et al. 1993)

As trade policies became increasingly inward looking, import substitution emerged as the principal industrial strategy. Inflation rates were quite high during most of this period, but began to moderate in the late 1970s. The mild externally oriented deregulations of the late 1970s occurred only after rice harvests improved and inflation was reduced to tolerable levels. The 1978 devaluation and the mild trade reforms (some reductions in tariffs and export taxes) were instituted after the Pertamina crisis in 1976–1977. However, the need to turn to a more externally oriented reform process was obviated by the second oil boom. Once again deregulation of trade and investment was halted, and industrial policy became inward looking with rice self-sufficiency and development of processing industries, especially plywood, assuming priority.

What was remarkable about Indonesian deregulation in the 1980s was that the momentum of reforms closely matched the seriousness of crises in the balance of payments. Limited real sector reforms in 1983–1985 gave way to more fundamental reforms during 1986–1989. Once again deregulation measures were instigated by external shocks (weakness of commodity prices, collapse of the oil market) and the compelling need to amass new sources of foreign exchange receipts in order to maintain credit standing in world financial markets. A strong response from foreign investors (foreign direct investment rose from $3.6 billion in 1986 to $16.2 billion in 1990) provided a resounding endorsement of the deregulation.[11] The sharp increase in private manufacturing investment, particularly by domestic investors, gave rise to huge increases in imports of capital and intermediate products. Moreover, imports of capital goods (with all transportation equipment excluded) rose from $2.3 billion in 1987 to $5.1 billion in 1990 and $6.7 billion in 1992.

Investment in sectors with comparative advantage was particularly strong: investment in textiles and wearing apparel showed the greatest advances in the period immediately following deregulation. This investment, in turn, resulted in a boom in manufactured exports that lasted from 1988 to 1993. The boom in investment, exports and growth resulted in some overheating and inflation that led policymakers to tighten monetary and fiscal policies beginning in the third quarter of 1991.

In the period following 1990, when oil prices again rose sharply, the momentum of deregulation again weakened and domestic concerns returned to the forefront of the policy environment. In 1991 and 1992, when relatively mild reform packages were announced, problems arose in the domestic banking sector. As short-term debt increased sharply between 1989 and 1991, the government sought to curb off-shore borrowing by both private and state owned enterprises and stepped-up prudential regulation of commercial banks.

In 1993 external factors once more came to command increasing attention. The passage of NAFTA and the successful conclusion of the Uruguay Round Agreement placed pressure on Indonesia to respond to external changes. Moreover, the plunge in oil prices and the decreasing net petroleum exports resulting from flat production and rising domestic consumption increased the importance of non-oil and gas exports and non-oil tax revenues.

Reasons for Success with Reforms

An important reason for Indonesia's success with reforms prior to 1997 was the practice of *sound macroeconomic management* that resulted in low inflation and a competitive exchange rate for the most part. The success in Indonesia is in marked contrast to failures in Latin America, where reforms were overwhelmed by destabilizing capital flows and high fiscal deficits. The government was able to steer clear of the main symptoms of "Dutch Disease" in the 1970s and beyond by avoiding prolonged periods of overvaluation of the Rupiah. A flexible exchange rate policy bolstered business competitiveness in tradables and helped offset the adverse impacts of domestic protection. Further, self-sufficiency in rice production through technological advances, substantial public investments and human capital formation were other key components of success.

The *widespread beneficial effects of deregulation policies* followed since the mid-1980s helped build public support for reforms as well. For example, employment induced by manufactured exports rose sharply to about 8 percent of total employment in 1989 from 3 percent of total labor employed in 1983. Such employment growth made it easier for the pro-reform group in government to win their battles with those who favored continued restrictions on trade, investment and financial policies.

The availability of a *skilled team of economic technocrats* who were often placed in influential positions of government and who pushed for deregulation in the mid-1980s certainly helped. Most often, the team of technocrats evaluated the options and arrived at a common, coherent view on the next steps in policy reform.

They demonstrated a *flexible and pragmatic approach* to policy reform, implementing change when necessary (such as with the major reform package adopted in response to the drop in the oil price) and correcting for errors in policy direction (such as the exchange rate) in a flexible and timely manner. Though special interests, especially those linked to the president's family, were also able to influence policy decisions and rules in their favor, the degree to which this occurred did not seriously and systematically compromise macroeconomic management and overall growth prior to 1997–1998. However, in the crisis of 1997–1998, there was a spectacular backlash against the Suharto government and its cronies that did collateral damage as well to the technocrats.

The *strong government commitment* to the development of agriculture, the allocation of sufficient budgetary and human resources to extend primary education throughout the countryside and on-going programs aimed at boosting health and family-planning all provided a fundamental basis for success when the reforms to open the economy began in earnest. *Getting the fundamentals right* during the past quarter century facilitated a strong supply response to incentives through technological innovations in agriculture, the exchange rate and, later, through the reforms of trade and investment.

All of the above combined to provide a high degree of *credibility* to the Indonesian reform effort, a factor that probably made all the difference between success and failure.

NOTES

1.   In an inflationary context this question becomes more complicated. Several authors have pointed out that the domestic financial market can only be deregulated if and when the fiscal deficit has been brought under control. This is because the existence of a large fiscal deficit must be financed by an inflation tax so that reserve requirements on banks can be kept high and interest payments kept low. Only by achieving this can the government continue to collect the same amount of "inflation tax." However, if reforms are sequenced such that the stabilization process is successfully carried out first then both the fiscal deficit and domestic inflation should already be under control.

2.   This view is not shared by all economists. In fact, Krueger (1984) has espoused the opposite view, suggesting that developing countries need access to considerable amounts of capital during the reform process, and that reliance on foreign funds will reduce the frictions that may emerge during major structural reforms. This analysis is based on the notion that adjustment costs associated with reforms will be lessened by increased availability of foreign funds. Therefore, logically, restrictions on capital imports should be lifted before trade reform is implemented.

3.   Frenkel (1982) states that second best considerations imply that it is preferable to deregulate the trade account before the capital account because the

degree of distortions involved will be much lower, and therefore so will be the welfare-reducing impact on the economy.

4.   Domestic private firms lodged complaints after the new foreign investment law of 1967 gave incentives to foreign private investors. Subsequently, in 1968, a domestic investment law was adopted giving similar incentives to domestic firms (Pitt 1986).

5.   These data exclude petroleum and banking investments.

6.   This assured plywood mills (which were often owned by forest concessionaires) a cheap supply of raw timber. Unfortunately, the ban led to gross inefficiencies and high volumes of wastage. It was not until 1988 that export receipts in plywood caught up with the dollar value of log and sawn timber exports of 1979.

7.   The development of natural gas itself was a major change. However, for much of the period in question gas was simply flared and gas finds were considered "dry holes" unless crude oil was also present. Development of gas exports required large investments and foreign technology to produce liquefied natural gas (LNG) for East Asian markets.

8.   It was repeatedly pointed out to the government of Indonesia that its great potential as an exporter of labor-intensive manufactures and non-oil natural-resource based products could not be realized under its highly protectionist trade policies and restrictive investment regulations until the mid-1980s. See for example Ariff and Hill (1985).

9.   Evidence to support this point can also be seen in the increasing discussions of labor conditions which reflected this concern. The level and intensity of labor action in 1993 and 1994 certainly contributed to the government's decision to substantially increase minimum wages in Jakarta and West Java, where most industry is concentrated. See Azis (1994) and Manning (1993).

10.   Sachs (1987) emphasizes the role of debt-forgiveness by foreign donors as giving a crucial support to stabilization in a manner that permitted resumption of growth. Implicitly, this debt-forgiveness was in response to reform measures such as "denationalization" of firms, openness to foreign investment and devaluation.

11.   The timing of the foreign investment deregulation couldn't have been better. Indonesia was able to "catch the wave" of booming investments from East Asia in the latter half of the 1980s. Data on the stock of FDI is based on summing inflows recorded in the balance of payments statistics as reported in Ramstetter (1992). Figures of realized foreign investment reported by BKPM (the Board of Investment) are a good deal higher than those estimated from the balance of payments, but both series show a substantial increase.

REFERENCES

Ariff, Mohammed and Hal Hill (1985), *Export Oriented Industrialization: The ASEAN Experience* (Sydney: Allen and Unwin Publishers).

Arndt W. Heinz and R.M. Sundrum (1984), "Devaluation and Inflation: The 1978 Experience" *Bulletin of Indonesian Economic Studies,* April, pp. 83–97.

Azis, Iwan J. (1994), "Indonesia" in John Williamson, (ed.), *The Political Economy of Policy Reform,* (Washington, DC: Institute for International Economics), pp. 385–416.

Balassa, Bela (1982), "Structural Adjustment Policies in Developing Economies" *World Development,* 10, pp. 23–38.

Bhagwati, Jagdish (1978), Foreign Exchange Regimes and Economic Development: Anatomy and Consequences of Exchange Control Regimes (Cambridge, MA: Ballinger Press).

Edwards, Sebastian (1989), *On the Sequencing of Structural Reforms* (Washington, DC: National Bureau of Economic Research, Working Paper No. 3137).

Edwards, Sebastian (1984), *The Order of Deregulation of the External Sector in Developing Countries* (Princeton, NJ: Princeton University Press, Essays in International Finance No. 156).

Edwards, Sebastian (1990), "The Sequencing of Economic Reform: Analytical Issues and Lessons from Latin American Experiences" *The World Economy,* 13 (1), pp. 1–15.

Frenkel, Jacob (1982), "The Order of Economic Deregulation: A Comment" in Karl Brumier and Alan Meltzer, (eds.), *Economic Policy in a World of Change,* (Amsterdam, The Netherlands: North Holland Publishers).

Frenkel, Jacob (1983), "Panel Discussion on the Southern Cone" *IMF Staff Papers,* 30 (1).

Krueger, Anne O. (1984), "Problems of Deregulation" in Arnold C. Harberger (ed.) *World Economic Growth,* (San Francisco, CA: International Center for Economic Growth).

Little, Ian M.D., Tibor Scitovsky and Maurice Scott (1970), *Industry and Trade in Some Developing Countries* (Oxford, England: Oxford University Press).

Manning, Chris and Joan Hardjono (eds.) (1993), "Labor: Sharing in the Benefits of Growth?" *Indonesia Update 1993,* (Canberra, Australia: Australian National University, Department of Political and Social Change Monograph Number 20).

McKinnon, Ronald (1991), *The Order of Economic Deregulation* (Baltimore, MD: The Johns Hopkins University Press).

Michaely, Michael (1991), "The Lessons of Experience: An Overview" in G. Sheppard and C. Langoni (eds.) *Trade Reform: The Lessons from Eight Countries,* (San Francisco, CA: International Center For Economic Growth).

Michalopoulos, Constantine (1987), "World Bank Programs for Adjustment and Growth" in V. Corbo, M. Goldstein and M. Khan (eds.) *Growth-Oriented Adjustment Programs,* (Washington, DC: IMF and World Bank), pp. 15–63.

Piggot, R.R., K.A. Parton, E.M. Treadgold and B. Hutabarat (1993), *Food Price Policy in Indonesia* (Canberra, Australia: Australian Centre for International Agricultural Research).

Pitt, Mark (1986), "Indonesia" in A. Choski and D. Papageorgiou, (eds.) *Economic Liberalization in Developing Countries* (Oxford, England: Basil Blackwell Publishers), pp. 6–196.

Ramstetter, Eric D. (1992), Foreign Direct Investment and Manufactured Exports from Developing Economies (Geneva, Switzerland: UNCTAD).

Sachs, Jeffrey (1987), "Trade and Exchange Rate Policies in Growth-Oriented Adjustment Programs" in V. Corbo, M. Goldstein, and M. Khan (eds.) *Growth-Oriented Adjustment Programs,* (Washington, DC: International Monetary Fund and The World Bank), pp. 291–325.

Thee Kian Wie (1993), "Reflections on Indonesia's Rising Industrial Nationalism" Paper prepared for the Conference on Indonesia: Contending Paradigms for the Future, Murdoch University, Fremantle, Australia, July.

Timmer, C. Peter and Walter P. Falcon (1975), "The Political Economy of Rice Production and Trade in Asia" in Lloyd G. Reynolds (ed.) *Agriculture in Economic Development,* (New Haven, CT: Yale University Press), pp. 373–410.

Timmer, C. Peter, Walter P. Falcon and Scott Pearson (1983), *Food Policy Analysis,* (Baltimore, MD: The Johns Hopkins University Press).

Williamson, John (1991), "On Liberalizing the Capital Account" *Finance and the International Economy,* edited by Richard O'Brien, AMEX Bank Review Prize Essays, (Oxford, England: Oxford University Press).

Williamson, John (1994a), "In Search of a Manual for Technopols" in J. Williamson, (ed.) *The Political Economy of Policy Reform,* (Washington, DC: Institute for International Economics).

Williamson, John (1994b), *The Political Economy of Policy Reform* (Washington, DC: Institute for International Economics).

World Bank (1987), *World Development Report 1987* (New York, NY: Oxford University Press).

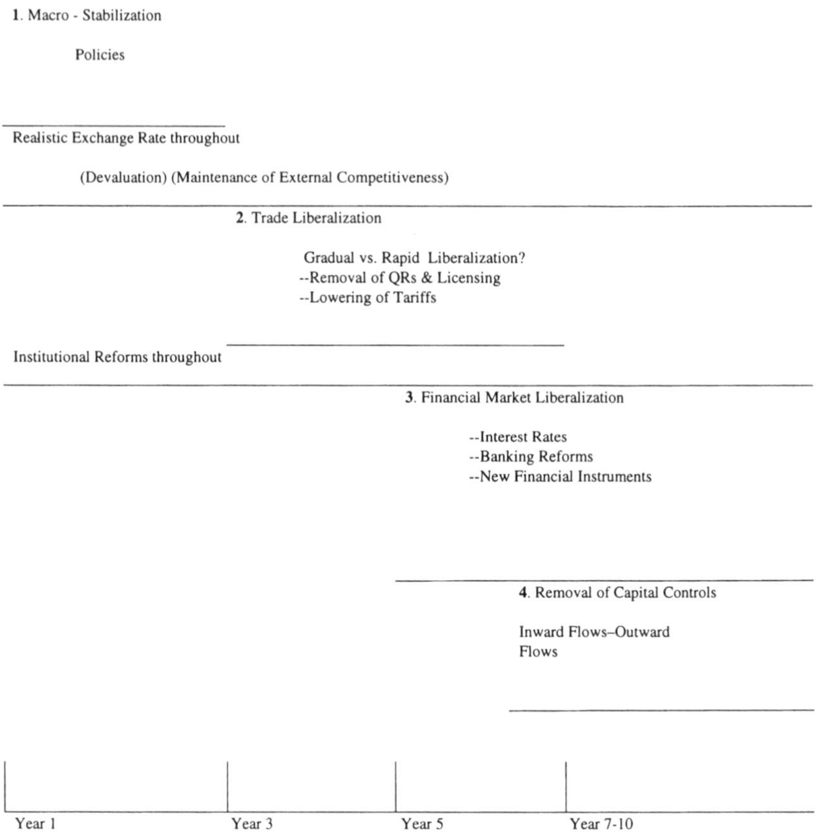

1. Macro - Stabilization

    Policies

Realistic Exchange Rate throughout

    (Devaluation) (Maintenance of External Competitiveness)

2. Trade Liberalization

    Gradual vs. Rapid Liberalization?
    --Removal of QRs & Licensing
    --Lowering of Tariffs

Institutional Reforms throughout

3. Financial Market Liberalization

    --Interest Rates
    --Banking Reforms
    --New Financial Instruments

4. Removal of Capital Controls

    Inward Flows–Outward
    Flows

| Year 1 | Year 3 | Year 5 | Year 7-10 |

FIGURE 2.1. CONVENTIONAL SEQUENCING OF ECONOMIC REFORMS

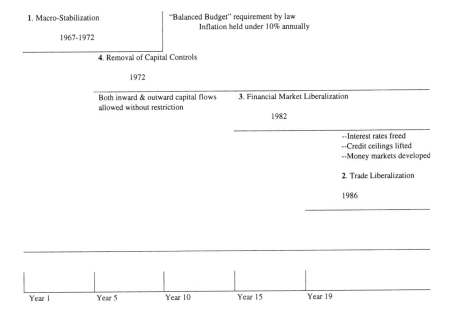

FIGURE 2.2. INDONESIA'S SEQUENCING OF ECONOMIC REFORMS

CHAPTER 3

Foreign Investment Policy: Evolution and Characteristics

Mari Pangestu

This chapter reviews the evolution and salient characteristics of direct foreign investment (DFI) in Indonesia in the three decades of the New Order government of President Suharto (1967–1998). In terms of evolution, DFI policy exhibited an early liberalization period till about 1970, followed by a sometimes ambivalent but mostly restrictive period till about 1985, and culminating in a significantly more open and receptive period after 1985. The focus of this chapter is on the last-mentioned period that featured some dramatic changes in policy and witnessed an equally dramatic surge in foreign investment and exports.

At the outset, a clear definition and understanding of DFI is desirable. Such investment is distinguished from portfolio investment in that it involves an equity stake which allows for influence over management.[1] DFI differs from other forms of foreign capital inflows in that it not only brings capital, but also technology, access to international markets, and management and marketing capabilities. It is sometimes accompanied by foreign borrowing (offshore financing) but domestic borrowing is also common.[2] The discussion below focuses on DFI in the manufacturing and services sectors that are approved through the Board of Investment. DFI in the oil and gas and financial services sectors is not included since these sectors are covered by different regulations and approval processes.

EVOLUTION OF FOREIGN INVESTMENT POLICY: 1967–1997

Foreign investment policy typically covers government policy over ownership and sectoral restrictions, performance requirements that DFI must fulfil, and incentives provided. The Indonesian government's dilemma of choosing between state and market orientation is reflected in foreign investment policy stances that swung from liberalization to restriction and back again depending on such considerations as the flow of oil revenues and the relative availability of foreign capital. When oil revenues were high or foreign capital plentiful, the policy stance was one of indifference at best. In other periods, when oil revenues were low and the supply of foreign investment restrained the policy stance typically shifted to greater receptivity to DFI. The rise and fall of nationalist sentiments also influenced the direction of DFI policy.

Liberalization in the Early Years: 1967–1970

In the wake of the hyperinflation and low business confidence that characterized the end of the Sukarno era in the mid-1960s, the New Order government moved early and decisively to restore macroeconomic stability and alter the orientation of the economy from state control to reliance on market forces. In parallel with macroeconomic stabilization and sweeping changes in the trade and incentive regimes, a more favorable stance was adopted towards private investment. Some nationalized enterprises were returned to previous owners, and a new law concerning foreign investment (Law no. 1, 1967) was instituted. This law provided a 30-year guarantee of non-nationalization and compensation. It also provided a wide range of incentives in the form of reduced or no taxes in priority areas, such as a two-year tax holiday and exemption of import duties and sales taxes for capital goods. Initially there were no restrictions on foreign ownership, although the wording of the law and implementing regulations made it clear that this was a temporary situation until such time domestic investments could fulfil the need. The spirit of the new investment laws, including a separate law for domestic investment, reflected the perennial dilemma faced by policy makers in Indonesia and developing countries in general, that is, the competitive pressure to obtain capital, technology and access to international markets to accelerate economic development on the one hand, and the threat of foreign domination of the domestic market on the other.

Despite the fact that the processing of investment licenses was quite complex at the time, as a result of the "open door" policy on foreign investment, 22 PMA (*Penanaman Modal Asing*—foreign investment company) owned projects were approved in 1967. By 1970, 177 PMA projects were approved, of which 37 were completely foreign owned (Hill 1988).

Restrictions, Liberalization and More Restrictions: 1970–1985

The closure of sectors to foreign investment began in the early 1970s. A growing number of sectors were considered closed to foreign investors based on the following criteria:

1. domestic entrepreneurs are deemed capable to undertake the activity;

2. activity is targeted for pioneering development of state enterprises because of its strategic nature; and

3. activity is targeted for small domestic entrepreneurs.

The main regulatory instrument during this period was the annual "Priority List of Investments" *(Daftar Skala Prioritas,* DSP) put out by the Board of Investment. The DSP had the advantage of making investment approval more transparent. Before the DSP investors had little idea of which sectors the government was promoting and which sectors were being reserved for domestic entrepreneurs (Hill 1988).

Nevertheless, there were many problems with the list. It was not sufficiently comprehensive, and the product definitions were not precise enough to clarify which sectors were open to foreign investment. Furthermore, the DSP list also regulated the production capacity and the number of licenses given were based on this. There were also no clear or consistent criteria to determine whether a sector should be open or closed to DFI, or to accurately calculate existing demand or capacity.

The second oil price increase in 1979, and thus the increase in the availability of foreign exchange revenues, ushered in another wave of restrictions on foreign investment. High economic growth and revival of foreign investor interest also meant that the government's concern about improving the investment climate declined. For instance, in 1981 there was a reiteration of divestment requirements along with moves to implement phase down requirements.[3]

In the early 1980s, Indonesia began to experience capital shortages due to the fall of oil and commodity prices. During the first adjustment period (1982–1985), appropriate macroeconomic stabilization measures, structural and resource mobilization reforms (e.g., tax and financial sector reforms), and measures to improve efficiency in customs, ports and shipping were undertaken. However, as discussed elsewhere (Bhattacharya and Pangestu 1993), trade and industrial policies became even more inward-oriented and subject to government intervention. Various import monopolies were introduced and domestic localization policies increased. Foreign investment policies also became more restrictive.

From 1980 onwards, more sectors were closed to foreign investors. The 1981 DSP included certain sectors that were reserved exclusively for "co-operatives." Industrial policy became increasingly protectionist and various local content programs were introduced especially in the automotive, machinery and electronics sectors. As a result, export-oriented investments were discouraged. At the same time, some supportive measures were also undertaken. The Board of Investment was made a one-stop service center, that is, the Board would facilitate the processing of all other related licenses for approval. While the one stop service constituted an improvement, in comparison with other countries Indonesia's approval process remained longer and more costly. For example, all approvals needed to be signed by the president.

The ambivalence in the investment climate facing foreign investors created by restrictions on full foreign ownership, divestment requirements, and lengthy approval procedures, affected investment adversely. The peak of the deterioration came with the closure of two large U.S. multinationals, Fairchild and National Semiconductor in 1985 and early 1986 respectively. The closure of these two plants was related not only to the worldwide slump in the electronics industry, but also the lack of government support and the deterioration in the incentive system.

Liberalization Renewed: 1986–1989

In 1986 the economy again suffered a series of external shocks due to a sharp fall in oil prices and an appreciation of the Japanese yen. Again appropriate macroeconomic stabilization measures (e.g., fiscal austerity and devaluation) as well as substantial real and financial sector reforms were undertaken. This liberalization was linked with efforts to promote non-oil exports and encourage private sector participation in the economy as part of efforts to diversify the dependence of the economy away from oil and government led growth.

The first set of deregulations were introduced in May 1986 with the objective of promoting export-oriented investments, investments in eastern Indonesia, and those in the capital market. First, the 20 percent minimum Indonesian shareholding requirement was relaxed to 5 percent for PMA projects that were "high risk" ventures, were located in remote areas (e.g., eastern Indonesia), that involved high technology, were export-oriented (i.e., exported 85 percent of their production), or required large capital expenditures (i.e., project costs above $10 million). The requirement to divest to Indonesian ownership for such projects remained 20 percent in five years and 51 percent in 10 years.

Second, it was confirmed that the license of joint ventures would remain valid for 30 years, and can be extended another 30 years if the PMAs increased their capital due to expansion or diversification. This cleared up some confusion and reassured foreign investors who were interested in re-investing in Indonesia on a minority partnership basis. Third, a PMA could now also obtain national treatment if it was at least 75 percent Indonesian owned (state and/or private), or if 51 percent of its shares were traded in the capital market, or if it was 51% Indonesian owned and if at least 20 percent of its shares were traded in the capital market. National treatment implies that a PMA can obtain the same incentives as an Indonesian venture. Some of these incentives include the subsidized export credit scheme, and lending from the state banks. However, it was clearly stated that national treatment does not change the PMA status of the company concerned.

Fourth, the definition of export oriented was changed from 100 percent to 85 percent of products exported. This definition was important as export oriented PMAs could enter into sectors deemed closed by the DSP, and obtain duty drawback facilities for their imported inputs used in export production. Allowing some sales in the domestic market was thought to provide flexibility to export oriented companies to overcome canceled exports and surplus inventories, and make it attractive for export oriented PMA companies who have Indonesian partners or who have a long-term plan to sell in the domestic market.

More deregulation was undertaken in December 1987. This time the conditions under which national treatment was accorded to PMAs was further relaxed to 51 percent (down from 75 percent) Indonesian owned, or 45 percent (down from 51 percent) Indonesian owned provided that 20 percent of its shares were sold in the capital market. Also, significant changes were made with regard to ownership and divestment regulations. The minimum Indonesian ownership at the time of formation of the company was lowered to 5 percent for PMA companies that exported 100 percent of their production with no further obligation to divest to Indonesian ownership. The general phase down requirement to 51 percent was extended from 10 years to 15 years. Furthermore, PMA companies with a minimum capital of $10 million or located in one of the provinces in East Indonesia or exporting at least 65 percent of their production could also be formed with a 5 percent minimum Indonesian share holding. Unlike the 100 percent export-oriented PMAs, there was a phase down requirement to 20 percent within 10 years and 51 percent in 15 years for these types of PMAs. There was also an indication of the flexibility with which the Board of Investment viewed the phase down requirements. The Board stated that it maintained the authority to extend the phase down requirements by another 5 years. The minimum capital investment needed for PMA companies was lowered to $250,000 based on employment creation, export production, support to the big industry, and non-competition with existing industries. Finally some trading activities were permitted for PMA, mainly related to the purchase of items required for production, exporting their own products, and purchasing and exporting products of other Indonesian companies.

In 1989 there was a liberalization of foreign ownership restrictions in certain areas. Full foreign ownership was allowed in the Batam Economic Zone with only a 5 percent divestment to Indonesian share holding in five years, and no further divestment requirement if the PMA exported 100 percent of its products. This was considered as a "trial balloon" for further liberalization of foreign ownership restrictions.

Over the 1985–1988 period, the DSP list was also significantly overhauled and became more transparent. First, the number of activities open to PMA was greatly expanded. In the 1986 DSP list the number of fields designated open to foreign investment was increased from 475 to 926. Some of the sectors that were newly opened were housing, hotels and garment manufacturing. Other important areas in the manufacturing sector that were opened up (which previously were considered "strategic") were chemicals, metallurgical industries and machinery. The opening up of the large number of sectors to PMAs reflected a major change in the policy environment from one where large sectors of the economy were reserved for domestic companies to one where greater emphasis was placed on attracting foreign investment for capital, technology and business know-how. The sectors that remained closed were in sectors related to "national security" and in small-scale industries.

Moreover, the previous imprecision in product definition in the DSP was removed by listing products according to ISIC categories. Investors could now turn to the ISIC code for more precise guidelines. Finally, the list no longer specified the production capacities or number of licenses that are allowed for investment.

There were also three additional measures introduced concurrently with the 1987 DSP list. First, to encourage modernization and restructuring, existing producers could expand up to 30 percent of their original capacity even if such activities were not listed as "open" in the DSP. Second, producers were also allowed to diversify into the production of "related items," where such production did not involve new capacity investment. Third, PMA companies could now invest their profits and other funds in new or existing domestic companies that could thereby obtain PMA status. The last measure increased the flexibility with which domestic companies could seek an "injection" of funds (e.g., through foreign institutional investors).

The most significant change during this time was the recognition that the last three categories of the DSP would function as a "negative list" for PMAs. Indeed, in May 1989 the DSP was replaced by a negative list. In principle, any sector not on the negative list was deemed "open" for PMA companies. The original negative list had 64 sectors closed for foreign investment (although some of these continued to be open under certain conditions such as export-orientation).

Liberalization Sustained: 1990–1997

After significant forward movement for three years, foreign investment liberalization efforts experienced a lull in the 1989–1992 period as the number of inquiries and project approvals increased. The economy was also booming with an average growth rate of 7 percent in 1989–1991. The rapid growth, the resulting high inflation (close to 10 percent per annum) and increased current account deficit necessitated macro stabilization measures. These measures included tight fiscal and monetary policies, as well as limits on foreign borrowing by state-related entities. A decline in foreign investor interest began around 1992, partly due to external factors such as the recession in Japan, Indonesia's largest investor and the diversion of funds to China, and partly due to a perceived decline in the investment climate in Indonesia. The government responded by introducing a number of facilitating measures.

A significant move came in the form of a 1992 decree whereby 100 percent foreign ownership was allowed for certain types of investment, and the requirement of divestment to Indonesian majority ownership was extended from 15 to 20 years. In addition, complete foreign ownership was allowed for PMAs with investments over $50 million, those located in eastern Indonesia and those located in a "bonded zone" with all of its production exported. The phase down requirement was also relaxed for these types of investments. For PMAs in the first two categories, the phase down requirements were 5 percent within five years and then 20 percent within 20 years. For those in the bonded zones, the phase down was 5 percent within five years and no further requirements thereafter.

The lower the minimum capital requirement on foreign investment of $250,000 was extended to labor-intensive operations defined to be employing more than 50 persons, export-oriented projects redefined to be exporting 65 percent of production, and supplier industries producing raw materials or intermediate goods. For such investments, the minimum Indonesian share holding was 5 percent with a phase down to 10 percent in 10 years and 51 percent in 20 years from the start of commercial production.

Under the October 1993 deregulation package, the authority to grant permits and licenses for land, building, operation and environment was moved from the state level to the regency (Dati II) level. While this decentralization and greater regional autonomy must be viewed positively and in line with the overall direction of government policy, care must be taken to evaluate whether the regions are in a position to process the regulations with efficiency and transparency. There remains a concern about the capabilities and training of officials at the district and regency levels to process complex regulations. As expected performance differs widely across the regional boards of investment.

A "big bang" in deregulation came in June 1994. Dramatic liberalization in sensitive areas concerning full foreign ownership and divestment of foreign ownership were undertaken. The push for deregulation appears to have come from increased competition for trade and investment in an increasingly competitive global environment. A deceleration in the growth of non-oil exports and a decline in foreign investment approvals in 1993 also provided impetus. In addition, international developments within the GATT (now WTO) and APEC influenced the thinking of policy makers. Finally, the policy makers were also responding to the strong reaction from the reversal in phase down requirements under the October 1993 package.

The 1994 changes were dramatic. First, new foreign investors (or existing ones) could now choose two alternatives in structuring their foreign investment: a joint venture with a maximum of 95 percent foreign ownership, or full foreign ownership. The full foreign ownership rule was more liberal compared to those of other countries in the region. The minimum capital requirement was also eliminated. Second, there was a substantial relaxation of the phase down requirement. For joint ventures set up with at least 5 percent Indonesian share holding, divestment of foreign shares was no longer mandatory. For companies set up with complete foreign ownership, divestment of some of the foreign shares was required after 15 years. The amount of divestment was not mandated.

Third, it was decided that the license for foreign investment (Article 18 in Law no. 1 of 1967) can be automatically renewed as long as it is perceived that the benefits to the economy and national development continue to persist. Fourthly, the government also clarified that foreign investments were no longer required to be located in designated Industrial Estates. Finally, the government officially opened up nine sectors previously deemed closed for foreign investment: ports; production and generation of electricity, telecommunications, shipping, air transport, drinking water, railways, atomic energy generation plants, and mass media.

The 1994 DFI package was complemented by a trade deregulation package in May 1995 that reduced the maximum import tax (tariff and surcharge) on vehicles to 200 percent and scheduled a reduction of the tariffs to 90 percent by 2003. This tariff cut would reduce vehicle prices and promote competitiveness in the domestic vehicle sector. For the first time, the government also announced a time schedule for tariff reductions for close to two thirds of tariff lines to reach 10 percent by 2003 The tariff reduction schedule was influenced by its commitments in AfTA. The 1995 package reduced the anti-trade bias by one-third (World Bank 1996), and together with the 1994 package went far in leveling the playing field for competition in Indonesia. Tariff reductions continued into 1996 leading to a fall in unweighted average tariff by nearly one percentage point to reach 14.2 percent.

As part of its commitment to the WTO in the area of Trade Related Investment Measures (TRMS), Indonesia also notified its local content policies which affected the automotive sector and milk production. However, the introduction of the national car program whereby P. T. Timor, a company owned by President Suharto's son, was the only company allowed duty free imports of inputs with the requirement that they would fulfill the local content requirements several years hence, became a major controversy. Indonesia was brought to the WTO Dispute Settlement panel by the major countries, and lost the case. By the deadline of January 1, 2000, Indonesia had eliminated local content requirements.

Policy Responses to the Recent Crisis (1998–1999)[4]

Indonesia was severely affected by the financial and economic crisis that began in the second half of 1997 due to a combination of vulnerabilities, policy missteps and institutional capacity weaknesses, further complicated by a serious political and social crisis. As a result, compared to other crisis-afflicted countered in the region, Indonesia experienced the largest economic contraction (14 percent in 1998), the slowest recovery, the highest real depreciation of the exchange rate, the worst banking crisis, significant deterioration in social conditions, and an ongoing crisis of confidence which persists despite a change of government. DFI is an important component of its recovery process but this time it will require more than just receptive DFI policies to revive much needed inflows.

Since Indonesia had already liberalized many restrictions prior to the crisis, the main policy responses concerning DFI consisted mainly of reducing the number of closed sectors. Only 16 sectors remain closed and 9 sectors are in public goods provision, which allows foreign ownership up to 95 percent. Restrictions on DFI in palm oil plantations, retail and wholesale trade have now been removed. Other policy changes with regard to DFI relate to allowing 100 percent foreign ownership in the banking sector (compared with maximum of 85 percent) and of listed shares (compared with 49 percent).

Under the IMF reform package, there was clear recognition that DFI policies alone will not attract DFI and a much wider policy response was needed to improve the overall competitive environment facing investors. The main reforms were in the areas of improving the legal and institutional framework, governance and competition policy. Indonesia has revised its Bankruptcy Law (April 1998), a law on Fair Competition (May 1999, implemented in 2000) and a fair trade commission, a new law on mergers, consolidation and acquisitions, corporate governance, and a program on legal reforms.

While policy reforms in response to the crisis have been comprehensive and progressive, Indonesia is still experiencing a net DFI outflow. There are a number of factors still seriously undermining investor confidence in Indonesia. They are inconsistent implementation of reforms, especially with institutional reforms such as the bankruptcy court; political instability and lack of security; and uncertainties with regard to implementation of the huge decentralization program whereby many policy areas, including investment will be conducted at the district level. The issue of nationalism has also reentered the debate as restructuring and sale of assets taken over by the government implies a redistribution of ownership, including foreign.

CHARACTERISTICS OF DIRECT FOREIGN INVESTMENT

Growth and Trends[5]

The Board of Investment (BKPM) provides data on approved foreign and domestic investment. In the early years of the Suharto government, foreign investment exceeded domestic investment approvals for a number of years. This was partly due to the large role played by the government as an investor in the years following the first oil boom, and the lack of substantial private resource mobilization. However, since the 1980s, approved domestic investment has tended to be much higher than foreign investment (Table 1), although the figures might be misleading since the realization of domestic investment is thought to be lower than foreign investment. Sectoral restriction was thought to lead to a rush for project submission because it was widely deemed that an approval might be worthwhile if the sector was closed by further restrictions.

The trends in DFI show a few periods of dramatic increase. In 1988 DFI approvals tripled to reach $4.4 billion; and then doubled again in 1990 to $8.8 billion.

The increase can be attributed to an increase in export oriented DFI in response to the improved investment climate and special incentives for exports. It can also be linked to the increased DFI outflows from Japan and other East Asian newly industrialized economies beginning in the mid 1980s as they experienced rising costs from the appreciation of their currencies. In 1992 DFI peaked again at $10 billion before declining in 1993 to $8.1 billion. The increase in approvals can be traced to the deregulation measures outlined above, while the fall was mainly due to diversification of investment funds to newly competitive China and a slowdown in fund inflows from major investors such as Japan.

Dramatic increases in DFI, as well as domestic investment approvals, occurred in the 1994–1997 period. The policy moves of 1994, the approval of a number of large projects in the chemical, paper and pulp and infrastructure sectors, and the boom experienced by Indonesia just prior to the crisis were the main explanatory factors. In 1994, DFI approvals almost tripled to $27.5 billion compared with 1992, and by 1995 had reached close to $40 billion before declining slightly to $30 billion in 1996. Even in 1997, since the financial crisis occurred in the latter half of 1997, approvals were still $33.8 billion.

The approved DFI data should be compared with the net DFI flow data from the balance of payments, which shows a much lower realized DFI number. The figures are net inflow figures and thus already factored in outflows for debt repayments and Indonesians investing abroad (which is a low number). The figures on net capital inflows show that prior to the deregulation in the mid-1980s, foreign capital flows mainly comprised of official foreign borrowing. Beginning in the late 1980s, private capital inflows comprising portfolio flows and DFI increased dramatically. This was due to the liberalization of both foreign investment and capital market regulations. The economic reforms and adjustments undertaken also created a better business environment for overall investment. From net DFI numbers, DFI peaked in 1996 at $6.2 billion compared with only $1-2 billion in the 1990-94 period. In 1997 DFI was still $4.7 billion, but has plummeted since then and Indonesia is still experiencing a net DFI outflow into 2000.

The major share of approved FDI went to the manufacturing sector and half of that amount went to the chemicals and pharmaceuticals sub sector, which can be expected given its oil and gas resources. Some of these large capital intensive projects were not realized or have been either down sized or postponed. The second largest recipient of approved DFI is the paper industry sector, also resource based. Other sub sectors that received DFI were food and beverages, and textiles. The latter has become increasingly export oriented with DFI playing a major role.

TABLE 1
TRENDS IN FDI APPROVAL AND NET CAPITAL FLOWS ($MILLIONS)

	Domestic Investment Approval	Foreign Investment Approval	Official Capital	FDI	Other Capital
1985	3,383	853	1,739	-308	-240
1986	3,438	848	3,074	-258	-1,033
1987	6,356	1,520	2,104	-385	-1,163
1988	8,423	4,411	1,965	-576	-169
1989	11,070	4,714	2,776	-682	-368
1990	30,662	8,751	633	1,092	3,021
1991	21,066	8,778	1,419	1,482	2,928
1992	14,454	10,323	1,112	1,777	3,582
1993	18,976	8,143	743	2,003	3,216
1994	24,625	27,353	307	2,108	1,593
1995	36,958	39,945	336	4,346	5,907
1996	30,013	29,929	-522	6,194	5,317
1997	18,772	33,833	2,880	4,677	-5,015
1998	9,337	13,563	9,762	-356	-12,651
1999	7,746	10,891	5,434	-2,778	-6,796
2000 (up to July)	1,553	6,087	1,286 (Q1)	-1,474	-477

Note: numbers for official, foreign direct investment (FDI) and other private capital flows are net flows.

Source: Domestic and Foreign Investment Approval from Board of Investment, and official capital, FDI and other capital from Bank Indonesia, Economic and Financial Statistics, various issues (Balance of Payments data).

Employment

The number of Indonesians working in approved foreign investment projects increased from 338,062 in 1985 to 2 million by 1995 (see Table 2). The sub-sectors that profited most in terms of employment were plantations, textiles, metal goods, chemicals and construction. The most labor-intensive investments were in the primary sector (except mining and fisheries) and manufacturing sectors: textiles, paper and pulp, food processing, and services; hotels, restaurants and construction. As for employment contributions by investing country, the main investors were Japan and the Asian NIEs. This is indicative of the more labor-intensive projects from these countries (especially South Korea and Hong Kong).

TABLE 2
EMPLOYMENT IN APPROVED FOREIGN INVESTMENT PROJECTS

	1967-1995			*1967-1985*		
	Workforce #	Workers/ Project	Value/no. workers ($000/ no. workers)	Workforce #	Workers/ Project	Value/no. workers ($000/ no. workers)
Primary	244,984	819	39	66,813	597	32
Secondary	1,563,268	738	43	233,577	517	49
Tertiary	226,522	268	111	37,672	267	38
Total	2,034,774	624	50	338,062	480	45

*up to January 1995

Source: Board of Investment (BKPM)

Exports

There are no published data that link realized exports and foreign investment. However, some evidence of the link between foreign investment and exports can be obtained from approved foreign investment data on export-oriented projects and data from the Survey of Industry (conducted by the Bureau of Statistics). Approved foreign investment became more export-oriented after 1985. In the 1967–1985 period, 56 percent of projects were export-oriented and by 1995, 64 percent were export-oriented. By 1995, the value of planned exports ($52 billion) from such projects was overshadowing the level of realized non-oil exports ($32 billion). Even if only 30 percent of the planned level were realized, about $15 billion worth of exports could be attributed to foreign investment. This is, of course, a very rough approximation. A high percentage of export-oriented products were in the fishery, food, textile, wood, paper, chemical, non-metal minerals, basic metal, and metal goods industries.

Countries that had a high percentage of export-oriented investment (over 70 percent) were Taiwan, South Korea, and West Germany. Other countries with high percentages (over 60 percent) were Japan, Switzerland, Hong Kong, and Singapore. However, the contribution to planned exports was dominated by Japan and the East Asian NIEs, with the United States and the United Kingdom accounting for slightly less than 10 percent of total contribution respectively.

Since 1990, the BPS *Survey of Industry* has asked firms to indicate what percentage of their production is exported and the results show that foreign firms are more export oriented (Table 3). In 1990 both domestic and foreign firms on average exported 17 percent of their production. By 1997 domestic firms exported only 23 percent of production compared with 32 percent for foreign firms. The more export oriented foreign firms also imported more inputs given the weak backward linkages of these export oriented firms. Foreign firms used more than double the imported inputs compared with domestic firms.

TABLE 3
COMPARISON OF EXPORT ORIENTATION OF DOMESTIC
AND FOREIGN FIRMS

SITC	% Output Exported Foreign			% Output Exported Domestic		
	90	93	97	90	93	97
311 Food Prod	4	14	46	12	19	24
312 Food Prod	8	34	17	21	14	7
313 Beverages	0	7	10	4	5	2
314 Tobacco	0	0	0	1	7	10
321 Textiles	19	36	26	15	16	19
322 Garments	58	81	43	39	45	31
323 Leather	11	28	80	46	36	15
324 Footwear	64	78	75	48	72	57
331 Wood Prod	55	61	72	46	54	51
332 Furniture	71	38	69	47	63	41
341 Paper Prod	20	23	19	6	18	15
342 Printing&Publ	0	22	0	2	4	3
351 Basic Chem	11	9	21	10	11	31
352 Other Chem	1	4	6	7	4	4
354	0	0	41	0	0	8
355 Rubber Prod	39	35	35	44	56	53
356 Plastics	10	23	33	9	11	17
361 Pottery&china	28	18	28	5	25	4
362 Glass Prod		4	6	6	37	30
363 Cement	0	0	2	12	5	5
364 Str.Clay Prod	0	40	0	1	1	16
369 Other Non Met	20	11	90	7	11	15
371 Basic Metals	2	35	20	11	13	9
372 Basic Metals	57	85	47	3	11	38
381 Metal Prod	18	35	23	3	5	8
382 Non Elec Mach	2	6	44	1	3	2
383 Elec Eqpt	25	51	38	8	17	14
384 Transp Eqpt	2	13	10	0	2	8
385 Prof Eqpt	2	28	69	13	9	57
390 Miscell	28	75	28	13	37	37

Source: Processed from Central Bureau of Statistics, Survey Industry

The sectors in which foreign investment contributed to a high percentage of exports were beverages (mainly beer); basic non-iron and steel metals; metal products, electrical equipment, and transportation equipment. The relocation of Korean and Taiwanese firms in the late 1980s and early 1990s have also contributed to the increase in exports of the textiles and garment firms. The relocation of these firms were motivated by rising costs in their own country, graduation of GSP and avoiding increased trade frictions with the major markets, especially the US. The role of foreign investment in emerging exports such as footwear and electronics has also been increasingly significant since the early 1990s and right up to the period before the crisis.

Performance of Foreign and Domestic Firms

Table 4 provides some indicators of performance between domestic and foreign firms. Foreign firms are much larger on average compared with domestic firms. In the early 1990s they were four times as large and by 1997 they were five times as large. A very rough picture of labor productivity is obtained based on value-added per worker. As can be expected, foreign firms on average have twice the labor productivity of domestic firms. However, over time, especially up to 1993, domestic firms were becoming increasingly productive and the differential with foreign firms was becoming less than twice. However, in the few years before the crisis, the trend reversed and foreign firms became increasingly productive again. One hypothesis for this trend is that domestic firms became increasingly domestic oriented whilst foreign firms became increasingly export oriented. Foreign firms also had a higher level of average wages compared with domestic firms, amounting to twice as much in most years. However, labor and capital intensity levels were about the same for both types of firms.

TABLE 4
COMPARISON OF PERFORMANCE BETWEEN FOREIGN AND DOMESTIC FIRMS (MANUFACTURING SECTOR ONLY)

Foreign

Yr.	Average Size	% Prod Exported	% Imp. Int. Input	Capacity Utilization	LP Rel.to Dom.Inv	% Non Prod Workers	Labor Intensity	Capital Intensity	Aver. Wage
90	451	17	53	67	248	20	15	85	3025
91	476	22	57	65	204	18	17	83	3134
92	524	35	57	64	187	17	18	82	3693
93	541	28	53	75	171	16	18	82	3843
94	578	32	51	75	184	15	17	83	4235
95	597	32	54	72	195	14	16	84	4864
96	581	35	52	76	198	15	15	85	5603
97	553	32	58	69	236	15	16	84	6278
Av.	538	29	55	70	203	16	16	84	4334

Domestic

Yr.	Average Size	% Prod Exported	% Imp. Int. Input	Capacity Utilization	LP Rel.to Dom Inv	% Non Prod Workers	Labour Intensity	Capital Intensity	Aver. Wage
90	149	17	24	70	100	18	19	81	1565
91	167	22	26	73	100	18	21	79	1903
92	169	22	24	70	100	18	22	78	2434
93	176	20	21	72	100	18	20	80	2495
94	176	24	24	74	100	18	19	81	2637
95	169	26	25	73	100	17	19	81	2903
96	158	26	24	76	100	18	18	82	3337
97	160	23	23	70	100	17	25	75	4091
Av.	166	22	24	72	100	18	20	80	2671

Source: Central Bureau of Statistics, Survey Industry

Given the higher export orientation as already noted, foreign firms had a higher proportion of their inputs which were imported or more than 50 percent and this was twice as much as domestic firms.

There are two possible explanations for the observed pattern of import-propensity. First, the foreign firms are part of an international production network, and when the parent company dominates the allocation of production and input selection, there would be a higher propensity to import inputs. Second, foreign firms export products of higher quality. This necessitates imported inputs since local inputs often do not meet international quality standards. Evidence from case studies suggests that both of these factors are at work in Indonesia.

CONCLUSIONS

Indonesia's DFI policies have shifted between being open and being more restrictive during the last three decades. These shifts have been linked to the availability of foreign exchange revenues from oil, exports in general and inflows of DFI. Since the mid-1980s, however, a more consistent policy direction can be observed in favor of greater receptivity to DFI. This stance, combined with deregulation in other areas, its potential large market, its comparative advantage in low cost labor and natural resources, made Indonesia an attractive destination for foreign investment. Right up to the recent crisis, the contribution of DFI to growth, exports and employment was increasing.

Indonesia has undergone a major economic, social and political crisis in the last few years and it is now still in the very early stages of a fragile recovery. In the short term DFI can certainly play a role in the recovery through contributing to exports, and providing much needed new investments, including taking over from distressed domestic firms and financial institutions to accelerate corporate and bank restructuring. DFI can also be beneficial in the medium term to facilitate market access, technological and human resource development that will be crucial to Indonesia's competitiveness in the global market. The current government has responded appropriately to the need to attract much needed new investment with a comprehensive policy reform package. The IMF led program includes the traditional response of removing remaining restrictions on DFI, but also recognizes the importance of other reforms. The comprehensive program of reforms includes structural reforms, competition policy, improving legal infrastructure, and corporate governance.

NOTES

1.   As a rule of thumb, a minimum of 10 percent ownership is deemed to lead to some control over management, and is used to distinguish between direct foreign investment and portfolio investment.

2. From the balance of payments perspective, the outflows associated with DFI are the dividends, repatriation of profits, interest payments and installments associated with the offshore borrowing, royalty, management, or technology license fees.

3. It was announced that for PMAs approved after February 1974, a 30 percent minimum Indonesian share holding must be reached by the end of 1981. It is not clear, however, whether this requirement was ever enforced. Further, for new PMAs a minimum of 20 percent Indonesian share holding requirement was put into effect.

4. See Pangestu (2000) for more discussion.

5. Data on DFI in Indonesia come from various sources. Approved investment data are available from the Board of Investment, the government agency that approves all foreign investment and domestic investment with facilities. Even though the data is only approved investments, the main advantage of this data is that one can get disaggregated information about sectoral breakdown, investor country origin, export-orientation, employment, and regional location. Estimated realized DFI can be obtained from Bank Indonesia data in the balance of payments which is based on their estimates of loans taken out by DFI. If one had access to the data, another way to estimate realized DFI would be through SGS since all duty free imports of machinery and equipment have to go through them.

REFERENCES

Bhattacharya, Amar and Mari Pangestu (1993) "Indonesia: Development Transformation Since 1965 and the Role of Public Policy" in D. Leipziger (ed.) *Lessons from East Asia,* Washington, DC: The World Bank.

Hill, Hal (1988) *Foreign Investment and Industrialization in Indonesia,* New York, NY: Oxford University Press.

Mari Pangestu (2000) The Potential Role of Foreign Direct Investment in Indonesia's Recovery, paper for the PAFTAD 26, *Globalization in the New Millennium,* Seoul, June 14–16, 2000.

CHAPTER 4

Deregulation and Total Factor Productivity: 1985–1992

Dipak Dasgupta, James Hanson,
and Edison Hulu

Theoretically, deregulation can improve the productivity of an economy through a number of channels. First, deregulation encourages resources to shift into more productive and internationally competitive sectors and out of protected and inefficient sectors. This "stock" effect is often missed in discussions of productivity gains focused on firms and "competitive" advantage, yet it remains at the heart of the matrix of gains from comparative advantage and international trade. Second, deregulation allows easier access to higher quality inputs, an effect which was an important source of productivity growth in Korea, for example (Feenstra et al. 1992). Third, deregulation encourages greater competition, by making it profitable to sell in the export market and necessary to face imports, rather that stagnate in a domestic, protected market. This forces firms to innovate to keep pace with the competition. Fourth, deregulation encourages foreign direct investment, which brings new techniques and management capacities. Fifth, financial deregulation, in particular, provides increased funds for smaller and more labor-intensive firms (see Harris et al. 1994), which allows them to expand and modernize.

All of these channels were evident in Indonesia during the deregulation of the mid-1980s. Therefore, it is reasonable to hypothesize that the total factor productivity (TFP) of the newly deregulated Indonesian economy would also increase. The rest of the paper examines the strength of this hypothesis. We find that TFP did indeed increase during the 1986–1992 deregulation period.

TOTAL FACTOR PRODUCTIVITY GROWTH: METHODOLOGY

To test for total factor productivity growth, this paper uses the now-standard "sources of growth" framework of Denison (1962), and Solow (1956, 1957). Under this approach, GDP growth is accounted for/attributed to growth in inputs and aggregate technical progress (aggregate improvements in total factor productivity).

More specifically, real GDP is assumed to be produced by factors of production such as capital and labor in a well-defined way—the so-called "aggregate production function." In its most popular "Cobb-Douglas" version, this function assumes that the ratio of the growth of GDP to the growth rate of each factor is constant.[1] It generates aggregate production which is linear in the logarithms of output and inputs. An additional restriction is often imposed: if all inputs are increased by the same proportion, then output would also increase by the same proportion.[2] This restriction makes the Cobb-Douglas a "constant returns to scale" function. In more complicated versions of the "production function" the relationship between the growth of each input and the growth of GDP is assumed to change in well-defined ways.

Aggregate technical progress, or an improvement in factor productivity, is also assumed to take place in well-defined ways. In the simplest version, total factor productivity is assumed to increase steadily, independently of the growth of the inputs. In more complicated versions, in addition to some overall growth of all the factors, each factor can be assumed to improve in productivity separately.

Some growth analysts have taken an additional step in trying to account for total factor productivity growth by relating it to improvements in the quality of the inputs. For labor inputs, wages may be taken to be a suitable measure of quality differences to the extent that they reflect the value that profit-maximizing firms assign in the labor market to various types of labor in the production of GDP.[3] Hence, an appropriate way to adjust for improvements in the quality of labor force is to weight the labor force data by the relative wages for each type of labor. For example, more educated laborers typically receive a higher wage, so if the number of educated laborers goes up faster than the labor force, then the average "quality" of the labor force would also improve.[4] A similar approach may be applied to different types of capital, but adjusting the capital stock for differences in quality requires substantial information on depreciation periods and the tax treatment of different types of capital goods.

TOTAL FACTOR PRODUCTIVITY GROWTH IN INDONESIA: DATA ISSUES

In order to estimate total factor productivity growth in Indonesia, we have to estimate real output (usually GDP), the capital stock, labor, and human capital. The rest of this section discusses the adjustments made in the standard Indonesian data. The data are presented in Table 4.1.

To begin, we have used *real GDP* data for the period 1978–1992 only. Data are available for earlier periods as well. However, the improvements in the national accounts estimates and the difficulties of reconciling two different bases (1973 and 1983) led us to use only the 1983 based data. We also checked our results by using a very rough estimate of a 1989 base GDP. In particular, we applied the real growth rates (in 1983 prices) of the 21 GDP sectors to the nominal sector-based GDP in 1989 and the results were similar to those reported below. As is well recognized, the real GDP has been somewhat underestimated after 1985 owing to underestimates of the fast growing industrial sector after deregulation. Moreover, real GDP growth might have also been underestimated due to more rapid construction of housing after the financial deregulation—the estimates of owner-occupied housing in the GDP accounts have grown much more slowly than construction. Adjusting the published GDP statistics for these underestimates would increase the estimated rate of technical progress/total factor productivity after deregulation. Despite this, we have chosen not to make any adjustments to the published GDP data.

TABLE 4.1
INDONESIA: GDP, CAPITAL LABOR, AND HUMAN CAPITAL INDICES, 1978–1992

Year	GDP 1983=100 (Rp. Billion)	Capital Stock/a 1983=100	Labor Adjusted (million)	Human Capital Indices
1978	58,133.0	162,990.8	51.68	1.000
1979	61,500.3	172,102.6	53.24	1.005
1980	66,722.7	183,648.9	57.51	1.011
1981	71,553.1	197,082.6	59.88	1.016
1982	71,360.7	211,437.2	61.51	1.022
1983	77,623.7	226,676.1	62.98	1.032
1984	83,037.4	240,439.0	65.09	1.042
1985	85,082.0	255,246.0	66.54	1.052
1986	90,080.5	271,562.8	68.37	1.061
1987	94,517.9	288,728.3	70.40	1.074
1988	99,981.5	308,154.6	72.37	1.079
1989	107,436.8	330,559.6	73.43	1.084
1990	115,216.5	356,679.9	75.85	1.104
1991	123,164.8	384,585.9	76.42	1.126
1992	130,909.0	415,145.2	78.52	1.128

/a Capital-Output ratio in 1985 = 3; and depreciation rates = 2%

Source: BPS and authors' estimates.

The *capital stock* was estimated using the now-standard "permanent inventory" method. Gross fixed investment, at constant 1983 prices, was then added to the base year capital stock figure. Depreciation was assumed to be constant. The gross fixed investment figures are the same as the national accounts figures, except for construction. In the case of construction investment, the national accounts figure for investment between 1978 and 1983 was slightly adjusted upward. This was done by adjusting the data on construction, using the ratio of construction output to GDP between 1984 and 1986, to maintain a constant ratio in the first part of the series. The base year capital stock was derived using a capital-output ratio of 3 to 1 in 1985.[5] The depreciation rates of 2 percent and 3 percent were used with the various base year capital stocks; 2 percent gave the most statistically significant results.

The *labor force* estimates were derived from SAKERNAS data. Estimation of the total labor force are made complicated by large variations of the numbers of mainly female unpaid household or agricultural labor in different surveys and censuses.[6] For paid workers and unpaid workers outside agriculture, SAKERNAS surveys were used directly with (logarithmic) interpolations for the years in which no surveys were done.

We also adjusted the reported number of household unpaid workers in agriculture. For this we assumed that data from 1976, 1986, and 1986–1992 were comparable. We then interpolated using a constant rate of decline in the ratio of unpaid workers in rice production and applied that to the estimated annual ratio to rice production. The resulting estimates of the labor force are shown in Table 1. The effect of this adjustment is to reduce the estimated growth in female and total employment. This effectively means that, compared to usual estimates, in our case more female workers in industry had previously been working as unpaid laborers in households or agriculture. In addition, we estimated the production function using only salaried workers.

The labor force data was adjusted for *human capital* changes. The estimated number of workers in each category of educational attainments (Table 4.2) was weighted by the wage in 1989 for each category (see McMahon and Boediono 1992). We assumed that the adjusted unpaid laborers had the same education distribution. Therefore wage acts as a weight in the SAKERNAS data for this group. The resulting total wage income each year (at 1989 relative wages) was then divided by the total number of workers to derive an index of human capital with 1989 weights. As noted above, the rationale for the human capital adjustment is that the wage differentials reflect the different productivity of each category of workers, owing to educational and experience differences.

ESTIMATES OF TOTAL FACTOR PRODUCTIVITY

Following Solow (1957), a simple Cobb-Douglas relationship was estimated for the period 1978–1992 to determine TFP growth. This formulation contained real GDP in 1983 prices, the labor force, adjusted for changes in education, and the real capital stock in 1983 prices. Although more sophisticated methods have been developed since Solow's path-breaking analysis, the small sample size and the construction of the variables make this simpler version more attractive for Indonesian data.

The estimated results are reasonable. GDP is found to be positively related to both inputs, with roughly constant returns to scale (technically, the sum of the estimated coefficients of adjusted labor and capital was very close to one). However,

Table 4.2
Indonesia: Number of Workers by Education, 1978–92 (Adjusted, Millions)

Year	No Schooling			No comp. Primary			Primary School			Junior High School			High School			Academy/University			Grand Total		
	M	F	Total	M	F	Total	M	F	Total	M	F	Total	M	F	Total	M	F	Total	M	F	Total
1978	6.96	8.20	15.16	12.39	4.77	17.16	9.17	2.76	11.93	2.75	0.77	3.52	2.28	1.04	3.32	0.44	0.15	0.59	33.98	17.70	51.68
1979	6.75	8.32	15.07	12.12	4.99	17.11	9.70	3.17	12.87	2.90	0.86	3.76	2.57	1.25	3.81	0.44	0.18	0.62	34.47	18.77	53.24
1980	6.76	9.01	15.77	12.22	5.59	17.81	10.58	3.89	14.48	3.16	1.03	4.18	2.99	1.59	4.58	0.46	0.23	0.68	36.18	21.33	57.51
1981	6.71	8.90	15.61	12.22	5.69	17.92	11.45	4.35	15.80	3.41	1.12	4.53	3.45	1.85	5.30	0.47	0.26	0.73	37.71	22.18	59.89
1982	6.49	8.77	15.26	11.91	5.80	17.71	12.07	4.86	16.93	3.58	1.22	4.80	3.88	2.15	6.03	0.47	0.30	0.78	38.41	23.10	61.51
1983	6.05	8.43	14.48	12.14	6.07	18.21	12.24	5.11	17.35	3.84	1.32	5.16	4.31	2.45	6.75	0.65	0.38	1.03	39.23	23.76	62.99
1984	5.70	8.08	13.78	12.52	6.32	18.84	12.55	5.36	17.91	4.16	1.42	5.58	4.83	2.78	7.60	0.90	0.48	1.38	40.65	24.44	65.09
1985	5.25	7.71	12.96	12.63	6.57	19.20	12.59	5.60	18.19	4.41	1.52	5.93	5.30	3.14	8.43	1.22	0.60	1.82	41.40	25.14	66.54
1986	4.45	6.64	11.09	10.38	6.65	17.03	14.72	7.64	22.36	5.00	2.03	7.03	5.55	3.50	9.05	1.34	0.46	1.81	41.44	26.92	68.36
1987	4.16	6.26	10.42	10.15	6.63	16.78	15.12	7.94	23.06	5.29	2.31	7.60	6.01	3.96	9.97	1.75	0.82	2.57	42.49	27.91	70.40
1988	3.98	5.88	9.86	9.84	6.29	16.12	15.60	8.98	24.58	5.64	2.53	8.18	6.75	4.16	10.91	1.73	0.99	2.72	43.54	28.83	72.37
1989	4.03	5.98	10.01	9.97	6.39	16.36	15.80	9.13	24.93	5.72	2.58	8.29	6.84	4.23	11.07	1.76	1.01	2.76	44.11	29.32	73.43
1990	3.79	5.43	9.22	9.61	6.20	15.81	17.10	8.97	26.07	6.45	2.71	9.15	7.56	5.00	12.56	1.91	1.13	3.04	46.43	29.42	75.85
1991	3.46	4.72	8.18	8.88	5.55	14.43	17.30	9.28	26.57	7.17	3.18	10.35	8.33	5.18	13.51	2.09	1.29	3.38	47.23	29.19	76.42
1992	3.47	4.81	8.28	9.27	5.83	15.09	17.26	9.31	26.57	7.24	3.24	10.48	8.66	5.78	14.45	2.26	1.39	3.65	48.17	30.35	78.52

M–Male; F – Female

Source: Authors' estimates, based on SAKERNAS.

the adjusted "labor" variable was not very significant in statistical terms (nor were the "labor" and the "labor quality index" separately). The estimated rate of technical progress over the whole period was not significant either.[7]

However, aggregate productivity growth after 1985 is statistically significant. The addition of a productivity growth term for 1985–1992 improves the rest of the estimated production function relationships a great deal, except that there still is no significant total factor productivity growth for the period 1978–1992. Dropping the (insignificant) total factor productivity growth term for 1978–1992 and assuming constant returns to scale, yields the following estimated production function:

(a)   GDP =   3.4 +   0.45 Capital +   0.55 labor   (Adj. for the market
                   (4.7)   (5.0)   (5.0)   value of education)

          +0.011 Annual Increase in TFP after 1985
          (2.4)

Note: R^2 (adjusted) = 0.971. Sum of Squared Residuals = 0.002583, Standard Error = 0.0147 where GDP, Capital and Labor (Adjusted) are in logarithms and the *t* statistics are expressed in parentheses below the coefficients.[8]

These results imply that Indonesian total factor productivity increased only after 1985, when the deregulation measures began. In particular, the 1979–1985 data suggests that there was no (statistically) significant increase in total factor productivity during that period—all of the growth in output can be reasonably explained by higher quantities of inputs.

According to equation (a), after 1985 GDP grew about 1.1 percentage point per year faster than can be explained by increases in physical capital, labor, and human capital. Thus, about 31 percent of the 3.8 percent annual growth in GDP per worker in 1986–1992 was directly due to higher productivity growth in the deregulation period. About 55 percent of this growth was due to additional capital per worker.[9] This, to some extent, was a result of higher investments during the deregulation period. Finally, about 14 percent was due to increased educational attainment of the labor force. As a result, the higher productivity after deregulation caused about 61 percent of the *increase* in the growth of GDP per worker.

These results make intuitive sense. Growth picked up after deregulation began in 1985, from 5.6 percent per annum during 1979–1985, to 6.4 percent per annum. The rate of investment also increased from 23.2 percent to 25.9 percent. However, the estimated growth of the labor force slowed after 1985 from 3.7 percent to 2.3 percent: as noted above, the substantial increase in paid labor, which is usually cited as rapid employment growth, reflects a shift from unpaid female labor in agriculture to paid labor in urban areas. And, although human capital grew somewhat faster, 1 percent per annum versus 0.7 percent per annum, the adjusted labor force growth declined after 1985. In sum, while GDP growth increased sharply after 1985, input growth increased very little. Therefore the higher output growth can only be explained by increases in total factor productivity after deregulation.[10]

A surprising result of this analysis is the low contribution of human capital increases to the growth in GDP per capita. Indonesia made a massive effort to broaden access to primary education, reflected in an average annual increase of 3.8 percent in the total years of schooling per capita between 1978 and 1992. However, the market value of that increase in schooling grew much less impressively—just under 1 percent per year. This difference reflects the low wage differential (less than 15 percent) that the labor market accords to primary graduates compared to workers without any schooling (information from the wage structure in 1989 and McMahon and Boediono 1992). In part, this low differential (in 1989) may reflect the large increase in the supply of workers with primary education, but it may also reflect differentials in learning achievements compared to the other East Asian countries (World Bank 1993).

Other recent analyses (Thomas and Wang 1993; World Bank 1993) suggest that in Indonesia total factor productivity growth accounted for smaller increases in per capita GDP growth than elsewhere in Asia. In part, this result may be due to an over-estimate of the growth of human capital in these studies through use of the "stock" value of the years of education, rather than the market value of education. Further, the inclusion of the estimate of Indonesia's residual inventory investment as part of "investment" creates upward biases in the estimation of physical capital growth. Both of these accounting processes would result in lower estimates of total factor productivity growth.[11]

CONCLUSION

Our total factor productivity analysis suggests that the post-1985 deregulation contributed to improved resource allocation and more rapid technical progress in the Indonesian economy. In addition, deregulation was associated with higher rates of gross fixed investment, which also contributed to faster growth.

NOTES

1.   This means that if there are two inputs (x and y) in the production process of widgets, and both of these inputs grow a rate z, then output of widgets (total product, or gross domestic product if widgets are the only products in the economy) would also grow at rate z.

2.   Returning to the previous example, if both x and y increase by a factor of m, then the production of widgets would also increase by a factor of m.

3.   This does not necessarily imply that worker's productivity is equal to their wage: if the proportionate differences between wages and productivity are equal across different classes of worker, only then will the relative wage will be an indicator of relative productivity.

4.   Standard labor force data is the simplest version of this—the weights of the different types of labor are the same.

5.   Base year capital stocks also were calculated using capital-output ratios of 2.0, 2.5, 3.5, 4.0, 4.5, and 5.0. Ratios 3 : 1 or 3.5 : 1 gave the most statistically significant results.

6.   See Korn (1992) and Oey-Gardiner (1993) for further discussions of this problem.

7.   Technically, there is a high degree of "collinearity" between the different variables, as is generally the case with this type of estimate. As noted above, generally the estimates based on capital-output ratios of 3 or 3.5 in 1985 with 2 percent depreciation rate gave the best fits. The estimated equation was:

(b)   GDP =   4.4 + 1.21 Capital + 0. 21 Labor (Adjusted for the market
                      (0.5)   (2.4)   (0.7)   value of education)

                      -0.032 Annual Increase in TFP
                      (0.8)

Note: R² (adjusted) = 0.995. Sum of Squared Residuals = 0.003310, Standard Error = 0.0173 where GDP, Capital and Labor (Adjusted) are in logarithms and the *t* statistics are expressed in parentheses below the coefficients. As noted, the "best" capital output-ratio was 3 (or 3.5) and the "best" depreciation rate was 2 percent. These results were considerably improved when a time-trend was added for the period after 1985.

8.   The sequential procedure to derive this equation was: first, the estimation of an equation using capital (capital-output ratio = 3, depreciation 2 percent), adjusted labor, a constant rate of technical progress in 1978–1985, and a constant rate of technical progress 1986–1992. In that equation, the coefficients of adjusted labor and the post-1985 time-trend were significant at the 10 percent level and capital at the 15 percent level, while the overall time-trend was negative and not significant. Jointly testing the hypothesis of constant returns to scale and a zero overall time trend, or testing sequentially the hypothesis of a zero time-trend and then constant returns to scale could not be rejected. The reported *t* statistics in equation (a) are for an estimate where the coefficients of capital and labor were forced to sum to one, that is, constant returns to scale. In that equation, the coefficients were 0.42 and 0.59 respectively, and both these estimates and the time-trend were significantly different from zero at the 90 percent level or above. The coefficients are robust: differentiating the data and re-running the regressions yields roughly the same coefficients, although the level of significance drops, as is usually the case.

9.   This is computed as the product of the (logarithmic) increase in capital per worker and the estimated output elasticity (0.45) of capital, divided by the (logarithmic) increase in output per worker.

10.   Note again that these results probably underestimate the increase in growth and productivity because they do not adjust for the underestimate of GDP growth in manufacturing and construction.

11.   Even with these low wage differentials, primary education has a high private rate of return. This is because primary age children do not work and the opportunity cost of attending school is essentially zero. The case is somewhat

different for junior secondary school age children who have to consider not only fees and earnings differentials, but also opportunity costs of lost casual earnings.

REFERENCES

Denison, E.F. (1962) *Sources of Economic Growth in the U.S. and Alternatives Before Us,* (New York, NY: Committee on Economic Development).

Feenstra, R.C. et al. (1992) "Accounting for Growth with New Inputs: Theory and Evidence," *American Economic Review,* 82 (2), (May), pp. 415–421.

Harris, John R., Fabio Schiantarelli, and Miranda G. Siregar (1994) "The Effect of Financial Liberalization on the Capital Structure and Investment Decisions of Indonesian Manufacturing Establishments," *World Bank Economic Review,* 8(1) (January), pp. 17–47.

Korn, Alex (1992) *Distinguishing Signal from Noise in Labor Force Data From Indonesia,* (Jakarta, Indonesia: Bappenas Development Project II, DAI).

McMahon, W.W. and Boediono (1992) *Education and the Economy: The External Efficiency of Education,* (Jakarta, Indonesia: The Ministry of Education and Culture).

Oey-Gardiner, Mayling (1993) *A Study of Women's Issues in Agricultural Transformation,* (Jakarta, Indonesia: Report for the World Bank).

Solow, Robert M. (1956) "A Contribution to the Theory of Economic Growth," *Quarterly Journal of Economics,* 70 (1), pp. 65–94.

Solow, Robert M. (1957) "Technical Change and the Aggregate Production Function," *Review Of Economic and Statistics,* 30 (3), pp. 312–320.

Thomas, Vinod, and Yan Wang (1993) *The Lessons of East Asia: Government Policy and Productivity: Is East Asia an Exception?* (Washington, DC: The World Bank).

World Bank (1993) *The East Asian Miracle: Economic Growth and Public Policy,* (Oxford, England: Oxford University Press).

CHAPTER 5

The Determinants of Indonesia's Non-Oil Exports

Dipak Dasgupta, Edison Hulu,
and Bejoy Das Gupta

INTRODUCTION

In the mid-1980s, Indonesia faced two large external shocks: a decline in the price of oil, its then principal export, and a large movement in exchange rates (i.e., the devaluation of the dollar vis-à-vis the yen) which increased its external debt. The country was then faced with the dual challenge of stabilization in the short-term and finding a new non-resource based engine for growth in the long-term. Indonesia met both challenges successfully. Among the most important factors in this was the expansion of non-oil exports.

Between 1985–86 and the crisis of 1997–98, the growth of non-oil exports was the foundation of Indonesia's success in macroeconomic stability, rapid economic and employment growth, rising productivity, and improved external creditworthiness. Indonesia's non-oil exports grew from about $5.9 billion in 1985, $26.6 billion in 1993—a nearly five-fold increase over 8 years. The share of non-oil exports went from about 30 percent to over 70 percent and oil and gas exports fell from $12 billion to $10 billion per annum.

The *composition* of non-oil exports also underwent dramatic change. Figure 1 shows the growth and diversification of non-oil exports between 1985–1993. The growth in the volume of exports also shows a *wave-like* pattern, as surging new exports captured previously untapped markets. In particular, the following trends emerged:

1. In 1985, much of non-oil exports originated from a *traditional* base of primary commodities and some manufactured products—rubber, coffee, tea, tin, aluminum, fertilizer, and others. These commodities together accounted for close to one-half of total non-oil exports or about $2.7 billion in 1985. But by 1993, their share in oil exports fell to about one-quarter, and in absolute terms, increased to only about $6.7 billion.

2. Two relatively new manufactured product groups—garments and textiles and plywood—grew more rapidly and became more prominent. These two broad categories accounted for about $1.7 billion (or 28 percent) of total exports in 1985. By 1993, the value of such exports had increased to about $11.3 billion (or 43 percent) of total exports.

3. Further, *diverse and new other manufactured and processed exports* such as footwear, furniture, handicrafts, processed food, palm oil, fisheries, electrical products, paper and paper products, and new mining products (copper and nickel)—grew at equally fast rates and resulted in a diverse export structure. These "other" products were worth $1.4 billion, or less than one-quarter of total non-oil exports in 1985. By 1993, their value had increased to $8.5 billion, or about one-third of non-oil exports.

The overall rate of recorded growth in non-oil exports in Indonesia was about 21 percent per annum, more than four times faster than world export growth. Indeed, Indonesia's non-oil export growth between 1980–1992 was higher still, about 30 percent per annum (Hill 1994), and was the fastest rate recorded among major countries.

By 1993, Indonesia had experienced a significant shift to non-oil exportables. The ratio of non-oil exports to GDP rose dramatically from 7 percent in 1985 to about 20 percent in 1993. How did Indonesia manage to sustain its non-oil export growth at such fast rates? What was the relative importance of world demand, as opposed to domestic supply factors? What role did large exchange rate devaluations of the 1980s play? How important were various price and non-price factors in sustaining exports? And how important were policy reforms such as the reduction of trade policy barriers, and the deregulation of foreign and domestic investment? These are some of the issues explored in this chapter.

Specifically, we attempt to quantitatively explain the determinants of Indonesia's non-oil export performance between 1985 and 1993. In the application to Indonesia, there are several relatively novel features in our analysis: (a) a separation of supply and demand factors, (b) a separation of the price and non-price factors, (c) a test for the importance of trade policies, (d) the utilization of quarterly data and associated variables, and (e) the use of "cointegration" techniques.

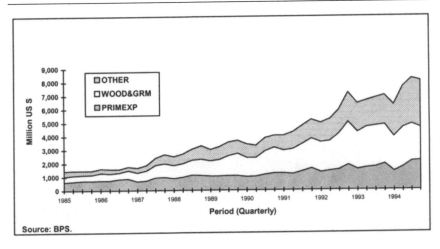

FIGURE 1. GROWTH AND COMPOSITION OF NON-OIL EXPORTS, 1985–1994

REVIEW OF THE EXISTING LITERATURE

The General Literature on Export Determinants

Early research on the determinants of export performance tended to focus heavily on world demand factors, with the supply of exports assumed to be highly elastic (Goldstein and Khan 1978). A country's export performance was likely to be good if the composition of exports was such as to face high income elasticities of demand and could penetrate markets with high incomes and high growth. If these factors held, then with even moderate world income growth, a country could export ever larger volumes without facing demand constraints.

For example, studies have shown that some industrial countries, notably Japan, have enjoyed high income elasticities of demand, in the range of 2.5–5.0 (i.e., a 1 percent change in world demand causes a 2.5 percent to 5.0 percent increase in demand for the country's exports). The studies have also found a high price elasticity of demand (estimates generally have a negative sign). Krugman (1989) has suggested that this phenomenon is attributable to Japan's ability to supply an ever more diverse range of manufactured products. Similarly, studies have sought to show that Korea, Taiwan, and Hong Kong, star-performers in exporting, have benefited by expanding their range of exports over time. Muscatelli, Srinivasan, and Vines (1992) estimated that Hong Kong's income elasticity of demand was 4.2. Still, it is clear that the "extreme small country" assumptions—that world demand does not matter—does not hold, except in a few empirical studies (Reidel 1988).

TABLE 1
NON-OIL EXPORTS, 1985–1993 (MILLIONS OF US$)

Year		Primary Commodities	Wood and Garment	Others	Total
1985	I	605.2	419.7	415.6	1440.5
	II	656.7	442.1	375.9	1474.7
	III	707.9	430.6	340.3	1478.8
	IV	700.8	451.7	322.3	1474.8
1986	I	720.5	575.9	325.7	1622.1
	II	724.3	523.1	330.5	1577.9
	III	821.1	493.3	262.4	1576.8
	IV	860.3	623.0	268.3	1751.6
1987	I	649.3	664.1	356.0	1669.4
	II	703.1	759.6	397.2	1859.9
	III	941.1	928.1	522.9	2392.1
	IV	971.9	999.8	685.5	2657.2
1988	I	884.0	964.7	654.5	2503.2
	II	971.6	1004.0	714.9	2690.5
	III	1125.7	1100.9	820.4	3047.0
	IV	1102.9	1192.5	1000.9	3296.3
1989	I	1058.3	1117.3	839.6	3015.2
	II	1053.8	1220.4	950.6	3224.8
	III	1084.9	1459.6	1009.2	3553.7
	IV	1076.1	1644.7	965.4	3686.2
1990	I	989.1	1418.5	996.7	3404.3
	II	1023.2	1368.2	910.9	3302.3
	III	1157.2	1732.8	970.3	3860.3
	IV	1247.0	1911.5	878.7	4037.2
1991	I	1250.8	1682.9	1093.4	4027.1
	II	1186.6	1840.5	1249.5	4276.6
	III	1383.5	2015.2	1350.9	4749.6
	IV	1601.2	2196.3	1394.3	5191.8
1992	I	1310.0	2217.7	1419.4	4947.1
	II	1412.2	2197.1	1622.8	5232.1
	III	1500.2	2652.1	1776.9	5929.2
	IV	1834.0	3174.1	2179.7	7187.8
1993	I	1511.3	2753.3	2114.3	6378.9
	II	1626.7	3002.8	1969.0	6598.5
	III	1686.7	3033.2	2067.1	6787.0
	IV	1907.5	2898.6	2174.8	6787.0
1994	I	1353.4	2558.3	2365.0	6276.7
	II	1662.3	2924.7	3002.3	7589.3
	III	2093.3	2752.6	3362.6	8154.5
	IV	2124.8	2754.6	3459.9	8339.3

Source: BPS.

Mody and Yilmaz (1994) suggest that demand functions for a country's exports may tend to systematically overestimate or underestimate actual exports because they ignore a strong country-specific *persistence* of exports. They show that for a pooled sample of 20 countries, from 1972 to 1985, there have been persistent (country-specific) undercounts or overcounts of export growth. In particular, for Indonesia and Turkey, the positive fixed rate effects (i.e., on a non-zero, country-specific dummy) were large. They attribute this to a process whereby buyers are attracted to sellers as exports increase and sellers become more reliable. While they cannot find a simple physical correlate, they use growth of telecommunications services as a proxy for this. They also provide indirect evidence to show that certain countries that have positive persistence effects (Group I countries). These differ from negative persistence effects countries in Group II countries, not because their price or income elasticities differ greatly (i.e., the composition of exports effect), but because during downturns in world demand, demand for Group II countries tend to fall sharply.

While the Mody and Yilmaz findings are interesting for cross-country comparisons, their findings could be stressing something else—that country-specific *supply* conditions (termed "reliability of exports," "diffusion effects of success in exporting," or "long-term contracting gains") matter. Indeed, they note country-specific fixed effects may be arising from the omission of adequate supply factors. To allow for the possibility of the simultaneous determination of export volumes and prices, a two-stage least squares (2SLS) procedure is used in the Mody and Yima paper, where the instruments are lagged exports, lagged relative export prices, lagged wages and world income, and lagged imports of capital goods. However, whether these add enough information on key supply factors is questionable.

A second strand of research became popular in the 1970s onwards, with emphasis on the modeling of the export supply response. Exports were supply-determined and export demand was not analyzed. As under small country assumptions, the price elasticity of world demand was assumed to be infinite, and world demand was assumed not to be a constraining factor. Generally, the higher the price elasticity of supply, and the higher the response to capacity, the better a country's export response. Typically, the price elasticity of export supply has tended to be high (ranging between 1.0 and 2.0, except for a few countries like Japan where it is as high as 3, or in Hong Kong where it is 5). Export supply price elasticity is generally greater (and of the opposite sign) than the demand price elasticity (which ranges between -0.6 to 1.6, except for a few countries like Japan and Hong Kong). This has provided the empirical support to real exchange rate changes as a policy tool to encourage exports. The two disparate elements were eventually combined in a simultaneous analysis of export demand and supply in Goldstein and Khan (1978), who applied the model to developed countries. Further work, using a simultaneous framework, and using cointegration techniques and error correction models, have since been extensively developed and applied to developing countries (Das Gupta 1990).

The Indonesia-Specific Literature on Export Determinants

Indonesia-specific research on export performance is sparse. Early work was done by Kincaid (1984), using quarterly data for the time period 1971 to 1981. It looked at the supply determinants of non-oil, non-timber exports, and estimated that the long-run price elasticity of supply was as high as 6 (i.e., a 1 percent change in export prices led to a 6 percent change in export volumes), and that the domestic supply capacity was also high at about 5. However, we have no means of assessing the impact of world demand factors, which presumably exercised significant influence on primary commodity exports.

More recent quantitative analysis has been done by Ahmed and Chhibber (1989), Ghosh (1993) and Woo et al. (1994). Ahmed and Chhibber used annual data for the period 1973–1987. They estimated two separate equations, one for non-oil manufactured exports and another for non-oil, non-manufactured exports.

For manufactured exports, they assume that world demand is unlikely to be a constraining factor (although world demand is used to instrument the 2SLS equation of export supply), and used value-added in manufacturing as an export supply proxy. Using the real exchange rate, they find a relatively low supply response to the price variable of about 1.0; and a large response (2.6) to the supply capacity variable. In the case of non-oil, non-manufactured exports, they assume that world demand is a constraining factor. The estimated function again uses the real exchange rate as the supply price variable (rather than the relative price of Indonesia's exports to world prices, for consistency with the overall econometric model for Indonesia) and world income, plus a dummy for a log export ban.

In effect, the function mixes export supply and world demand factors. Their findings are a low supply price elasticity (0.2), a high world income elasticity (1.5), and a negative effect of the export ban on logs. It is difficult to generalize from the Ahmed and Chhibber equations about the key determinants of Indonesia's non-oil exports. But one conclusion would be that fast growing exports from Indonesia (i.e., manufactured exports) basically respond to supply factors—depreciating real exchange rates and expanding manufacturing capacity.

Ghosh (1993) turns explicitly to world demand factors. However, the time-period studied is not cited. The demand price elasticity (Indonesia's export unit values relative to import prices in export markets) for non-oil exports is estimated to be about -1.0, and that for world income (world imports) is estimated to be a relatively high 2.0. However, no supply factors or simultaneous modeling techniques are applied. Cointegration tests are provided, supporting the existence of a long-run relationship between the volume of exports, relative prices, and world income. The implication is that Indonesia's export performance depends strongly on world income and, to a lesser extent, on external price competitiveness.

Woo et al. (1994) estimate an equation for the growth rate of non-oil exports as a function of the change in the real exchange rate, the change in real GDP, and a time trend. Theirs is a supply function, with no world demand constraints. The price elasticity of supply to real exchange rate changes is low at about 0.3 (e.g., a 40 percent real devaluation would increase exports by only 12 percent), while that to supply capacity is relatively high at about 1.3, although there is a negative time trend factor (1.6 percent p.a.) for the latter case. The estimation period is 1971–1980, and does not cover the recent deregulation period. Nevertheless, the authors claim that, " . . . the 1983 and 1986 devaluations and the trade reforms created a wide variety of new manufactured exports . . . (p. 141)." Elsewhere, they give high regard to real exchange rate policies, while discounting the importance of world demand factors. They write, " . . . the real GDP of industrial countries grew by only 2.7 percent in 1983, compared to 3.4 percent in 1979, but the increase in Indonesia's non-oil exports was nonetheless large . . ." Real exchange rates and trade policies are hypothesized to have been the most important determinants of non-oil export growth after 1983, although the actual estimated export supply function would suggest a modest supply response.

It appears from the above that the determinants of the extremely rapid growth of Indonesia's non-oil exports are far from clear. In one case (Ghosh), world demand factors are emphasized as being significant, while in others they are not (Woo et al.). In other studies, supply factors are emphasized. The price elasticity of supply and real exchange rates policies to elicit a supply response are strongly stressed. Nevertheless, the weight of evidence is in favor of low price elasticities. Most authors estimate these to be between 0.2 to 1 (the exception being Kincaid at 6.0). Therefore, it is doubtful that real exchange rate devaluations could alone have accounted for the nearly five-fold increase in the volume of exports between 1985–1993. Export supply capacity variables have clear and strong effects, although not much is said about what policy factors may have influenced them. Some gaps, therefore, still remain in the literature.

THE MODEL: DEMAND AND SUPPLY DETERMINANTS OF EXPORTS

In order to estimate the determinants of aggregate non-oil exports, it is essential to model both demand and supply factors. As we have seen, through the "small country" assumptions, the literature has often emphasized supply factors at the expense of demand factors. However, small country assumptions often do not hold, especially in the context of a country like Indonesia which has significant world market shares in primary commodities, as well as in some manufactures (e.g., plywood). On the other hand, world demand factors can also be exaggerated. Consequently, both supply and demand factors should be considered separately and included in an ideal simultaneous model.

Following Das Gupta (1990), the demand for Indonesia's exports is specified in this chapter as a function of Indonesia's export prices relative to world export prices (i.e., external competitiveness), and exogenous shifts in world real income or activity. The structural equation is:

(1) $\quad X_d = a_0 + a_1(P_x/P_w)_t + a_2Y_t.$

Here:

X_d = Export Demand,

P_x = Price of Indonesia's Exports,

P_w = World Prices;

Y = Level of Real Income or Activity in Export Markets, and

t = Time Period.

The expected sign of the coefficient of price (a_1) is negative, and that for income (a_2) is positive.

The supply of exports is specified to be a function of Indonesian export prices relative to domestic prices, domestic supply capacity, and changes in trade policies. In addition, two short-run factors are considered: (a) a dummy variable for 1992–1993, D, to capture the effects of over-reporting of exports, and (b) an excess domestic demand variable, ED, which reduces short-run supply of exports. Ignoring these short-run factors, an increase in export prices relative to domestic prices increases the profitability of exporting, and hence the supply of exports. Export supply is also hypothesized to increase with an increase in domestic supply capacity or investment. A third factor is the stance of trade policies. Since trade policy barriers act as disincentives to exporting (relative to selling in domestic market), export supply is expected to increase as trade policy barriers are lowered. The structural equation is:

$$(2) \qquad X_s = b_0 + b_1\,(P_X ner/P_d)_t + b_2(INV)_t + b_3(TPV)_t.$$

Here:

X_s = export supply,

P_X = export price,

ner = nominal exchange rate,

P_d = domestic aggregate price level,

INV = investment,

TEL = infrastructure capacity variable (e.g., telephone lines), and

TPV = trade policy variable reflecting the stance of current trade restrictions.

The expected signs of coefficients are as follows: relative prices (b_1) positive, productive capacity (b_2) positive, and trade policy restrictiveness (b_3) negative. In the estimations provided later, we use alternative specifications of the supply function, in which the INV variable is replaced by an alternative infrastructure supply capacity variable, TEL.

The above equations provide the structural description of a simultaneous model. In this setup, export volumes and prices are endogenous and in equilibrium export demand is equal to export supply. Since it might take time for supply to adjust, the supply equation might contain leads or lags.

THE DATA

Quarterly time-series data were obtained for the period 1985–1993 from the *International Financial Statistics* (IFS) for "world activity level" and "world prices," and from the *Quarterly Statistical Indicators* (BPS) for all other variables.[1]

Volume of Exports (Xt). This variable was calculated from disaggregated quarterly data on non-oil export volumes (BPS), broken up into 10 principal product groups (Xti). The total volume index was calculated by a weighted index,

$$X_t = \sum_i^n X_{ti} / \sum_i^n w_i.$$

with the value of product exports in total non-oil exports in 1990 (wi) chosen as the individual weights:

Export Price Index (Px). The total export price index was proxied by the unit value of total non-oil exports (in U.S. dollars).

World Prices (Pm). World prices were proxied by the import price (U.S. dollars, 1985 = 100) of the United States. Since more than 95 percent of Indonesia's total exports are denominated in U.S. dollars, and since the United States is a major price setter for world exports, this was chosen as the main indicator of world prices. An alternative procedure could have been a weighted indicator of import prices in major industrial country markets. However, the effects of cross-currency movements are a source of large disturbances, and the index was therefore not used. Instead, another world price indicator, the MUV index (manufacturing unit value of industrial products exported to developing countries), was chosen as an alternative world price indicator.

Domestic Price Variable (Pd). The domestic price level was measured by the quarterly cost-of-living (CPI) index.

World Income (Y). The level of real income in 5 industrial countries (United States, Japan, Germany, France, and United Kingdom) for which data was easily available–appropriately weighted by their share in total exports from Indonesia—was chosen as the indicator for world income. This indicator could have been expanded to include other countries, but the indicator is not that sensitive to the choice of countries, once these 5 large industrial countries are included.

Domestic Supply Capacity (INV). The sum of past four quarters of total investment (i.e., previous one year of investment), starting with one quarter previous to the current quarter, was used as a proxy for domestic supply capacity. While the lags between investment and supply capacity may indeed be much longer, it was felt that such an index would nevertheless reasonably well capture the impact of investment on capacity, since current investment would reflect to some extent, the investment and supply buoyancy. Other alternative measures—such as an electricity supply index and the index of manufacturing output—were also constructed and yielded similar results.

Domestic Supply Capacity (TEL). The number of licenses issued for new telephone connections was used as an alternative supply capacity variable, as a general proxy for improvements in physical infrastructure services. This is because investment (or manufacturing output, or non-oil GDP) is sometimes difficult to interpret as a supply capacity variable, because these variables also could be reflecting domestic demand conditions, as much as supply factors. Only annual data were available on telephone lines, and were transformed into quarterly values, using straight-line interpolation between years.

Excess Domestic Demand (ED). The difference between trend GDP and actual GDP is used as a short-run excess demand measure.

Dummy Variable for Over-reporting of Exports (D). The dummy variable takes the value 1 for all quarters between 1992 second quarter and the last quarter of 1993; and zero otherwise.

Trade Policy Barrier Index (TPI). The weighted average share of domestic manufacturing production covered by non-tariff barriers was chosen as the main indicator or proxy for the extent of trade policy barriers (see Figure 2). Its reverse is interpreted as the impact of deregulation on exports. No quarterly data were available for such an index and yearly values were chosen, with the date of annual deregulation packages (usually in June each year) used to change the value of the index.

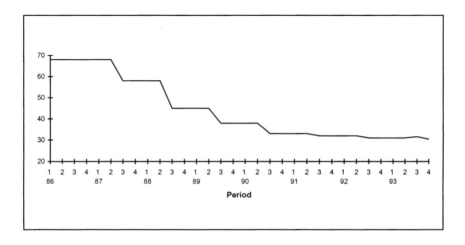

FIGURE 2. TRADE POLICY BARRIER INDEX, 1985–1994

THE RESULTS: SINGLE EQUATION
DEMAND AND SUPPLY FUNCTIONS

World Demand for Indonesia's Non-Oil Exports

The estimated world demand equation is shown below, estimated without simultaneous restrictions: The estimated equation results suggest that, ignoring simultaneity, the income elasticity of the world demand for Indonesia's non-oil exports is high at about 2.7. This is broadly consistent with an earlier estimate (Ghosh 1993) which suggested an elasticity of 2.1. This is also consistent with the evidence from Brazil (Carvalho and Haddad 1982), Greece and Korea (Balassa et al. 1986). The price elasticity of demand for Indonesia's non-oil exports is also high (about -2.8) and is over twice the size of Ghosh's estimate (-1.04). Such a high price elasticity is closer to the estimates for manufactured exports from Greece (Balassa et al. 1986), and Hong Kong (Reidel 1988). The price and income elasticities found here are not dissimilar to estimates for industrial countries reported in Goldstein and Khan (1978) and Das Gupta (1989) who also used quarterly data. In aggregate, world demand does not appear to be a major constraint on Indonesia's exports.

$$(3) \quad \ln(X_d)_t \quad = \quad -3.194 \quad + \quad 2.722 \ln(Y_w)_t \quad - \quad 2.771 \ln(P_x/P_M)_t$$

$$(-1.3) \qquad\qquad (17.9) \qquad\qquad\qquad (-6.1)$$

$$R^2 = 0.92, \ CRDW = 1.94 \ \text{and} \ ADF = -4.25*{}^2$$

Supply of Indonesia's Non-Oil Exports

All variables, other than the dummy variable for 1992–1993, in the equation for supply of exports appear to be non-stationary with unit roots, but stationary after first differences. The estimated equations shown below report the results for the supply of Indonesia's non-oil exports.

As evident, the null hypothesis of non-cointegration is rejected from the *CRDW* statistic and other tests in both estimated equations. An equilibrium relationship appears to exist between non-oil export supply, the relative price of exports (with a two-quarter lag), export supply capacity variables, and the trade policy variable. The price elasticity of supply is relatively low (between 0.34 and 0.40), and there appears to be a lag of about two quarters (different lag structures were tried and this yielded the best estimates). This estimate is similar to those reported for Indonesia earlier and those for other countries such as India (Das Gupta 1990). The elasticity of the export supply to past investment variable is positive but low. An alternative specification using telephone lines (lagged by four quarters) as a supply capacity variable causes the elasticity to increase to about 1.25. This estimate is similar in magnitude to that for other countries. The elasticity of the trade policy variable is negative and high: a 1 percent decline in the coverage of non-tariff barriers to imports would imply a 0.5 percent improvement in exports.

(4) $\ln(X)_t$ =   -0.469   +0.164 ln($SUMLINV$)$_t$ +0.339 ln(P_x/P_d)$_{t\text{-}2}$ - 0.563 ln(TPI)$_t$+0.312 D
                            (-0.02)   (2.6**)   (2.2**)   (-3.4*)   (4.8)

$R^2 = 0.96, CRDW=1.82, ADF= -4.9**$

(5) $\ln(X)_t$ =   -0.772 +1.25ln(TEL)$_{t\text{-}2}$- 0.397 ln(P_x/P_d)$_{t\text{-}2}$ - 0.492 ln(TPI)$_t$ - 0.851ED_t
                            (-0.68)   (12.3)   (3.7*)   (-5.8)   (-2.4*),

$R^2=0.98, CRDW=2.06, ADF=-5.5*$

The plots of the estimated and actual export demand and export supply functions are shown in Figures 3 and 4. The single-equation estimates appear to predict well actual exports for Indonesia.

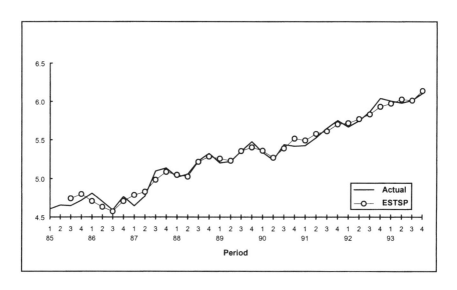

FIGURE 3. ESTIMATED AND ACTUAL EXPORT SUPPLY

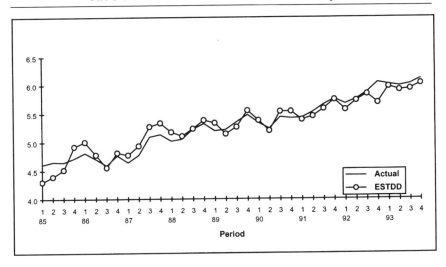

FIGURE 4. ESTIMATED AND ACTUAL EXPORT DEMAND

$$(6) \qquad \ln(X_d)_t \quad = \quad -1.691 \quad + \quad 3.236 \ln(Y_w)_t \quad - \quad 3.971 \ln(P_x/P_M)_t$$

$$\qquad\qquad\qquad\qquad (-0.4) \qquad\quad (16.0) \qquad\qquad\qquad (-5.7)$$

$$R^2 = 0.92, \; CRDW = 1.92 \text{ and } ADF = -4.25*$$

A SIMULTANEOUS MODEL OF DEMAND AND SUPPLY OF EXPORTS

Export Demand

Export volumes and prices are endogenous in the simultaneous system formed by the export demand and supply functions. We thus use two stage least squares procedure (2SLS), where the instruments used for the endogenous relative price variable are: current world income, sum of investment in the previous four quarters, the non-tariff barrier index. All instruments are expressed in logs.

The estimated equation is shown below. The biggest change from the previous single-equation estimate is that the export-price demand elasticity increases to -4.0 from -2.8. The world income elasticity coefficient also increases to 3.2 from 2.7. The implication of these changes is that after correcting for simultaneity, export demand for Indonesia's exports in world markets seems to be much more elastic to prices and income. Consequently, if Indonesia maintains its external competitiveness, world demand is not a major constraining factor for its exports. Conversely, if price competitiveness is weakened, Indonesia will suffer from a large decline in the volume of exports. On the other hand, world income growth will lead to large increase in Indonesia's exports. In the event of a slowdown in world income growth, Indonesia can still maintain high growth in exports by improving its price competitiveness.

Export Supply

For export supply, we instrument export prices by world income, sum of investment from the previous four quarters, the index of non-tariff barriers, telephone lines, and the dummy variable D in a 2SLS setup. The estimated equations are shown below. The main changes from the single equation estimates provided earlier are that: (a) the supply price elasticities increase to between 0.4 and 0.6 (from 0.3 and 0.4 earlier) and (b) the coefficient of the non-tariff barrier index drops marginally. The other coefficients for supply capacity variables (*INV*, or *TEL*) remain about the same.

(7) $\ln(X_s)_t$ =   -1.345   +0.157 $\ln(SUMLINV)_t$ +0.607 $\ln(P_x/P_d)_{t-2}$ - 0.499 $\ln(TPI)_t$ +0.359 D
                         (-0.68)   (2.4**)   (2.1**)   (-2.7*)   (4.5)

         $R^2 = 0.96$, $CRDW = 1.82$, $ADF = -4.9**$

(8) $\ln(X_s)_t$ =   -0.712 +1.26$\ln(TEL)_{t-2}$ - 0.372 $\ln(P_x/P_d)_{t-2}$ - 0.479 $\ln(TPI)_t$ - 0.748ED_t
                         (-0.46)   (11.3)   (2.3*)   (-4.7)   (-2.2*),

         $R^2 = 0.98$, $CRDW = 1.93$, $ADF = -5.1*$

The main effects of the simultaneous model are, thus, to both raise the demand price elasticity of exports and the supply price elasticity of exports compared to the single equation estimates. The predicted and actual export volumes and prices are shown in Figures 5 through 7. In Figure 5, predicted export volumes follow the actual values and pick-up the turning points reasonably well (given that these are quarterly data). Figure 6, which shows the price of exports relative to U.S. import prices, indicates a slowly declining trend. This is suggestive of increased competition in world markets and demand effects as Indonesia's volume of exports increases dramatically over time, faster than world income shifts. Figure 7, which shows the export prices converted to Rupiah relative to domestic prices indicates the very large gains initially from the 1986 devaluation.

Indonesia enjoyed the maintenance of these gains until 1990. However, from 1991 onwards, falling world export prices and nominal exchange rate adjustments that failed to keep up with rising domestic inflation and costs led to the fall in relative export prices.

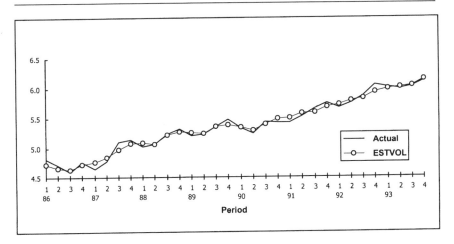

FIGURE 5. PREDICTED *(ESTVOL)* AND ACTUAL EXPORT VOLUMES (SIMULTANEOUS MODEL)

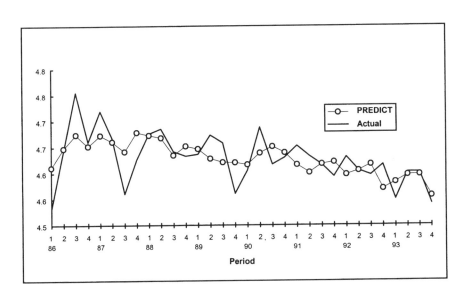

FIGURE 6. ACTUAL AND PREDICTED EXPORT PRICES (RELATIVE TO US IMPORT PRICES)

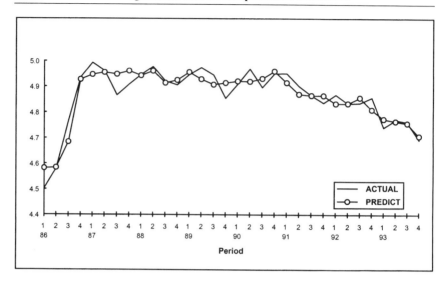

FIGURE 7. ACTUAL AND PREDICTED EXPORT PRICES (RELATIVE TO DOMESTIC PRICES)

GOVERNMENT POLICY AND EXPORT PERFORMANCE

Exchange Rate Policy

The literature puts strong emphasis on the role of exchange rate policies in boosting non-oil exports. In August 1986, the Rupiah was devalued vis-à-vis the U.S. dollar by about 43 percent. Coming close behind a large (20 percent) nominal devaluation in September 1983, the effect of the 1986 devaluation strengthened incentives to exporters. The effect of the "weighted real exchange rate" change vis-à-vis a basket of currencies was even larger since the dollar also depreciated against other currencies.

To determine the importance of the 1986 devaluation on exports, we ran a simulation with a 20 percent (instead of a 43 percent) nominal devaluation in 1986 (and nominal and real exchange rate adjustments thereafter from this base that follow the actual historical path of exchange rates). The main policy question here is: to what extent was devaluation *necessary*?

Figure 8 indicates in line *PLTEDVOL* the predicted volumes of exports in our model and line *SLTEDVOL* shows what the predicted volume of exports would have been with a 20 percent lower real exchange rate devaluation in 1986. As is evident, the effect is significant: export volume in the final period (fourth quarter 1993) would have been some 14 percent lower, equivalent to some $3 billion in lower export earnings. The loss in export earnings over the entire period, 1987–1993, would also have been large. Still, the *overall* impact remains relatively small (and becomes increasingly smaller over time). *While the 1986 devaluation boosted exports in the base year, over time its effect became progressively less important, and the volume of exports grew due to other factors.*

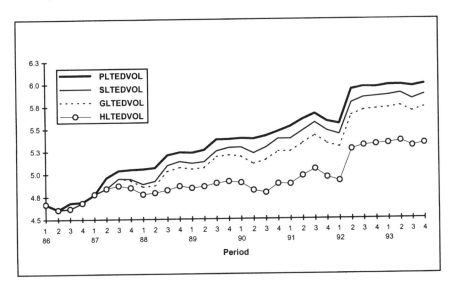

FIGURE 8. SIMULATION RESULTS FOR FACTORS OF EXPORT GROWTH

Investment Deregulation

To identify the impact of investment deregulation, we ran a second simulation with a lower exchange rate path. We lowered investment between 1987 and 1988 to 90 percent of the actual value, and to 80 percent of the actual value from 1989 onward. Line *GLTEDVOL* in Figure 8 shows what the simulated exports would have been under such a scenario. As is evident, the quantitative impact of lower investment growth is about the same as the lower exchange rate simulation. While the impact is significant, it does not slow-down export growth dramatically.

Therefore, the simulation suggests that investment deregulation played a significant and large role in boosting non-oil exports. However, its quantitative impact was nevertheless small compared to other possible factors.

Trade Deregulation

To gauge the impact of trade policy deregulation, we ran a third simulation with lower exchange rates and lower investments. We assumed that no reduction in trade barriers occurred. Line *HLTEDVOL* in Figure 8 shows what the simulated exports volume would have been in the absence of any reduction in trade barriers. It is arguable whether this simulation exaggerates its effects compared to other policy variables, such as exchange rates and investment deregulation. However, between 1983 and 1985, under a difficult external situation, Indonesia had raised trade policy barriers as an alternative way to manage its balance of payments. Consequently, a scenario of unchanged trade policies was indeed a possibility. The simulation reveals that with existing trade policies there would have been very little growth in non-oil exports. Consequently, exports in 1993 would have been some 31 percent lower. *The simulations suggest that trade policy changes were the most important influences on Indonesia's non-oil export growth between 1985–1993.*

˙NOTES

1.   All variables in the estimated equations were expressed in logarithms, implying the assumption of constant elasticities.

2.   (*) means significant at the 1 percent level and (**) at the 5 percent level. The numbers in parentheses are *t* statistics. *CRDW* refers to the Durbin-Watson statistic and *ADF* to the Augmented Dickey-Fuller test.

REFERENCES

Ahmed, Sadiq and Ajay Chhibber (1989) "How Can Indonesia Maintain Creditworthiness and Non-Inflationary Growth?" *Policy Planning and Research Working Paper No. WPS 291,* (Washington, DC: The World Bank).

Balassa, Bela et al. (1986) "Export Incentives and Export Growth in Developing Countries: An Econometric Investigation," in *World Bank Development Research Department Discussion Paper 159.*

Carvalho, J.C. and C.L.S. Haddad (1982) "Brazilian Export Growth: Estimating the Export Supply Response, 1955–74," in A. Krueger (ed.) *"Trade and Employment in Developing Countries,* (Chicago, Illinois, NBER/University of Chicago Press).

Das Gupta, Bejoy (1989) "Determinants of Exports from Developing Countries: Exchange Rate Policies and Exports in the 1980s," in R. O'Brien and T. Datta (eds.) *International Economics and Financial Markets,* (London, England: Oxford University Press).

Das Gupta, Bejoy (1990) *"Exports and Exchange Rate Policy: The Case of India,"* D.Phil Thesis, (Oxford, England: University of Oxford).

Ghosh, Swati (1993) "Indonesia's Vulnerability to the External Environment—An Assessment," Background paper (mimeo), (Washington, DC: The World Bank).

Goldstein, Morris and Mohsin S. Khan (1978) "The Supply and Demand for Exports: A Simultaneous Approach," *Review of Economics and Statistics,* 60.

Hill, Hal (1994) "Indonesia's New Order—The Dynamics of Socio-Economic Transformation," (Australia: Allen and Unwin Publishers).

Kincaid, G. (1984) "A Test of the Efficacy of Exchange Rate Adjustment in Indonesia," *IMF Staff Papers No. 31,* (Washington, DC: International Monetary Fund).

Krugman, Paul (1989) "Income Elasticities and Real Exchange Rates," *European Economic Review,* 33.

Mody, Ashoka and Kamil Yilmaz (1994) "Is There Persistence in the Growth of Manufactured Exports—Evidence from Newly Industrializing Countries," Washington, *Policy Research Working Paper No. 1276,* (Washington, DC: The World Bank).

Muscatelli, V.A., T.G. Srinivasan, and D. Vines (1992) "Demand and Supply Factors in the Determination of NIE Exports: A Simultaneous Error Correction Model for Hong Kong," *Economic Journal,* 102.

Reidel, James (1988) "The Demand for LDC Exports of Manufactures: Estimates from Hong Kong," *Economic Journal,* 98.

Woo, Wing Thye, Bruce Glassburner, and Anwar Nasution (1994) *Macroeconomic Policies, Crises, and Long-Term Growth in Indonesia, 1965–90,* (Washington, DC: The World Bank).

CHAPTER 6

The Impact of Deregulation on the Manufacturing Sector

Farrukh Iqbal[1]

    Given the conventional association of trade and investment deregulation with exports of manufactured goods, one can assume that the regulatory regime shift that took place in Indonesia during the 1980s would have had a major impact on the country's manufacturing sector. This is documented and assessed in this chapter through a comparison of changes in key manufacturing sector characteristics over two periods: 1980-85, which captures the before-deregulation situation and 1986–91, which provides a sense of the after-deregulation situation. Structural details of the sector can be assessed through annual industrial survey data put out by the *Biro Pusat Statistik* (BPS). For our present purposes, the cleaned and revised series to 1991 is analyzed so as to get a sense of the initial impact of the deregulation on the manufacturing sector.[2] In particular, we look at growth in output, employment and exports as well as changes in the structure of the manufacturing sector in terms of firm size and concentration.

    As already noted in earlier chapters, the second half of the 1980s in Indonesia was characterized by a series of deregulatory measures that provided incentives at the microeconomic level for enhanced export activity. This was supported by a macroeconomic stance that was also consistent with export orientation. The results of this newly coherent combination of microeconomic and macroeconomic policies were both striking and quick. Four features stand out over the period 1986–1991:

TABLE 1
TRENDS IN SELECTED MACROECONOMIC VARIABLES

	Real Growth		Shares	Shares
	1980–1985	1986–1991	1985	1991
GDP	3.9	6.5		
Non-oil GDP	5.7	7.0	77	80
Manufacturing GDP	1.1	13	16	20
Total Fixed Investment		13.2		
Private Fixed Investment		15.4	13.5	19
Total Exports	-1.1	15		
Non-oil Exports	1.3	21	32	55
Manufactured Exports	n.a.	30	8	23

Source: World Bank.

GDP Growth Jumped. The economy grew at the rate of 6.5 percent as compared to a rate of only 3.9 percent during the previous five years. This is even more remarkable given that, by and large, this period was one of "soft" oil prices.

Private Investment Surged. Private (fixed) investment soared, rising at an average rate of 15%. The share of fixed private investment in GDP increased from 13.5% in 1985 to over 19% by 1991.

Non-Oil Exports Boomed. Non-oil exports increased from around $6 billion dollars per annum in 1985 to over $15 billion dollars, rising at an annual rate of around 21 percent and increasing their share of total exports from 32 percent to 55 percent.

Productivity Grew. While the contribution of total factor productivity growth was negligible before 1985, recent research suggests that almost one-third of the growth in GDP per worker during 1986-1992 was due to such productivity growth (see Chapter 4).

Rising Importance of Manufacturing Sector

The above characteristics of the post-1985 experience have one element in common: they are all related to sharp growth in the manufacturing sector and especially among sub-sectors producing manufactured exports. The share of the manufacturing sector in total output rose from 16 percent to 20 percent: this was the biggest structural shift among all economic sectors over this period. An even more remarkable shift occurred in the structure of exports: manufactured exports grew at the rate of 30 percent per annum, raising their share of total exports from 8 percent to 23 percent in the short span of five years.

Indonesia's experience is consistent with that of many other East Asian countries that had taken the outward-oriented path earlier. In particular, the experience of these countries suggests that openness to trade boosts growth as well as total factor productivity. The reasons why one might expect exports (especially of manufactured goods) to help increase productivity have been amply explored elsewhere.[3] Engaging in such exports helped the East Asian high performance economies move towards the international best practice frontier more rapidly (thus increasing their technological efficiency) while improving the allocation of their resources (thus increasing their allocative efficiency). Both processes helped produce high rates of productivity and economic growth. In this, these countries were also helped greatly by improvements in the quality of their human capital made possible by earlier investments in education.

As far as the causes of the extraordinary burst in non-oil export growth concerned, similar factors have been important in Indonesia as elsewhere in East Asia in earlier decades. Empirical analysis for the Indonesian case (see Chapter 5) supports two conclusions: first, that trade-boosting policies (including export promotion through duty drawbacks and exemptions, reduction of tariffs and non-tariff barriers, the maxi-devaluation of 1986 and increasing receptiveness to foreign investment in the export sector) together explain most of the growth in non-oil exports that has been experienced since 1985 and, second, that duty exemption, reduction and non-tariff measures had, by themselves, a rather substantial influence on the rate and pattern of non-oil export growth.[4]

STRUCTURAL CHANGES IN THE MANUFACTURING SECTOR

Patterns of Growth in Employment

It is sometimes claimed that deregulation is harmful to the interests of the domestic labor force. At one level this view is easy to disprove for the case of Indonesia. Our results show that labor began to gain from deregulation right away as overall employment grew more rapidly in the latter half of the 1980s than in the earlier half. This was due in part to extremely rapid employment growth in the manufacturing sector. Employment in manufacturing rose at an annual rate of 13 percent during 1986–1991; this is more than one and a half times the 8 percent rate recorded during 1980–1985.[5] In Indonesia's labor-abundant context, employment expansion is probably the most important determinant of labor incomes. To the extent that wage-labor incomes are an important dimension of poverty (at least in urban areas), it is very likely that deregulation helped relieve the conditions of poverty and near-poverty in Indonesia in the period between 1985 and the crisis of 1997–98.

TABLE 2
EMPLOYMENT GROWTH IN MANUFACTURING SECTOR

Sector	Employment Growth 1980-1985	Employment Growth 1986-1991	Employment Share 1985	Employment Share 1991
Food	4.0	5.1	30	22
Textiles	7.7	16.9	23	26
Wood Products	21.4	20.5	11	14
Paper	10.8	7.1	3	3
Chemicals	9.9	15.8	14	16
Nonmetals	13.6	15.8	6	6
Basic Metals	16.3	9.1	1	1
Metal Products	7.0	12.1	11	11
Miscellaneous	16.8	34.2	1	1
Weighted Average	8.1	12.8		

Source: BPS, Backcast data.

A closer look at details of employment growth across manufacturing sub-sectors shows the following features:

Faster Employment Growth Was the Norm. Employment growth was higher in most sub-sectors during 1986–1991 than in the previous five years. At the 3-digit level, 20 out of 28 sub-sectors experienced faster employment growth. A similar result obtains at the 2-digit level (see Table 2). So the figures reflect broader tendencies in the economy rather than the experience of only a few sectors.

Employment Growth Linked to Export Orientation. Employment growth was most rapid in the more export-oriented sub-sectors. For example, employment growth was most rapid in textiles, wood products and miscellaneous items. These are also the three sub-sectors with the highest share of exports to output. The link between employment growth and export orientation was tested more rigorously through regression analysis. This showed a positive and significant correlation between rate of employment growth and export share by sector at the five-digit level.[6]

Structural Change Occurred. As a result of the above trends, the three most export-oriented sectors within manufacturing increased their share of total employment from 35 percent in 1985 to 41 percent in 1991. The share of the three least export-oriented sectors (food, paper, and nonmetallic minerals) decreased from 39 percent to 31 percent. However, this decline was entirely restricted to the food sector, whose share fell from 30 percent to 22 percent. By 1991, the textile sector surpassed the food sector to become the biggest employer in manufacturing.

Patterns of Growth in Value-Added

The manufacturing sector experienced a much higher rate of growth in value-added during 1986–1991 than in the earlier half of the 1980s, 18.4 percent compared to 10.4 percent.[7] When combined with the data on employment growth, this suggests that labor productivity (value-added per worker) increased faster during 1986–1991 than in the earlier period.

A closer look at the details of value-added change within the manufacturing sector reveals the following trends:

Higher Value-added Growth Was the Norm. Most manufacturing sub-sectors participated in the higher growth of the latter half of the 1980s. At the 2-digit level, 7 out of 9 sub-sectors experienced more rapid growth. Only the wood products and basic metals sub-sectors experienced less rapid growth. In the case of the wood products sector, this was largely due to the fact that it had grown at a very rapid pace in the first half of the 1980s following the ban on log exports that stimulated the domestic plywood processing industry.

There Was No Clear Link with Export Orientation. While the three most export-oriented sub-sectors (textiles, wood products and miscellaneous) increased their share in total value-added from 23 percent to 27 percent, there was no clear link between growth in value-added and export orientation. Several sectors with low export orientation also experienced high value-added growth.

TABLE 3
VALUE-ADDED GROWTH IN MANUFACTURING

Sector	Value-added Growth 1980-1985	Value-added Growth 1986-1991	Value-added Share 1985	Value-add Share 1991
Food	6.1	11.9	34	26
Textiles	12.9	21.7	13	15
Wood Products	25.4	22.8	9	11
Paper	18.4	29.5	3	5
Chemicals	4.9	22.3	15	16
Nonmetals	15.7	19.2	5	5
Basic Metals	78.2	6.0	7	5
Metal Products	7.8	25.5	13	16
Miscellaneous	19.3	46.3	1	1
Weighted Average	10.4	18.4		

Source: BPS, Backcast Data.

Patterns of Investment and Export Orientation

Indonesia progressively relaxed restrictions on foreign investment after 1985. More and more areas were opened up, minimum investment requirements were lessened, and procedural steps for approval and registration were reduced. Together with other changes in the overall environment (such as the realignment of exchange rates after the Plaza Agreement of 1985), these measures were successful in attracting a large inflow of foreign investment into Indonesia. During 1986–1992, about $6.3 billion of foreign investment was received. The pace of change can be appreciated from the fact that while foreign investment doubled from 0.2 percent of GDP to 0.4 percent during 1980–1985, it more than tripled in the next five years to 1.4 percent of GDP.

A notable feature of foreign investment after 1985 was its export orientation. Two pieces of evidence show this. First, according to the foreign investment approval data published by the Investment Coordinating Board (BKPM), there was a pronounced increase in the number and proportion of approvals for export-oriented projects during 1986–1989. In 1986, 38 percent of approved projects (19 out of 50) were designated export-oriented. By 1989, this proportion had risen to 79 percent even though the number of projects also increased sharply to 294 (Thee 1994).[8] Second, a survey of Japanese investors in Indonesia shows that, whereas in 1986 their export to sales ratios were less than 4 percent on average, by 1992 this had risen to over 16% (Kawaguchi 1994).

The rise in the economic importance of manufacturing was also reflected in investment data collected by the BKPM.[9] The share of manufacturing in total domestic investment rose from 43 percent in 1985 to 66 percent in 1989; that in total foreign investment rose from 80 percent to 90 percent over the same period.

TABLE 4
INVESTMENT AND EXPORT PATTERNS IN MANUFACTURING

Sub-sector	Share in Foreign Investment 1985	Share in Foreign Investment 1989	Share in Foreign Investment 1993	Share of Exports in Total Output, 1992
Food/Beverages	0	5	2	15
Textile/Footwear	0	12	5	34
Wood Products	0	2	0	55
Paper	4	2	15	
Chemicals	39	53	14	19
Nonmetallic Minerals	0	4	1	11
Basic Metals	8	2	2	25
Metal Products	28	6	14	18
Misc.	0	0	0	61
Memo Items				
Manuf. in Domestic Invest.	43	66	61	
Manuf. in Foreign Invest.	80	90	42	

Source: Investment approval data from BKPM; Export data from BPS.

Effects by Size of Firm

A common belief or perception is that deregulation only benefits larger firms. There are several reasons to expect why this might be a natural concomitant of the change process. First, financial markets in developing countries tend to be relatively underdeveloped; in such a context, firm size confers advantages both in terms of access to bank funds as well as command over own resources. To the extent that deregulation creates opportunities for growth through investment in new areas, one might expect larger firms to seize opportunities faster on account of their superior financial position. Second, to the extent that deregulation generates opportunities for growth through export-orientation, there is a premium on access to information and the ability to use such information. Larger firms are better placed to obtain information about foreign demand and also in a better position to hire the skills needed to use such information. Small firms are more likely to benefit through becoming integrated with larger firms in sub-contracting and other out-sourcing relationships. In other words, smaller firms are more likely to participate through a "trickle down" process.

Analysis of changes in the size-distribution of Indonesian manufacturing firms during the 1980s shows a complex pattern in which both large and small firms appear to have benefited from deregulation. Table 5 shows transition probabilities or probabilities that firms will have grown or reduced in size over a given period. Comparisons are made between the periods 1980–1985 and 1986–1991 to see if deregulation has affected these probabilities. The comparison shows the following main patterns:

Probability of growing larger. The probability of growing in size increased for all size groups except for the very small. Proportionately, it increased the most for large firms. For the very small, there was no change in the probability of growing larger relative to the earlier period.

Probability of growing smaller. The probability of growing smaller increased for relatively smaller firms but decreased for relatively larger firm.

Probability of exit. The probability of exit (which essentially connotes bankruptcy) increased for all size groups but the increase is proportionately greatest for large and very large firms. The suggests that (a) the risks of doing business have increased under deregulation, and (b) those who have a higher probability of growing under deregulation also face an increased probability of failure.

TABLE 5
TRANSITION PROBABILITIES (IN PERCENT)

Size Group	Prob. of growing bigger		Prob. of growing smaller		Prob. of exit	
	1980–1985	1986–1991	1980–1985	1986–1991	1980–1985	1986–1991
Very Small	12	12	32	37	32	37
Small	21	26	36	38	17	23
Medium	9	14	23	24	11	17
Large	20	30	29	26	3	13
Very Large			33	28	4	11

Note: Size is defined in terms of number of workers as follows: Very small = 20-49; Small = 50-99; Medium = 100-499; Large = 500-999; and Very large = 1000 plus.

Source: BPS, Backcast Data.

A focus on transition probabilities alone is insufficient to capture the dynamics of growth and change among firms. For one, such a focus misses developments within given size groups. Analysis of data on employment by size of firm suggests that smaller firms have increased their share of total manufacturing employment during 1986–1991. Thus, where firms with less than 50 workers accounted for 11 percent of total employment in 1986, their share had gone up to 13 percent by 1991. At the other end of the size distribution, the share of employment accounted for by very large firms dropped from 32 percent in 1986 to 26 percent in 1991. It would thus appear that the dominant pattern among very small firms was one of substantial employment growth. This pattern was, however, spread over a large number of firms so that relatively few of them became large enough to graduate into higher size categories.

ISSUES IN DOMESTIC COMPETITION

Restrictions on Domestic Competition

Deregulation of external trade and investment promotes productivity growth through providing a source of competition to domestic entrepreneurs. But such measures alone may not be sufficient to generate adequate competitive pressure. Some parts of the economy may be naturally protected from external competition (e.g., the non-tradable sectors) and these may be of considerable importance to overall economic performance. In some other cases, even if trade is possible, it may only be profitable for a relatively narrow range of goods and services, leaving a large segment of domestic production to the discipline of the domestic market alone.[10] In still other cases, unrestricted trade may be put off until a political consensus is reached in its favor. In all these cases, a direct focus on domestic competition is probably more relevant than a focus on trade policy. Vigorous domestic competition can also make possible the development of export capacity. In many East Asian countries, export success was due in large measure to the discipline imposed by stiff domestic competition, which honed the design, production and marketing expertise of domestic producers and assisted them in exporting.

In Indonesia, restrictions on domestic competition were pervasive in the 1980s and 1990s, hobbling the growth of progressive, efficiency-seeking enterprise. Such restrictions took the form of cartels, price controls, entry and exit controls, exclusive licensing, public sector dominance, and *ad hoc* interventions by government in favor of specific firms and sectors. Some restrictions were imposed by the national government, others by local government units, and still others by trade and business associations (often with official sanction). The table below provides a sampling of the variety and scope of such restrictions in the Indonesian economy.

TABLE 6
RESTRICTIONS ON DOMESTIC COMPETITION (PRIOR TO 1997)

Type of Restriction	Sectors in Which Prevalent
Cartels	Cement, Glass, Plywood, Paper
Price Controls	Cement, Sugar, Rice, Autos
Entry and Exit Controls	Plywood, Autos
Exclusive Licensing	Clove Marketing, Wheat flour Milling
Public Sector Dominance	Steel, Fertilizer

Cartels. Many Indonesian industries were organized as cartels with controls on prices, outputs, entry and exit enforced through trade associations. Such industries were typically characterized by a sharp dichotomy with relatively efficient firms at one extreme and inefficient, high cost firms at the other. The two types of firms co-exist because of cartel rules that prevent price competition within the sector from driving the inefficient firms into bankruptcy. This was the case, for example, in textiles, cement, and the paper and pulp industries. The cost of supporting inefficient firms is passed on to consumers in the form of higher average prices for the goods produced by the relevant industry. Often, government supports the cartel arrangements because they protect state-owned enterprises in the sector; this was the case, for example, in the cement sector where state owned cement manufacturers tended to be the high-cost, low-profit producers.

Exclusive Licensing. A good example of restricting competition through exclusive licensing is provided by the case of clove marketing. Here existing competitive arrangements in marketing were abrogated by government and sole rights for distribution of cloves were given to one company that was supposed to act on behalf of growers to obtain higher prices for them. This government-sponsored monopsony failed. After an initial period of high prices, the scheme resulted in excessive production by growers and a reduction of purchases by cigarette manufacturers who are the main users of cloves in Indonesia. According to one study, in 1991 alone, this arrangement involved a loss of Rp. 62 billion for clove farmers (who had to destroy surplus stocks when the monopsony buyer failed to buy them up) and cigarette manufacturers (who had to pay high prices to the same intermediary acting as a monopolist seller). The company, on the other hand, made a profit of Rp. 25 billion on the arrangement. The overall welfare loss to society is estimated to have been around Rp. 21 billion. These are static loss estimates; over time, losses due to lowered investment in clove growing and cigarette manufacturing (and higher investment in relatively inefficient substitute activities) could be several times higher.[11]

Government-Business "Cooperation." Ad-hoc interventions by government in favor of large or otherwise influential business groups were fairly common in

Indonesia during the Suharto period. Such interventions took the form of government equity participation in large commercial projects with one favored group or another, the provision of special credits, favoritism in the procurement practices of public enterprises, or the outright grant of exclusive licenses to produce, import, and sell in certain regions. Often, the stated justification for such interventions was the need to build a strong domestic private sector that can compete internationally. Unfortunately, such interventions typically have the opposite effect. By decreasing domestic competition they promote inefficient firms. By providing large benefits to the chosen few, they generate rent-seeking behavior in the private sector.

There are many examples of non-transparent transactions between government and selected private groups under the Suharto government. In the textile and paper industries, some private groups were allowed to buy public enterprise assets at very low prices without an open and transparent divestiture process. The converse also happened: the public sector purchased private assets at significantly inflated prices (relative to the market). For example, government purchased the shares of a large business group in a cement company at prices roughly three times the going market value of the shares. Government also purchased the shares of a private partner in the Cold Rolling Mill Indonesia company at a price equivalent to three times the prevailing market valuation.

Consequences for Structure

The above-mentioned policies and practices indicate that there were (and still are) significant pockets of monopoly and oligopoly in the Indonesian economy. While it is difficult to document this empirically for all the major sectors, it is possible to do so for the manufacturing sector. The table below shows levels of concentration in sub-sectors of manufacturing as measured by the share of the top four firms in total output. Among the interesting features are:

> *High Degree of Concentration.* The average level of concentration is rather high by international standards. Indonesia's average of 47 percent for the manufacturing sector is higher than what is typically observed in industrialized economies. For example, it is higher than the concentration ratio of 22 percent for the United Kingdom and 36 percent for the United States.

> *Domination by Oligopolies.* By international standards, an industry is considered oligopolistic if its four firm concentration ratio is above 40 percent. Using this definition, it would appear that the majority of Indonesia's manufacturing sub-sectors in 1991 were characterized by an oligopolistic market structure: 7 out of 9 sub-sectors had concentration ratios above 40 percent.

The concentration data reported here must be interpreted with caution. The data available from the BPS are on an establishment basis and do not provide ownership information. Some sub-sectors may be highly concentrated by ownership but this would not be captured by the BPS data if owners operate several different firms in the same sector. Lack of competition may also not be captured if the sector is characterized by a cartel of many equally large players. A case in point is plywood. During the Suharto era, this sub-sector was dominated by a cartel that controlled entry and sales in international markets. However, the BPS data show that plywood was a relatively competitive sector with a concentration ratio of only 0.13 (at the 5 digit level). Anecdotal information suggests that this is an underestimate of the true concentration in the sector on an ownership basis. In any case, the cartel nature of the sub-sector makes it automatically non-competitive.[12]

TABLE 7
CONCENTRATION RATIOS IN MANUFACTURING
(SHARE OF TOP FOUR FIRMS; IN PERCENT)

Sub-Sector	Conc. Ratio: 1985	Conc. Ratio: 1991
Food	59	62
Textile/Footwear	25	24
Wood Products	13	16
Paper	44	50
Chemicals	46	45
Nonmetallic minerals	76	58
Basic Metals	82	72
Metal Products	50	57
Miscellaneous	72	49
Weighted Average	50	47

Source: BPS, Backcast Data.

Structure and Performance

Theory suggests that the lack of competition should lead to economic inefficiency. At the empirical level it is difficult to show this link convincingly for Indonesia because accurate sectoral efficiency data (such as total factor productivity measures) are not available. However, an indirect method may be employed. This is to examine the correlation between export orientation and concentration by sector. Export-orientation provides a defensible measure of efficiency since exporters have to compete in unfettered international markets. Those who succeed are likely to be those who are most efficient and keep close to international best practice in their product and process technologies. The table below shows that there is a broad negative correlation between export-orientation and concentration. Sub-sectors with above-average degrees of concentration tend not to be heavily engaged in exporting, presumably because they are unable to compete in open and unprotected markets.

More sophisticated statistical analysis confirms the above. A regression model based on 118 sub-sector observations at the 5 digit level shows a statistically significant negative link between concentration ratios and export shares.[13] Such results must be interpreted with caution, of course. While the negative relationship between concentration and export orientation holds at the aggregate level, this does not imply that it must hold for every single sub-sector as well. Furthermore, as already noted, for some sub-sectors, such as plywood, the concentration data may not reflect the true degree of competition.

TABLE 8
CONCENTRATION AND EXPORT ORIENTATION

	High Export Orientation	Low Export Orientation
High Concentration		Non-metals
		Metal Products
		Chemicals
		Paper
		Food
		Basic Metals
Low Concentration	Wood Products	
	Textiles/Footwear	

Notes: High concentration refers to cases where sub-sector concentration (four firm ratio in 1991) is greater than industry weighted average of 47 percent; high export-orientation refers to cases where the share of total output going to exports is greater than the industry average of 25 percent (in 1992).
Source: World Bank staff calculations.

Effect of Deregulation. The correlation between export orientation and concentration suggests another hypothesis, namely, that deregulation should have reduced overall concentration by increasing the share of the export-oriented sub-sectors. Indeed, the data show that this has been the case. Overall concentration declined from an average of 50 in 1985 to 47 in 1991. This reflects a decline in concentration for 15 out of 28 sub-sectors at the 3-digit level. Thus deregulation has been competition enhancing on balance as one might have expected from theoretical considerations also.[14]

NOTES

1.   The author is indebted to Dr. Anggito Abimanyu for help in organizing the manufacturing sector data on which much of this paper is based.

2.   The process of cleaning and revising the data included the following: conducting new backward-looking surveys to collect information on firms that were missed or were not properly recorded in earlier surveys; estimating data for non-surveyed establishments; and making adjustments for undercoverage. Because of the emphasis on establishing accurate information for earlier years, the revised series is commonly known as the "backcast" series.

3.   The conceptual and empirical link between exports and productivity growth is covered in detail in the World Bank publication *The East Asia Miracle* (1994). The main assertion here is that exporting helps firms acquire best-practice knowledge through such channels as the purchase of new equipment, direct foreign investment, technology licensing, transfer of non-proprietary technology, and buyer-generated information on quality, design and process.

4.   The export-promoting role of the BAPEKSTA scheme and of reforms in customs administration should not be overlooked. The use of BAPEKSTA facilities grew rapidly after 1986. For example, whereas in 1987 only 494 firms were registered as "beneficiaries" of duty drawback and exemption facilities, by 1991 this number had grown to over 3,000. Similarly, the value of imports covered rose from around $200 million in 1987 (on a realized rather than approved basis) to almost $7 billion in 1991. Less easy to quantify but of significant importance also were the reforms introduced in customs administration. These consisted mainly of reducing the scope of inspections by customs personnel. A presidential decree ("Inpres 4") removed the authority of customs to inspect and process shipments valued at more than $5,000 transferring these functions to a private surveying company. This change brought about a substantial reduction in import clearing times (reportedly from three weeks to a few days on average) and costs (reportedly around 25 percent).

5.   The employment level and growth figures shown by the Backcast series of the Industrial Surveys differ from those shown by other sources. For example, census data report a total manufacturing employment level of 5.8 million in 1985 and 8.2 million in 1990; the relevant figures from the Backcast series are 1.9 million and 2.8 million respectively. Two factors probably contribute the most to this discrepancy. One is that the Industrial Survey data cover only those firms in the formal manufacturing sector which have an employment level of at least 20 people. The other is that the survey data probably cover less than the full universe of larger (that is, above 20 people) manufacturing firms.

6.   The cross-sectoral regression model consisted of employment growth over 1986–1991 as the dependent variable and share of exports to output as

the independent variable. The coefficient estimate of 0.11 was measured with a standard error of 0.03, thereby showing statistical significance at the 1 percent level.

7.   The BPS Backcast data provide a higher estimate of manufacturing sector growth than the national accounts, especially for the latter half of the 1980s. Consistency checks with other variables (such as the rate of growth of manufactured exports or electricity consumption) suggest that the national accounts data underestimate the true rate of increase in manufacturing sector output and thereby underestimate the true growth rate of the economy.

8.   A similar trend is seen in domestic investments registered at BKPM. Export oriented investments by domestic firms rose from 53 percent of the total in 1986 to 73 percent in 1989.

9.   These data are reported on an approval basis and cover only those projects for which special exemptions (on duties and taxes) have been requested from BKPM. They should not be confused with investment as defined and reported in the annual national accounts.

10.   Both theoretical and empirical considerations may be used to argue that trade liberalization, while important, may not be sufficient to generate desirable competitive effects. Among theoretical considerations it is generally argued that competitive effects of tariff reductions vary with the elasticity of the import supply curve. If imports are domestic price-inelastic, they will not provide much competition to domestic producers. Among empirical considerations one might note the following: the possibility of anti-dumping actions, the existence of inter-firm collusion and of restrictions on distributor arrangements and the possibility of foreign firms wishing to join in a domestic cartel rather than competing.

11.   Another example of government-sponsored restrictions on competition is provided by the wheat flour milling industry. This industry was dominated by a powerful private business group that controlled around 85 percent of flour milling capacity in the country. This group benefited significantly from exclusive licenses and special credits granted to it by government agencies that allowed it to buy out potential competitors. The group's virtual monopoly was protected by two government regulations: one which prevented the import of flour and another which restricted new investments in flour milling to projects exporting at least 65% of production.

12.   Concentration ratios for the various plywood-related industries grouped under wood products (at the 5-digit level) are Sawmills 0.18, Molding and Building Components 0.24, Plywood 0.13, Laminated Board and Decorative Plywood 0.78, and Wood Containers 0.77. The weight by output and value-added is by far the greatest for plywood which accounts for the weighted average for the group being under 0.20. By way of comparison, note that the concentration ratio for plywood, hard board and particle board mills in Malaysia is also relatively low, at around 0.22.

13.   The bivariate regression of concentration ratio (as dependent variable) and export share (as independent variable) provides a coefficient value of -18.9 for the independent variable and a standard error of 8.1. This implies that the coefficient estimate is statistically significant at the 1 percent level.

14. A similar result is found by Bird (1999) who reports concentration in Indonesian manufacturing to have declined to a level of 41 by 1994. Of course, a better test of the theoretical expectation that trade and investment deregulation leads to greater competition would involve price convergence data as well as price-cost margin data. Surveys of domestic and international prices for a range of goods suggest that price convergence has occurred since the mid-1980s. No data on price cost margins and imports by sector are available to test whether import penetration has reduced profits and squeezed rents.

REFERENCES

Bird, Kelly (1999) "Concentration in Indonesian Manufacturing, 1975-93," *Bulletin of Indonesian Economic Studies*, 35(1) April, pp. 43–73.

Kawaguchi, Osamu (1994) *"Foreign Direct Investment in East Asia,"* (Washington, DC: The World Bank, East Asia Regional Discussion Paper.

Thee Kian Wee (1994) "Intra-Regional Foreign Investment in Indonesia," *University of Gadjah Mada Business Review,* November.

Urata, Shujiro (1994) "Trade Liberalization and Productivity Growth in Asia: Introduction and Major Findings," *The Developing Economies, Special Issue: Trade Liberalization and Productivity Growth in Asia,* 32 (4), December.

World Bank (1993) *The East Asia Miracle: Economic Growth and Public Policy,* (New York, NY: Oxford University Press).

World Bank (1997) *Indonesia: Sustaining High Growth with Equity,* (Washington, DC: The World Bank), Internal Report No: 16433–IND.

World Bank (1994) *Stability, Growth and Equity in Repelita VI,* (Washington, DC: The World Bank), Internal Report No: 12857–IND.

CHAPTER 7

The Impact of Deregulation on Employment and Earnings

Nisha Agrawal

The significant transformation in the regulatory regime in the mid-1980s affected many aspects of the Indonesian economy. In particular, changes in the incentive regime caused shifts in the wage structure, the employment structure and average labor productivity. This chapter examines how these indicators of labor market performance changed as the reforms were implemented.

The key to the changes was the fact that, with deregulation, Indonesia was in a position to take advantage of its vast endowment of low-cost, low-skilled labor because the industries for which new and larger markets emerged initially were simple and labor-intensive. The pattern of growth that subsequently emerged was labor-friendly. Employment increased, especially paid employment, which grew by 4.6 percent per annum between 1986–1990. In contrast, in the four-year period prior to that (1982–1986), paid employment fell slightly (at an annual average rate of 0.02 percent), resulting in a net loss of 1.5 million paid jobs. During the second half of the 1980s, employment in manufacturing grew especially rapidly, by 8.5 percent per annum. While, due to the labor-surplus nature of the Indonesian economy, real wages did not show any noticeable increases until the early 1990s, average real labor earnings increased as labor entered more productive and higher-paying jobs both across and within broad sectors. This increase in earnings, combined with the increased participation of women in the labor force, was one of the major factors contributing to a substantial reduction in poverty in Indonesia that continued to take place through the period in review.

LABOR-RELEVANT CHARACTERISTICS OF THE EXPORT AND FOREIGN INVESTMENT BOOM

As Table 1 indicates, the composition of manufactured exports changed dramatically between the first and second half of the 1980s: the rate of growth of *labor-intensive* exports doubled while that of *resource-intensive* exports halved. Thus, the pattern of exports that emerged in the post-reform period was strongly consistent with Indonesia's comparative advantage in labor-intensive activities. During the second half of the 1980s, labor-intensive manufactures increased over eight-fold, from just over $800 million in 1985 to about $7 billion in 1991. As a result, the share of labor-intensive manufactures in the exports of all manufactures rose from 39 percent in 1985 to 58 percent in 1991.

Table 2 shows that the rate of growth of exports of most labor-intensive manufactures increased substantially in the post-reform period. The most spectacular growth in exports was recorded in two items: footwear, which grew at 123 percent per annum in the second half of the 1980s, and furniture, which grew at 95 percent per annum. The growth of footwear exports, in particular, was most remarkable, rising from only $8 million in 1985 to almost $1 billion in 1991, and quadrupling between 1989 and 1991. Table 2 also shows that despite the rapid growth in a number of items, the bulk (almost three-fourths) of labor-intensive exports in 1991 still consisted of a small number of commodities, in particular textiles, clothing and footwear. Textile and clothing exports doubled between 1989 and 1991, an astonishing performance in view of declining OECD growth rates and tightening quotas. They quickly become Indonesia's major manufactured export, accounting for one-third of the total, and easily surpassing plywood, which was the dominant export item of the 1980s.

TABLE 1
GROWTH OF MANUFACTURED EXPORTS IN INDONESIA, 1980–1991
($MILLIONS)

	1980	*1985*	*1991*	Increase per annum 1980–85	Increase per annum 1985–91
Total Exports of All Manufactures	501	2,044	11,816	32%	34%
Labor Intensive Manufactures	297	807	6,814	22%	43%
Resource Intensive Manufactures	119	992	3,488	53%	23%
Capital Intensive Manufactures	85	245	1,514	24%	35%

Source: Adapted from Hill (1992).

TABLE 2
SELECTED LABOR—INTENSIVE MANUFACTURED EXPORTS
IN INDONESIA, 1980–1991 ($MILLIONS)

	1980	1985	1991	Increase per annum 1980–85	Increase per annum 1985–91
Labor Intensive Manufactures —of which	297	807	6,814	22%	43%
Clothing	98	339	2,265	28%	37%
Fabrics	43	227	1,552	39%	38%
Yarn	3	13	204	34%	58%
Footwear	1	8	994	52%	123%

Source: Adapted from Hill (1992).

Since 1987, and up to the crisis of 1997, there was a dramatic increase in both domestic and foreign investment in Indonesia. This surge in investment occurred in response to the improvements in a previously unattractive investment and trade regimes. Most striking was the rise in investment in Indonesia by Asia's four NIEs—Korea, Taiwan, Hong Kong, and Singapore (Hill 1990). For decades, big companies in the industrialized West, and more recently, Japan, had been moving their manufacturing operations to lower-wage areas such as the four NIEs. But as wages rose there, these countries began to lose their comparative advantage in labor-intensive manufacturing. Not only did investment from the Western countries begin to move then to other lower cost countries, such as Indonesia, but the NIEs themselves began to shift some manufacturing operations overseas to such countries.

The government of Indonesia took several steps to encourage foreign entrepreneurs, especially from Japan and the Asian NIEs, to invest in Indonesia. In recognition of the fact that many potential investors from these countries were small, labor-intensive firms seeking to relocate their operations because of rising costs in their own countries, the Indonesian government in May 1989 reduced the minimum amount of foreign investment required from $1 million to $250,000. This step undoubtedly contributed to an increased flow of direct investment by Japanese, Korean and Taiwanese small- and medium-scale industries (Wie 1991).

TABLE 3
APPROVED FOREIGN INVESTMENT IN INDONESIA, 1986–1992

	1986	1987	1988	1990	1992
Total Amount of FDI approved ($m)	848	1,481	4,409	8,750	10,313
Number of Projects	93	130	145	432	305
Percentage Asian —of which	na	30%	63%	78%	65%
—Japan	na	14%	17%	18%	16%
—NIEs	na	15%	45%	58%	44%

Source: Wie (1991).

Table 3 illustrates the dramatic rise in the number and total amount of approved foreign direct investment (FDI) projects between 1986 and 1992. Over this period, the total amount of FDI approved per annum rose by over ten-fold. The number of projects approved per annum also increased dramatically, from 93 in 1986 to 305 in 1992. Asian countries, already an important source of investments, substantially increased their share of the total in the second half of the 1980s. Thus, in 1987, Asian countries accounted for only 30 percent of all projects approved in Indonesia, but by 1992, their share had increased to 65 percent. In 1992, the NIEs were the dominant foreign investors in Indonesia, accounting for almost 44% of all projects, with Japan accounting for another 16 percent.

The availability of cheap and abundant labor in Indonesia was obviously an important motivating factor for foreign investors, especially the NIEs, to invest in Indonesia. Using indices of value-added per worker in various industries as a measure of labor intensity, Wie (1991) found that the bulk of the FDI of the NIEs was concentrated in labor-intensive activities. For example, data from 1990 show that 99 of the 102 approved Korean and 94 of the 97 approved Taiwanese manufacturing projects were located in labor-intensive industries. Furthermore, 64 percent of Korean projects and 43 percent of Taiwanese projects were located in *highly* labor-intensive industries.

IMPACT ON EMPLOYMENT AND EARNINGS

Impact on Employment

The impact of the reform program on total employment is difficult to judge. For Indonesia, the usual labor force measures of employment and unemployment are not very illuminating. Total employment in Indonesia is largely supply-determined, growing at around the same annual rate as the labor force (3.5 percent during the 1980s). Thus, inspection of the total employment series tells us nothing about what happens to labor demand in Indonesia. The unemployment rate is also not a good indicator of the labor market situation: it has remained more or less constant through the 1980s, never rising above 3 percent during the 1982–1990 period. What is more indicative of changes in the Indonesian economy's demand for labor is changes in wage employment. As Table 4 indicates, wage employment grew at an average rate of 4.5 percent per annum over the 1986–1990 period—a sure sign of an improvement in the economy's demand for labor. The table also shows the very fast growth of wage employment in agriculture and manufacturing and the even faster growth in trade and restaurants, partly derived from the growth in other sectors, and partly reflecting the rapid expansion of international tourism.

TABLE 4
WAGE EMPLOYMENT BY SECTOR IN INDONESIA, 1986–1990

	1986 ('000)	1990 ('000)	1986–90 Annual Growth
Agriculture, Forestry, etc.	3,531	4,876	8.4%
Manufacturing	3,105	4,296	8.5%
Trade & Restaurants	789	1,1169	10.3%
Public Services	7,283	7,300	0.1%
Other	2,872	3,435	4.6%
Total	*17,580*	*21,076*	*4.6%*

Source: Adapted from Godfrey (1993).

The post-1986 boom clearly had a major effect on formal sector wage employment creation in Indonesia, and both male and female workers benefited from this boom, *though the gains were larger for female workers*. Table 5 reveals that the number of male employees in the manufacturing sector rose by 14 percent between 1982–1986. During the next four years, this number rose by a further 32 percent. The rate of job creation for female workers in the manufacturing sector also increased substantially in the post-reform period: during 1982–1986, the number of manufacturing sector jobs for women increased by 13 percent, whereas during the following four years, the number of jobs increased by a staggering 53 percent. As a result, while the share of female workers in the manufacturing workforce remained unchanged at 32 percent between 1982–1986, during the next four years it grew to 35 percent.

TABLE 5
NUMBERS EMPLOYED AND REAL EARNINGS IN
MANUFACTURING IN INDONESIA, 1982–1990

	1982	1986	1990	Increase 1982-86	Increase 1986-90
Male					
No. of Wage Employees ('000)	1,852	2,113	2,779	14%	32%
Real Earnings Index	100	102	112	2%	10%
Female					
No. of Wage Employees ('000)	879	992	1,517	13%	53%
Real Earnings Index	100	114	124	14%	9%

Source: Adapted from Godfrey (1993).

Impact on Earnings

Table 5 also shows that between 1982–1990, female workers in the manufacturing sector gained substantially more than their male counterparts in terms of real earnings: while male earnings grew by 12 percent over the entire period, female earnings grew by twice as much. Furthermore, the earnings for male workers in the manufacturing sector remained more or less constant in real terms between 1982–1989, before beginning to rise between 1989 and 1990. Female employees in the manufacturing sector, in contrast, experienced a growth in their real incomes in both the pre- and post-reform period, though again, a substantial part of their growth in earnings also occurred in the last year.

This trend is confirmed when we examine wage data instead of earnings data. Thus, the growth in employment between 1986 and 1989 in the manufacturing sector was achieved without a substantial increase in the real wage for either sex, which is consistent with the "unlimited labor-supply" model. By 1990, however, the labor market had begun to tighten in response to rising labor demand and we begin to get some evidence of an increase in real wages in the manufacturing sector in Indonesia. Indeed, real wages in agriculture also appear to have turned sharply upwards in 1992, while a similar steep upturn in construction wages in some cities seems to have started a year earlier (Godfrey 1993).

Despite the rapid growth in employment in the manufacturing sector in Indonesia since the mid-1980s, it needs to be kept in mind that the sector employed a relatively small share of the country's workforce. Thus, in 1990, the manufacturing sector in Indonesia accounted for only 10 percent of total employment, whereas the comparable share was 20 percent in Malaysia, and 17 percent in China, which has a significantly lower income than Indonesia. One reason for the smaller share of manufacturing sector employment in Indonesia as compared with other countries was the relatively recent growth of this sector in Indonesia. Another contributory factor, however, was the still incomplete process of internal and external deregulation of some of sectors, such as food processing, that have strong backward linkages to labor-intensive activities in agriculture.

REFERENCES

Godfrey, Martin (1993) *"Employment Planning Within the Context of Economic Reforms—A Case Study of Indonesia,"* Working Paper No. 39, World Employment Program Research, ILO, Geneva.

Hill, Hal (1990) "Foreign Investment and East Asian Economic Development," *Asian-Pacific Economic Literature,* 4 (2), September.

Hill, Hal (1992) "Manufacturing Industry," in A. Booth (ed.) *"The Oil Boom and After: Indonesian Economic Policy and Performance in the Soeharto Era,"* (Singapore: Oxford University Press).

Republic of Indonesia (1994b) *The Human Resources Profile of Indonesia,* (Jakarta, Indonesia: Department of Manpower).

Republic of Indonesia (1994c) *Indicator Ekonomi,* (Jakarta, Indonesia: Bureau of Statistics [BPS] Monthly Statistical Bulletin).

Republic of Indonesia (1993) *Manpower and Employment Situation in Indonesia, 1993,* (Jakarta, Indonesia: Department of Manpower).

Republic of Indonesia (1994a) *Statistic Indonesia: Statistical Yearbook of Indonesia for 1993,* (Jakarta, Indonesia: Bureau of Statistics [BPS]).

Wie, Thee Kian (1991) "The Surge of Asian NIE Investment into Indonesia," *Bulletin of Indonesian Economic Studies,* 27 (3), December.

CHAPTER 8

Sulawesi's Cocoa Boom: Lessons of Smallholder Dynamism and Hands-off Policy[1]

Akihiko Nishio *and* Takamasa Akiyama

Indonesia's cocoa sector expanded dramatically during 1980–1994 with production rising at a compounded average rate of 26 percent per annum, taking the level of output from 10,284 tons to 271,127 tons and making Indonesia the world's third largest cocoa producer after Cote d'Ivoire and Ghana. Exports of cocoa beans reached $166 million in 1993, making this one of Indonesia's major agricultural exports. The objective of this chapter is to discuss the reasons for the sector's phenomenal expansion. Two conclusions emerge from our analysis. First, a major factor behind the sector's growth was the *relative lack of government intervention* in the production and marketing of cocoa. Second, government nevertheless played an important role in providing adequate infrastructure to make the cocoa business a profitable one for smallholders to enter. These conclusions are based on an investigation of cocoa farming and distribution on the island of Sulawesi that accounts for the bulk of Indonesia's production.

While there are three categories of cocoa producers in Indonesia, namely, smallholders, private estates, and government-owned estates (PTPs), about 80 percent of incremental production during 1980–1994 came from smallholders whose share in total output increased from 10 percent in 1980 to 27 percent in 1985 and 72 percent in 1994. This was clearly the most dynamic producer group in the system and is also the focus of this chapter.

PRODUCTION OF
SMALLHOLDER COCOA

Cocoa plants were introduced to Java early in the eighteenth century. By 1930, production had risen to around 1,500 tons. Cocoa was produced mainly by plantations in East Java, owned by Dutch companies. This was fine or flavored cocoa, not the bulk cocoa that Europeans appreciated. From early on these cocoa plantings were very seriously affected by the cocoa pod-borer, especially in East Java where cocoa cultivation was abandoned in 1936. The Dutch estates in West Java were not affected by this pest, but they were effectively neglected during and after World War II. Thus, production remained marginal until the early-1980s. Although smallholder cocoa production had started in Maluku, Sulawesi and other islands, total smallholder production was only 1,058 tons in 1980.

Following high world cocoa prices in the late-1970s and early-1980s that were prompted by a sharp reduction in output from West Africa, the mid-1980s saw a phenomenal expansion in cocoa acreage and production by Indonesian smallholders. Total smallholder acreage expanded nearly 30-fold between 1980 and 1994, from 13,125 ha. (hectares) in 1980 to 389,946 ha. in 1994, and total smallholder production increased from 1,058 tons to 196,235 tons during the same period (see Figure 1). This large production increase also took place mainly on the island of Sulawesi, which accounted for 77 percent of total smallholder production in 1994.

This rapid expansion was due to several factors including: low cost of labor; abundance of suitable land; proximity to Malaysia; a highly competitive marketing network in Sulawesi; government aid; and the growth of extensive coconut plantations which were ready to receive cocoa trees as an intercrop (Ruf 1993a). In addition one must note the entrepreneurial and innovative skills of the smallholders, many of whom are Bugis, a people originating in South Sulawesi. A large number of Bugis went to work in plantations in Sabah, Malaysia, in the late-1970s in response to the growing demand for labor there. While working in these plantations, they not only acquired the know-how to grow cocoa very efficiently, but also gained capital for their own future efforts.[2]

A small number of these farmers returned to Sulawesi and started cocoa farming. The dissemination of know-how and the remittance of capital from Sabah contributed to the expansion of cocoa production in Sulawesi. So too did the supply of seeds from PTPs and private plantations that expanded operations in the late-1970s. Initially, the smallholders planted cocoa in South Sulawesi, but later many moved to Southeast Sulawesi (except Pakue in Southeast Sulawesi where cocoa had been grown for a long time), where land was more abundant. Population density is estimated to be 5/ha. in Southeast Sulawesi, which is much lower than 200/ha. in South Sulawesi. Smallholders often sold their farms and houses in South Sulawesi to invest in Southeast Sulawesi and grow cocoa on a monocultural basis.[3]

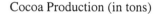

Cocoa Production (in tons)

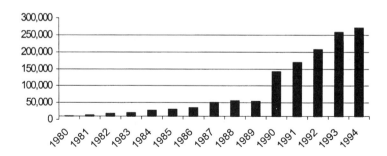

Source: Directorate General of Estates, Republic of Indonesia; Indonesia Cocoa Association.

FIGURE 1. COCOA PRODUCTION AND ACREAGE IN INDONESIA 1980–1994

An important contributing factor was the relatively good transport infrastructure. For an export crop like cocoa, transport infrastructure is essential. In many areas where smallholder expansion took place, adequate roads or ports or both were available. Public infrastructure investments, including some through the Transmigration Programs, were clearly important to cocoa acreage expansion.

Innovative and efficient production methods, coupled with the low cost of labor, suitable climate and soil, has kept the cost of production of Indonesian smallholders among the lowest in the world. This is one of the most important reasons why Indonesia's smallholders have been able to expand cocoa production at a very high rate in spite of declining world cocoa prices in the 1980s and early-1990s in U.S. dollar terms. Ruf (1993b) provides comparative data on costs of production, marketing, and taxes in the major cocoa-producing countries to show that Indonesia enjoyed the lowest "cost upon leaving the country" in the late 1980s.

MARKETING OF SMALLHOLDER COCOA

In contrast to the "marketing board" system to be found in many African cocoa producing countries in the 1980s (see Varangis et al. 1990), Indonesia has had an essentially unrestricted distribution system dominated by competitive private agents. Smallholders have a choice of selling their cocoa to village collectors ("pengumpul"), middlemen ("pedagang"), exporters, cooperatives, or estates. The first two are the most common choices since they operate in virtually every village. Collectors and middlemen do not need licenses or permits for their business. Most of the village collectors are themselves cocoa farmers, and collect cocoa from other cocoa farmers in the same village to sell to middlemen. Middlemen are generally merchants often engaged in other businesses, such as managing village retail shops. They buy cocoa from farmers and collectors, arrange transport operators to move the cocoa to major ports, and deliver it to exporters. Competition among collectors and middlemen is fierce. Farmers often sell to several collectors, and change collectors depending on prices. Similarly, collectors often change the middlemen they sell to, and middlemen change exporters. Price information is widely available. Information on prices in the New York Exchange is transmitted through radio by ASKINDO (Indonesian Cocoa Association) to all exporters, who in turn transmit it to middlemen and collectors. The Provincial Government of South Sulawesi transmits the cocoa prices prevailing in Ujung Pandang via regular radio bulletins. Farmers also listen to BBC radio broadcasts (in Bahasa) of cocoa prices.

The unrestricted and competitive marketing system for cocoa has had two notable outcomes. One is that domestic cocoa prices in Indonesia have tracked international prices very closely and the other is that marketing margins have been kept low. The first outcome can be seen in Figure 2 which shows movements in domestic (f.o.b. at Ujung Pandang) and world (ICCO Indicator Price) prices. The second result is shown in Table 1 which compares farmers' shares in f.o.b. prices for cocoa in major producing countries.

Farmers' share of export prices for cocoa is also higher than those for other agricultural commodities in Indonesia. In the province of South Sulawesi, the average farmers' share of the f.o.b. price for cocoa was 89 percent in January 1995 (see Table 3), which was considerably higher than the shares for cashew nuts (78 percent), Arabica coffee beans (77 percent), and nutmeg (68 percent).[4] The only commodity which has rivaled cocoa in South Sulawesi is Robusta coffee (92 percent), another deregulated commodity. It is worth noting that farmers' shares of export prices for some commodities in certain areas are significantly lower, such as for cassava in Lampung where farmers only received 18 percent of the f.o.b. price in 1988.

Three factors explain the high farmers' share of export prices for Indonesian cocoa: low marketing and distribution margins resulting from intense competition among traders under a free trade regime; a relatively good transport infrastructure which has kept transportation costs low in the major producing areas; and lack of large government levies such as export taxes.

Low marketing/distribution margins have played a major role in ensuring high farmgate prices. It has been argued that the low margin is a reflection of an efficient marketing/distribution regime, capitalizing on market forces particularly in terms of fostering competition among traders. As can be seen from Table 3, the gross marketing/distribution margin for cocoa, as residual of the farmers' share, was 11 percent of the f.o.b. price in South Sulawesi in January 1995. This is considerably lower than Arabica coffee (23 percent), cashew nuts (22 percent), and nutmeg (32 percent). It should be pointed out that the f.o.b. prices per kilogram of Arabica coffee and nutmeg at the time were higher than cocoa's by 3 times and 1.14 times, respectively, suggesting that cocoa's relatively low gross marketing/distribution margin is not merely an arithmetical result of its high value per kilogram.

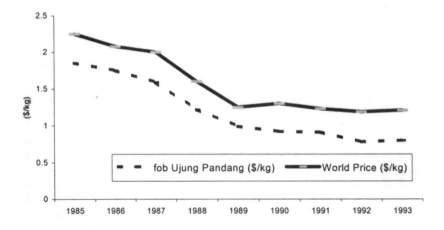

Source: Dinas Perkebunan South Sulawesi; World Bank (1995).

FIGURE 2. MOVEMENTS OF F.O.B. UJUNG PANDANG PRICES AND WORLD PRICES OF COCOA

TABLE 1
COMPARISON OF FARMER'S SHARE OF F.O.B. PRICES FOR
COCOA IN MAJOR PRODUCING COUNTRIES

Country	Farmers' Share	Marketing Boards
Indonesia	89%	No
Brazil	94%	No
Nigeria	82%	No
Ghana	63%	Yes
Cameroon	52%	Yes
Cote d'Ivoire	50%	Yes

Note: Indonesia's figure is based on January 1995 data in South Sulawesi. For all other countries, averages for 1980-1988 were used. Note that marketing boards were abolished in many African countries during the 1990s.

The efficiency of the marketing/distribution regime for cocoa and its benefits to farmers become clearer when contrasted with the cases of other commodities, for which inefficiencies in marketing/distribution are well known. The case of dried cassava ("gaplek") produced in and exported from Lampung in Sumatra is an example of monopsony/oligopsony situations and high transport cost, where the distribution margin was estimated to be as high as 82 percent of the f.o.b. price in

1988 (CASER 1992). While the margin includes the cost of drying fresh cassava, it is much higher than in East Java (47 percent). In Lampung, the farmers in a given area can only sell to a very limited number (often only one) of large traders/processors, in many cases under practices of advance payment before harvest, and they are not even allowed to see the pricing process including "rafaksi" (price deduction based on starch content, impurities content, etc.) and weight. Transport costs are also high (35–40 percent of the marketing margin.) due to the bulkiness and perishability of cassava, and to poor road infrastructure.

TABLE 2
COMPARISON OF FARMERS' SHARE OF F.O.B. PRICES FOR SELECTED EXPORT COMMODITIES FROM SOUTH SULAWESI

Commodity	Farmer's Share
Cocoa beans	89%
Coffee beans (Robusta)	92%
Cashew Nuts	78%
Coffee beans (Arabica)	77%
Nutmeg	68%
Memo Items	
Cassava (Lampung, 1988)	18%[a]
Cassava (East Java, 1988)	53%[a]
Sugar (Indonesia, 1992/93)	47%[b]
Copra (Central Sulawesi, 1995)	73%[c]

Source: Dinas Perkebunan, South Sulawesi.

Note: The period is January 1995. (a) Source: CASER (1992). Calculated as share of farmgate price for fresh cassava and export price for dried cassava. The margin therefore includes cost of drying (b) Source: World Bank estimates. Calculated as share of wholesale price minus taxes. (c) Estimated by World Bank mission in February 1995, assuming weight loss of 10% through redrying by exporter.

Sugar is an example of heavy government intervention, where the farmgate price (and the ex-mill price) is fixed by the government, and all sugar produced by the mills is required to be sold to BULOG except in Sumatra and the Eastern Islands where 50 percent and 75 percent of the output, respectively, can be sold directly to the market. The farmer's estimated share of the wholesale price (since sugar is not exported) is only 47 percent (considering that on average 38 percent of farmers' sugar output is kept by the mills as processing fee). But more importantly, farmers in major cane production areas are obliged to grow cane by the government, although rice would generally have higher returns (by 28 percent according to one estimate).

Among other commodities, copra farmers in Central Sulawesi receive advance payments before harvest from traders and processors who have established long-term relationships with farmers (similar to the dried cassava case in Lampung). The farmgate price is 73 percent of the f.o.b. price, reflecting the implied interest rate, and it is still substantially higher than dried cassava in Lampung, partly because its value per kilogram is much higher (by 8–9 times in 1994). Coffee presents an interesting case. After an export quota system was dismantled in 1989, gross marketing margins fell sharply from 30–40 percent to 8 percent because of increased competition. The above comparison of marketing systems for different commodities is summarized in Table 3.

The transportation of cocoa from production areas to export points in Sulawesi is accomplished at relatively low cost because of the availability of good roads. This is a major contribution made by public investment and it provides Indonesian cocoa farmers a big source of advantage over their counterparts in other major cocoa producing countries such as Ghana and Nigeria. The availability of good roads was also an important factor in the expansion of cocoa production in Cote d'Ivoire and Malaysia during the 1980s. The pattern of production in Sulawesi has followed the pattern of transport infrastructure. Cocoa production has expanded most in areas with good roads and/or sea-lanes (e.g., the Pakue area in Southeast Sulawesi) to Ujung Pandang and least in areas with poor road access, such as the southwest corner of Southeast Sulawesi.

Finally, the absence of export taxes also keeps the marketing margin low in comparison to that found in African countries, such as Ghana and Cote d'Ivoire, where export taxes were a prominent feature of the cocoa sector during the 1980s.

CONCLUSIONS

The rapid expansion of Indonesia's cocoa production in the last 10 years was mainly due to large production increases by smallholders in South and Southeast Sulawesi. While the climate and soil in Sulawesi and local entrepreneurial attitudes were vital for the development of this sector, the relative lack of government intervention, prudent macroeconomic policies and provision of good infrastructure were also very important. The "hands off" approach taken with regard to cocoa is especially notable because it differs from the approach taken with respect to many other commodities such as cassava, sugar, and cloves.

TABLE 3
COMPARISON OF MARKETING SYSTEMS FOR SELECTED COMMODITIES

Commodity	Selling Options for Farmers	Availability of Price Information for Farmers	Government Interventions	Gross Marketing Margins[b]
Cocoa (S. Sulawasi) (case of free market)	Can choose among a large number of collectors, who in turn sell to different middlemen.	Price information readily available. Local prices broadcast locally. World prices broadcast by BBC Indonesian service and by ASKINDO.	Retribution charges in certain regencies and 10 percent import tariff. VAT of 10 percent has been imposed since April 1995.	11% (50% in SE Sulawasi in 1980, before cocoa boom)
Robusta Coffee (S. Sulawasi) (case of free market)	Can choose among a large number of collectors, who in turn sell to different middlemen. During the export quota period beans eventually sold only to exporters with quota.	Price information readily available. Local prices broadcast locally. World prices broadcast by BBC Indonesian service and by AEKI.	De facto ban on export of low-grade coffee. (Export quota existed between 1981 and 1989.) VAT of 10 percent has been imposed since April 1995.	8% (30-40% in 1989, just when export quota was being dismantled)
Dried Cassava (Lampung) (case of monopsony/ oligopsony and high transport cost)	In many areas, a small number of (often only one) large buyer/ processors exist (oligopsony/monopsony). Price basically deter-mined by the buyer.	Very little price information available. The processes of price deduction (rafaksi) based on starch content, etc., and weighing are often kept confidential.	Export quota for the European market.	82% (reflects price deduction, cost of drying, high transport cost)
	Can sell only to the nearest mill in TRI[a] areas, at a price fixed by GOI. Farmers not receiving TRI credit can sell to anyone at any price (mostly in upland areas in E. Java).	Farmgate (provenue) price fixed by GOI, and announced annually at the beginning of next year's cane planting season.	Heavy interventions. Farmers in TRI areas obliged to plant sugar cane (i.e. cannot plant other crops with higher returns, namely rice) and to sell to mills at fixed prices. Mills in Java must sell all the sugar to BULOG at fixed prices. BULOG is also the sole importer of sugar, and conducts market operations to keep prices at certain levels.	53%
Copra (C. Sulawasi) (case of long-term farmer/buyer relationships based on credit advance).	Most copra sold to one trader/processor, who provides advance to the farmer before harvest. The rest is sold to spot markets.	Little price information available.	Retribution charges in all regencies of the province.	27% (reflects cost of re-drying, implicit interest on advance payment)

Notes: /a Smallholder Cane Intensification Program, started in 1975.
       /b Derived from Table 3 above.

NOTES

1.   A fuller version of this chapter was previously published in the Bulletin of Indonesian Economic Studies, 33 (2), August 1997. Permission to reprint is gratefully acknowledged.

2.   Plantations in Sabah have invested heavily in agronomic research and their yields are the highest in the world.

3.   Older farms tend to do more "mixed" culture. For instance, Jamal and Pomp (1993) reports that the majority of cocoa producing smallholders surveyed in the regions of Mamuju and Polewali in South Sulawesi engaged in mixed culture.

4.   It should be noted that the figures in Table 3 are the average based on cocoa from a number of locations, some of which are several hundred miles from the export port of Ujung Pandang.

REFERENCES

Center for Agro-Socioeconomic Research, CASER (1992) *Cassava Marketing in Indonesia.*

Direktorat Jenderal Perkebunan (Directorate General of Estates) *Statistik Perkebunan Indonesia, 1984–89,* (Jakarta, Indonesia: The Government of Indonesia).

Direktorat Jenderal Perkebunan (Directorate General of Estates) *Statistik Perkebunan Indonesia, 1990–92,* (Jakarta, Indonesia: The Government of Indonesia).

Jamal, Sofyan and Marc Pomp (1993) "Smallholder Adoption of Tree Crops: A Case Study of Cocoa in Sulawesi," *Bulletin of Indonesian Economic Studies,* 29 (3).

Ruf, Francois (1993a) "Indonesia's Position Among Cocoa Producing Countries," *Indonesian Circle,* 61, June.

Ruf, Francois (1993b) "Comparison of Cocoa Production Costs in Seven Producing Countries," *The Planter,* 69 (807), June.

Varangis, Panos, T. Akiyama and M.E. Thigpen (1990) "Developments in Marketing and Pricing Systems for Agricultural Export Commodities in Sub-Saharan Africa," (Washington, DC: The World Bank Policy Research Working Paper No. 43).

World Bank (1994) *Indonesia: Environment and Development,* (Washington, DC: A World Bank Country Study).

World Bank (1995) *Commodity Markets and the Developing Countries,* (Washington, DC: A World Bank Quarterly, Commodity Policy and Analysis Unit).

World Bank (1990) *Indonesia: Sustainable Development of Forests, Land, and Water,* (New York, NY: The Oxford University Press).

CHAPTER 9

Costs and Benefits of Soymeal Deregulation

Jacqueline L. Pomeroy

INTRODUCTION

In November 1988, the government of Indonesia (GOI) issued a regulation covering the domestic soybean and soymeal markets. The stated purposes of the regulation were to sustain a stable price and to establish a domestic source of supply. To accomplish these goals, the Ministry of Finance (MOF) established a series of prices and fees that would regulate the procurement and production of soybean meal. Procurement responsibility was transferred to the Bureau of Logistics (BULOG) which had broad authorities in Indonesia to buy and sell strategic agricultural commodities and foodstuffs. Domestic production was encouraged by setting a domestic price substantially above the international price of soymeal and erecting an effective ban on meal imports. However, only one domestic producer was permitted to operate, a producer with strong political links.

This regulation was changed three times between 1988 and 1995 (see Table 1). The first deregulation in 1991 substituted a tariff and large surcharge for the previous ban on imports. The second deregulation in 1993 eliminated the surcharge but required a minimum 40 percent domestic purchase ratio. A subsequent change in 1994 eliminated the 5 percent tariff and reduced the minimum domestic purchase ratio to 30 percent. This chapter presents estimates of the welfare changes that arose from these regulatory adjustments. These estimates, in turn, permit an assessment of the cost to the country of having had regulations that effectively created and supported a domestic monopolist in the market for soymeal.[1]

Since the preparation of this chapter, the political position of the monopolist and the parameters of the soymeal market have changed. Recent changes in regulatory arrangements are not reviewed since the purpose is primarily to illustrate the effects of certain types of regulations such as import bans, tariff surcharges and domestic content requirements which prevailed in Indonesia's soymeal sector during 1988–1995.

TABLE 1
SUMMARY OF SOYBEAN AND SOYMEAL REGULATION

YEAR	SOYBEANS	SOYMEAL
1988	Private imports banned, full import control given to BULOG. Beans crushed for a fee set by MOF, with BULOG retaining ownership. No controls over sale of domestic production.	Private imports limited and strictly controlled by license. BULOG sells to end users at prices set by MOF.
1991	Private imports banned. BULOG retains control over imports as before. No controls over sale of domestic production.	Private imports freely permitted with 5% tariff & 35% surcharge BULOG sells at price set by MOF
1993	Private imports banned. BULOG retains control over imports as before. No controls over sale of domestic production.	Private imports permitted with 5% tariff and with proof of 40:60 domestic: imported purchase ratio. BULOG sells at price set by MOF.
1994	Private imports banned. BULOG retains control over imports as before. No controls over sale of domestic production.	Private imports permitted with 0% tariff and with proof of 30:70 domestic: imported purchase ratio. BULOG sells at price set by MOF.

The principal use of soybeans in Indonesia is as soybean "meal," which is used as an input into the production of feeds. These are directed mainly to the poultry industry with secondary demands arising from fish cultivation and cattle feedlots. During the 1980s, rapid urbanization and income growth in Indonesia was shifting protein demand toward mass-produced meat sources, especially poultry. This shift was reinforced by the removal of government policies discouraging large-scale poultry operations. As private sector poultry production rapidly expanded as a result, so too did demand for animal feeds. Animal feeds use a number of inputs such as corn meal and soybean meal, although the high price of soymeal in Indonesia discouraged its use in favor of other protein sources.

Under the initial regulation of 1988, BULOG was the sole importer of raw soybeans. Control over imports enabled the government to sustain a high farm support price as well as to determine the price structure for crushing the beans into meal. There was only one approved producer of soymeal in Indonesia who commenced production in 1988 at the same time as the ban on private soybean imports was introduced. After importing the beans, BULOG paid the domestic monopolist a fee set by the Ministry of Finance to crush the soybeans. BULOG retained ownership of the resulting meal and sold it to the feedmills at a price also set by the MOF. In addition to its crushing fee, the crusher retained and was free to sell the soybean oil that is a by-product of the crushing process.

In 1991, BULOG was selling the soybean meal produced by the domestic crusher to feedmills in Indonesia at a price approximately 50 percent above the world price (c.i.f. China). This and other prices were administratively set by MOF, and any losses were covered out of the MOF budget.

The domestic monopoly soymeal producer was a relatively high cost producer, despite having a new crushing facility and world-class equipment. In addition, it was an exceptionally capital-intensive operation by Indonesian standards: the original capital investment was valued at around $50 million, with estimates of total employment at the plant never exceeding 350 workers.[2]

Although the intention of establishing the facility was to displace all import demand for soybean meal, even at the high domestic price soymeal demand was greater than the domestic crusher's output. Thus, there was a need for additional supply from imports, and on an exceptional basis, BULOG did permit imports of soymeal. For example, several feedmills were permitted to import soymeal at the basic 5 percent tariff while the 35 percent surcharge was waived, and payment of the tariff was deferred for one year. Nonetheless, the overall high price lowered the total quantity of soymeal demanded by feedmills considerably.

These regulations sustained a high soymeal price and frustrated the feedmills in Indonesia, who responded by buying limited amounts of the available domestic producer's meal and supplemented it with corn meal and other less desirable protein sources for poultry feed. Their preference was clearly to see imports enter the Indonesian market and force the domestic monopolist to compete with world prices. The government recognized this problem, and in June 1991 the Ministry of Finance announced that soymeal imports would be unrestricted and subject only to regular administrative procedures and a 5 percent import duty.

Our calculations indicate that it was quite likely that such a comprehensive deregulation would have forced the domestic monopolist soymeal producer to close down. Recognizing this possibility, BULOG effectively continued the import ban by simply refusing to issue any import licenses. Even so, in June and July some feedmills entered into contracts to import meal pending approval of their applications for letters of credit. Clearly, a serious conflict had emerged that required some resolution. The resolution that emerged was a compromise in which MOF decided to apply an import surcharge of 35 percent over the basic 5 percent tariff level but import licenses were to be provided without restriction. Further, BULOG lowered its selling price by 5.7 percent to a level that made domestic meal more competitive with meal imported under the tariff. The reduction in price provided some benefits for Indonesia. However, the tariff sustained a very high price for soymeal, continued to distort demand for soymeal and other feed ingredients, and thus to impede the development of an efficient poultry industry.

WELFARE ANALYSIS OF REGULATORY CHANGES

The welfare effects of the regulatory changes introduced in 1991 and 1993 were analyzed with the help of a standard partial equilibrium model.[3] The main assumptions of the model are:

1. Policy is designed to ensure that the domestic monopoly firm can produce at full capacity, with any meal imports acting as a residual supply source.

2. Under any policy regime Indonesia would be a small importer of meal, meaning that it has no ability to influence the world price of soymeal through varying its imports.

3. In the short run (e.g., one year), the demand curve for soybean meal in Indonesia reflects only the ability of feedmills to shift the mix of soybean meal in their feeds, for given levels of output. The demand curve has a constant elasticity over the relevant price ranges.

4. The domestic monopoly has constant marginal operating costs, which include its depreciation allowances, while its fixed costs consist solely of debt service.

Base Case Estimates

Under the price and production parameters that prevailed in 1991 before regulatory changes were made, the consumer subsidy arising from the controlled price was around Rp. 2.9 billion. Feedmills that were allowed to import soymeal (up to 10 m. kg.) also enjoyed an effective subsidy amounting to Rp. 1.8 billion. MOF suffered a budgetary loss on soybean acquisition that was only minimally offset by the present value of the tariff payments. By our estimates, the budgetary loss was some Rp. 13.6 billion per year. The domestic monopoly crusher's profits are estimated at Rp. 26.13 billion. Note, however, that "social profits," or those gains to society from soybean crushing and the sale of meal and oils, properly exclude any consideration of fixed costs. Thus, "social profits" equal the monopolist's revenues less variable costs, or Rp. 45.94 billion. Some of these results are detailed in Table 2.

The relevant question to ask is not the *level* of welfare under a particular policy (total welfare at a particular equilibrium is difficult to calculate in any event), but rather how welfare *changes* as policies change. The policy that provides the largest gain in welfare relative to the initial regulated equilibrium would be described as the best choice for the economy.

Estimated Effects of the 1991 Policy Changes

The new support package issued in July 1991 adopted changes in two main areas. First, BULOG's selling price for the domestic monopolist's meal was lowered to Rp. 580 per kg. We assume that BULOG was allowed to reimburse MOF based on this lower price. Second, all firms were given authority to import soybean meal, ending BULOG's status as sole importer. However, since imported meal was far cheaper than the domestic crusher's, even under the new price structure, GOI chose to erect a 35 percent surcharge duty on top of the existing 5 percent tariff. This 40 percent total tariff was sufficient to keep the domestic firm's soymeal competitive with the imported alternative.

TABLE 2
SHORT-RUN ACTIVITY LEVELS AND WELFARE CHANGES IN THE
INDONESIAN SOYBEAN MEAL MARKET FROM POLICY CHANGES, 1991

	1988 Policy	1991 Policy	Deregulation
Price (Rp/kg)	615	580	442
Production (m kg)	249	249	0
Consumption (m kg)	259	306	492
Imports (m kg)	10	57	492
Tariff, Tariff Surcharge (%)	5	40	5
MOF loss on Sovbeans (Rp bn)	-13.74	-22.46	0
Tariff Revenue (Rp bn)	0.17	9.36	10.08
Domestic Monopolist's Profits (Rp bn)	26.13	26.13	0
Changes In:			
Consumer Surplus (Rp bn)	-	9.89	64.919
Other Importers Cost Savings (Rp bn)	-	-1.77	-1.77
Domestic Producer Surplus (Rp bn)	-	0	-45.94
MOF Budget (Rp bn)	-	0.48	23.65
(Tariff Revenue)	-	9.20	9.91
(Procurement)	-	-8.71	13.74
Net Economic Efficiency Gain (Rp bn)	-	8.61	40.93

In computing the welfare changes of the shift to the "1991 Policy" in Table 2, we adopt Rp. 580 as the new domestic price. This lower price generates higher consumption at 306 m. kg. and sustains the domestic producer's full output. Thus, imports rise to 57 m. kg., by our estimate. These greater imports and the higher tariff combine to raise tariff revenue substantially. However, the lower price also commits MOF to a larger procurement loss (assuming fixed soybean import prices) because of its lower payment from BULOG.

With the new price and production parameters we estimate consumer surplus to rise to Rp. 9.89 billion per year. However, by eliminating the preferential treatment for feedmill importers, the previous Rp. 1.77 billion gain on this account disappears. The domestic crusher's operation is unaffected by the change (it remains fully protected) so neither its profits nor the producer surplus (revenues less variable costs) change under the new policy. There is a small rise in the budgetary loss absorbed by MOF as the gain in tariff revenue is more than offset by the rise in procurement costs. Overall, we compute the total welfare gain to be some Rp. 8.61 billion in the first year as a result of the lower price. This illustrates the powerful effect of going from an import ban to a tariff-based scheme.

At the same time, however, the policy change sacrifices a great deal of potential welfare benefits that could have been achieved by full deregulation, as shown in the third column of Table 2. Deregulation (that is, free imports subject to 5 percent tariff, we also assume that MOF and BULOG would withdraw from the market and expect the domestic crusher to pay for its soybean needs, though at cheap world prices rather than at expensive domestic prices) would lower domestic price to Rp. 442 per kg. (by 28 percent). Resulting substitution into soybean meal by feed mills should raise consumption dramatically, to 492 m. kg. Such a change would have achieved substantial gains in consumer surplus benefits. As suggested in Table 2, these gains to consumers would amount to almost Rp. 65 billion. Further, by significantly raising imports of soybean meal, MOF would gain substantial tariff revenue as well, compared to the situation under the previous policy. This revenue gain is reinforced by the fact that MOF would no longer need to absorb a budgetary loss on the procurement of soybeans for the local crusher's operation. All this illustrates the substantial welfare consequences of maintaining regulations that essentially supported the domestic monopolist. Full deregulation would essentially force the high-cost domestic monopolist out of business.

Estimated Effects of the 1993 Policy Changes

As part of its June 1993 deregulation package, the GOI announced a change in policy applied to imports of soymeal which included eliminating the 35 percent tariff surcharge on imports. The surcharge was replaced, however, by a requirement that 40 percent of the soybean meal purchased in Indonesia be locally produced. The remainder could be imported freely, though such imports would remain subject to the same basic 5 percent tariff as previously.

In late June 1993 the price of imported soymeal c.i.f. China was reported to be $240 per metric ton, or Rp. 499 per kg. at an exchange rate of Rp. 2,080 per dollar. The port handling and local transport cost for imported soymeal was then estimated at roughly 15 Rp. per kg.. Thus, with the original 35 percent surcharge in effect, the local cost per unit of imported soymeal was Rp. 713 per kg., while the price of locally-produced soymeal remained fixed at Rp. 615 per kg.[4]

With the change in policy, the local marginal cost of soymeal to feed millers becomes a blend of the costs of local soymeal (40 percent) and imported soymeal

(60 percent). As the unit cost of imported soymeal falls to Rp. 539 per kg. after the surcharge is removed, the blended cost is thus Rp. 569 per kg. This cost is 20.2 percent lower than the unit cost of imported soymeal prior to the reform.

The impact of the 1993 policy reform on economic efficiency in Indonesia was certainly positive, especially considering feedmillers' willingness to rapidly expand soymeal consumption at a lower price (recall the estimated price elasticity of demand is -3.2). Model-based results (reported in Table 3) show losses to the government but gains to soymeal users and consumers in general. There was no impact on the domestic monopolist's profits. The government loses surcharge revenues but gains additional tariff revenues for a net loss of Rp. 12.5 billion. The welfare gain to soymeal users was Rp. 36.8 billion. The net gain in economic efficiency to Indonesia was Rp. 24.3 billion.

As noted above, the gain to soymeal users under this policy is estimated at Rp. 36.8 billion annually. Although these benefits accrue directly to the feed millers who use the soymeal, just as with previous policy changes competitive market forces should allow part of these gains to be passed on to poultry growers and consumers in the form of lower prices. Thus, it should be reiterated that these estimates are conservative in that they reflect only changes in soymeal inclusion rates in poultry feed. Expansions in the production of feed would entail further benefits.

Because we assume that the local producer continues to produce at its capacity output level, there is no additional local production with this policy change and no resulting impact on the firm's revenues or costs. The domestic firm thus remains fully protected. To estimate the producer surplus per unit to the domestic producer, we start with the crushing fee received from BULOG minus variable costs per kg. of soymeal, estimated at a constant Rp. 31 per unit of soymeal (based on Maskus and Usmanto 1992, adjusted for inflation). Added to this is the value of the retained soybean oil generated as a by-product of the crushing. Based on a June 1993 f.o.b. price of soybean oil of US $520 per metric ton, this generates revenues of approximately Rp. 243 per kg. of soymeal produced. Net producer surplus for the local facility is thus estimated at Rp. 247 per kg.[5]

TABLE 3
WELFARE EFFECTS OF 1993 POLICY CHANGES

Imported Soymeal, China c.i.f June 1993 (Rp./kg.)	539
Blended Meal Price (Rp./kg.)	499
(40% domestic, 60% imported)	
Maximum Imported : Domestic Meal Ratio	1.5 : 1
Changes In:	
Consumer Surplus (Rp. bn)	36.8
Domestic Producer Surplus (Rp. bn)	0
MOF Budget (Rp. bn)	-12.5
(Tariff Revenue)	-12.5
(Procurement)	0
Net Economic Efficiency Gain (Rp. bn)	24.3

CONCLUDING OBSERVATIONS

Looking back at market conditions and changes in GOI soymeal policy between 1990 and 1994, it is possible to discern a strategy that tried to maintain the viability of the domestic monopolist while reducing somewhat the implicit taxes imposed on soymeal users. Starting from a situation in which imports were effectively banned, the GOI first tried to reduce the economic cost of the restriction by going from bans to tariffs, that is, instituting free imports with a high surcharge. This enabled feedmillers to increase production in order to meet rapidly growing demand for their product, while at the same time providing reasonable assurance as to the continued viability of the sole domestic producer.

The economic costs and market distortions resulting from the surcharge policy, however, continued to grow along with the demand for animal feed. Moreover, there was some apprehension that even with the price of imports higher than the domestic meal price, feedmillers would move to imports at the expense of the domestic crusher. The move to the 40 percent domestic content requirement and elimination of the surcharge can be seen as an attempt to minimize the overall welfare costs while maintaining a protected environment for the domestic firm (recall that the net costs to the government actually increased because of the substantial reduction in tariff revenues).

The costs to Indonesia of supporting the domestic monopolist were substantial. As the welfare computations for the 1991 complete deregulation case show, national welfare would have risen overall by Rp. 40.93 billion (in 1991 prices), the largest such gain available from any potential policy changes. *One interpretation of this finding is that GOI was annually investing Rp. 40.93 billion ($21 million) of Indonesia's scarce resources in order to sustain the operation of a plant that was worth just over twice that sum.* Shifting to the alternative surcharge policy improved the situation, but still sacrificed substantial potential gains. Comparing the welfare gains available under the 1991 policy change and under complete deregulation reveals that the GOI chose to spend Rp. 32.32 billion (40.93–8.61) to support domestic soymeal production.

The 1993 change to a 40 percent domestic content requirement resulted in a further gain of Rp. 24.3 billion (at 1993 prices) to the Indonesian economy, with consumers gaining Rp. 36.8 billion but at an estimated budgetary cost to the GOI of Rp. 12.5 billion. The subsequent reduction of the domestic content requirement to 30 percent would have reduced the growing distortion resulting from increased domestic demand in a manner that would be neutral to the interests of the domestic producer and cost the GOI the 5 percent lost tariff revenue. The domestic crusher would remain assured of demand for its full capacity output, and the GOI would retain its commitment to procure soybeans at the market price in order to sustain that level of output.

Effects on Employment

It is interesting to ask if these trade barriers to protect the domestic monopolist could be justified as a means of promoting domestic employment. From the data available on employment related to the soymeal sector, it appears that this could not have been a very powerful motivation for the regulations used. First, the domestic monopolist was an exceptionally capital-intensive firm. With only 350 employees, the capital labor ratio in the firm was approximately $143,000 (at its apparent capital value of $50 million), which was higher at the time than that of the average manufacturing industry even in the United States. Further, the vast majority of workers employed were unskilled and earning only the minimum wage. In terms of the number of "jobs saved" by the trade barrier, taking the estimate of the first-year net gains available from the 1991 deregulation, the net costs per job of the previous policy were some Rp. 117 million ($60,000), which far exceeded the average annual wage for unskilled labor in Indonesia.

Moreover, protection for the domestic firm in the form of high domestic prices for soymeal very likely precluded the development of more jobs in more competitive industries than it created in that firm. Additionally, there would be employment gains, perhaps quite substantial, in the poultry industry as a result of deregulation in soybean meal. Although these gains are not estimated here, we note that Indonesian poultry operations tend to be labor-intensive and their expansion, therefore, could be expected to significantly enhance employment.

NOTES

1.   This chapter draws substantially from work completed for the Ministry of Trade and the TIP Project, including Maskus, Pomeroy, Parker, and Bailey (1991), Maskus and Usmanto (1992), and Marks (1994). The empirical results reported in this chapter are derived from the model used in the referenced papers.

2.   It is important to note that domestic soymeal quality differs from imported meal. Its protein content was reportedly evaluated at some 41 percent to 42 percent (world standards are 45 percent to 47 percent) with an oil content of greater than 2 percent (world standards 1 percent). The domestic firm, however, was a reliable supplier in quantity terms, suggesting that local feedmills were willing to pay a small premium for its meal to compensate for the risk in experiencing delays in deliveries of imported meal.

3.   Maskus, Pomeroy, Parker, and Bailey (1991) extend the analysis to a longer-run period, allowing for shifts in demand. We limit our analysis here to the short-run welfare effects.

4.   The MOF had previously raised the price back up to Rp. 615 from its 1991 level of Rp. 580.

5.   There were increases in the summer of 1993 in the world prices of soybeans and soybean products due to changes in external conditions, notably the flooding in the central United States of America, and agricultural development and increased soymeal utilization in South China. Sensitivity analyses performed for these calculations suggest that the magnitudes of the welfare effects are substantially invariant to these changes.

REFERENCES

Marks, Stephen V. (1993) "Indonesia's 1993 Soybean Meal Import Policy Reform: Impacts on Prices, Quantities, and Economic Welfare," *USAID/EPSO/ Jakarta*, August.

Maskus, Keith E., Jacqueline L. Pomeroy, Stephen Parker, and Laura Bailey (1991) "Welfare Costs of Indonesia's Import Restrictions on Soybean Meal," *USAID/EPSO/Jakarta,* August.

Maskus, Keith E. and Paulus Usmanto (1992), "Soybean Meal Deregulation and its Impact on the Feed and Poultry Industries in Indonesia," *USAID/ EPSO/Jakarta,* June.

CHAPTER 10

The Indonesian Cement Industry: A Case for Modified Regulation

Herb Plunkett *and* Anwar Pasinringi[1]

The cement industry in Indonesia has often experienced seasonal shortages and high prices. This has bought forth widespread public criticism of the industry and its regulatory arrangements. There have been accusations of cartel control, hoarding and speculation, and calls for the industry to be deregulated. Cement is considered a strategic commodity because of its importance to the building and construction sectors and the centrality of these sectors in the Indonesian economy. The aim of this chapter is to describe the regulatory arrangements that prevailed in the mid-1990s, outline some important economic features of the demand and supply of cement, and discuss the consequences of some alternative regulations.

REGULATORY AND ECONOMIC ASPECTS

Existing regulatory arrangements in the Indonesian cement industry have three distinguishing characteristics: (a) use of guiding prices, (b) use of distribution quotas, and (c) a mix of private and state-owned firms.

Guiding Prices

Guiding prices for sacks of cement, known locally as HPS prices, are established at the retail level in major cities of each province. Although the HPS prices are not binding on retailers, they act as a form of price regulation because producers incur considerable public and political pressure when retail prices rise above the guiding prices, particularly in large industrial areas. At times of low demand they may act as a collective floor price for producers. The HPS prices are meant to cover representative costs of production and transportation as well as distributor and retailer margins and applicable government taxes. They are periodically reviewed and re-set but sometimes up to two years can pass between formal reviews.

Typically, there is no clear relationship between HPS prices and trade. In principle, in a competitive market, import parity prices should provide a ceiling to domestic prices and the export parity equivalent or marginal costs of production should provide a price floor, in the absence of the existing export control provisions. There is a pattern, however, to the deviation of retail prices from HPS benchmarks: the deviation is least in capital cities near cement plants and highest in capital cities far from existing cement plants. These features of the cement market are most evident outside of Java. This is also the pattern of prices that could be expected in a competitive cement market with fluctuations in the level of demand.

The basing of the HPS on the ex-factory plus freight cost from the nearest cement plant mimics a pricing feature that would occur under a deregulated and more competitive market. However, it does not necessarily mimic its efficiency, as the created competitiveness is not driven solely by commercial considerations. In deregulated and more competitive markets, the nearest producer would become the dominant supplier and price leader. Other producers would absorb the additional costs of transport in order to compete in the market, and the demand for their cement would be more price-elastic. In the short-run, producers would be willing to absorb additional transport costs from more distant markets until the marginal revenue no longer exceeds their marginal costs, including additional transport costs or the opportunity cost of exporting.

Distribution Quotas

The control of the geographic distribution of cement is the most important element of the existing regulation. Under current arrangements, distribution quotas are established monthly for each cement producer at meetings involving government officials and representatives from the Cement Producers Association of Indonesia. These quotas are based on the installed capacity of each producer. By negotiation, each producer is assigned delivery quotas to particular provinces based on plant location, historic supply and the cement market situation in each of the 27 provinces. Quotas are also specified for exports.

One objective of distribution quotas is to ensure that two or more producers supply each market area, thereby creating a degree of competition. While this gives buyers an alternative source of supply and provides some restraint on producer behavior, it is not a pattern that would emerge in an open market driven by competition among a few suppliers. Another objective is to ensure that *all* domestic markets are supplied. This is negotiated collectively and enforced through the issuing of licenses for exports. The Ministry of Trade only issues licenses when it is satisfied domestic supply is assured. Producers can fill their domestic market quotas directly from production or indirectly by importing cement and clinker to produce cement.

While the existing regulatory arrangements may meet the objectives of equitable supply across regions, they involve higher costs, especially from transportation. In a deregulated and more competitive market, more external trade would occur and there would be less cross-hauling within Indonesia. Producers favorably located with respect to export markets would export more and reap the additional benefits of being a regular long-term supplier, delivering less to distant Indonesian markets, which would have to import more on a long-term basis. Additionally, some producers would export more on a seasonal basis to spot markets in order to better utilize their production capacity during the off-construction period.

The Distribution Process

To ensure that their supply requirements are met in their assigned market areas, producers appoint distributors. The market areas of distributors are not regulated by the Government and, in principle, they can sell in other market areas depending on market conditions. In practice, distributors are reluctant to sell in other markets or handle competitive imports of cement for fear of jeopardizing their longer-term commercial relationship with producers who appoint them. There are no protective tariffs on imports, but the existing regulatory arrangements are not conducive to the easy entry of new participants in cement imports. The number of distributors a producer appoints depends on the size of the market allocation in the region. Producers can also sell directly to large contractors.

The Government does not control distribution and retail margins. Typical margins for these activities during nominal market periods are included in the calculated HPS prices. However, during periods of cement shortage, when retail prices exceed the HPS prices, the margins are more varied. The non-government producers monitor retail prices and change delivered prices to ensure that most of any increase in retail prices is returned to them. The government-controlled producers do not benefit in the same way since there is pressure on them to continue to charge only the ex-factory return implied by the HPS prices. Under such circumstance, distributors of cement from government-controlled producers are likely to receive most of the market increase in the price of cement.

The Demand for Cement

The demand for of cement fluctuates throughout the year. It tends to be higher in the second half of the year than in the first half. Typically 45 percent of the deliveries are made in the first half of the year and the rest in the second. This split in level of demand reflects the difference between the wet and dry seasons, and is accentuated by the budgetary allocation of development funds. There is also typically a sharp drop in demand in the month of "Idul Fitri," when deliveries are 70 percent or less of average monthly demand.

The Economies of Scale

The economies of scale in cement production imply that when choosing plant capacity, producers face a downward sloping long-run average total cost curve. Thus it is cheaper to supply the geographically dispersed markets from a few large geographically dispersed plants than from many small plants. On the other hand, the low value-to-volume ratio, which creates the high transportation costs, imply also that it may be economically rational for certain strategically-located smaller higher-cost plants to exist to supply isolated markets.

In sum, because of the geographic dispersion of markets for cement, the relative importance of transportation costs and marked economies of scale, the cement sector has a "natural" inclination to become a geographically-concentrated oligopolistic sector. This inclination is reflected in the structure of the cement industry. For example, there are only nine cement producers in all of Indonesia and the industry has a very high four-firm concentration ratio of 88 percent (assuming the government owned companies are regarded as separate firms).

ALTERNATIVE POLICIES

To better understand the economic implications of the existing regulatory policies, it is useful to analyze an alternative. The most obvious alternative is an unregulated cement market.

The Economics of an Unregulated Market

With an unregulated market there would be no geographic restriction on the distribution of cement either domestically or for export, and no government control over prices. Similarly, there would be no control over investment in the industry, other than the generally applicable environmental and foreign ownership requirements. Producers would be free to choose the markets in which they sold and the prices they set. Distributors and users of cement would be free to develop mutually acceptable arrangements with producers and among themselves. There would also be no artificial barriers to entry or exit from the industry.

With freedom to trade internationally and domestically, it could be expected that export parity would act to set a floor price and import parity a ceiling price to domestic prices. Since transport costs are an important part of the total cost of cement, there could be a relatively wide margin between these two prices.

In an unregulated market, producers could be expected to adjust their deliveries to improve their profitability. While this would result in some important changes in regional distribution, the majority of production would continue to be distributed to existing nearby markets. The improved profitability would come in part from a reduction in transport costs currently absorbed by producers to fulfill deliveries to distant markets. As a result of the adjustment, some producers would further develop their export markets on both a seasonal and a permanent basis. The north and eastern areas of Indonesia would initially increase their reliance on imports. In individual markets, it is likely that the nearest dominant supplier would become the price leader and other suppliers would have to match those prices to compete.

Producers could be expected to sell more in nearby markets as they can charge higher prices because demand is less price elastic and would absorb freight to compete in more distant markets, including exports, where price in more elastic. In other words, producers would develop a dual pricing structure. The competition between producers for profitable sales, and from imports in certain cases, would act to limit such price discriminating monopolistic behavior by individual producers. The continuation of high prices in significant regional markets, would signal the opportunity for profitable new regional investment in the industry. In this way the competitiveness in markets would be preserved and enhanced on the basis of market criteria.

Compared to ex-factory pricing alone, consumers as a group would be better off because they will not only be assured of being able to buy cement on an "ex-factory plus freight" basis, but also be able to buy on a "delivery" basis when it is cheaper. Producers also would be better off because they can contract and expand their geographic markets to better use their production capacity.

The economic intuition, as prefaced above, is that cement producers will price discriminate by charging a higher net (ex-factory) price to better recover their overheads in markets closer to their plants and a lower net price in markets further away from their plants where they have to pay for freight to compete. In other words, the addition of a uniform price is "Pareto-superior" to ex-factory plus freight pricing alone.[2]

As a result of fluctuations in demand, the existing pattern of seasonal variations in prices and variability in prices based on distance could be expected to continue. However, regional shortages are likely to be less pronounced as there would be less constraints on individual initiatives to profit from alleviating those shortages. Under the existing system, responses to unexpected increases in demand are delayed as producers have to renegotiate and adjust supply collectively.

The HPS prices would become irrelevant and the existing reporting require-ments on the industry, especially the twice monthly census of stocks at all levels in the distribution chain, would serve little purpose in the control of the industry. Producers would develop their own market information systems.

The Political Economy of Deregulating Cement

The above discussion of what might occur in Indonesia with an unregulated cement market is a general description of the current situation of the industry in the United States. Generally, markets are competitive with firms readily entering and exiting specific regional markets in the short-run. There are also no barriers to entering or exiting the industry in the longer run. However, the current situation in the United States did not evolve without government intervention. The U.S. government successfully prosecuted the industry in 1948 under anti-trust laws for collusive market behavior ("FTC vs. Cement Institute" 333 US 683, 1948).

Since 1902, the U.S. cement industry operated under a multiple "basing point" system of pricing.[3] Under this system, buyers are quoted only delivery prices determined on the basis of a price at a selected number of geographically dispersed sites ("basing" points) plus freight to the buyer from the nearest site, irrespective of the location of the cement plant that supplies the buyer. This system allowed producers located at a distance from the reference site to price discriminate and collect "phantom freight" from nearby sales. Most economists believe that this system of pricing served to increase industry collusion in cement as well as other declining cost industries, such as steel, which adopted similar systems (Haddock 1982; Karlson 1990; Koller and Weiss 1989).

Since the successful prosecution of the cement industry, cement has been offered for sale in the United States on an f.o.b. factory basis as well as a delivery basis. Regional markets have become more competitive since large plants were established in the East and Midwest with distribution terminals in distant markets. The economies of scale have enabled large producers to compete in distant markets, increasing competition, reducing regional market concentration and reducing cement prices.[4] Weiss (1989) has documented the strong general relationship between concentration in markets and increases in prices.

The danger with a complete deregulation of the cement industry is that in the resulting unregulated market collusive practices like those that existed prior to the successful prosecution of the industry in the United States could develop in Indonesia. In particular, larger firms could temporarily reduce prices in certain markets to drive-out smaller firms.[5] Thereafter large producers could more easily collude with each other to increase prices. While an increase in market shares for firms which have new low-cost production techniques and lower prices should be encouraged, a merger of firms or a temporary lowering of prices in selected markets to acquire market shares should be avoided.

In the absence of a policy to maintain competition and prevent the acquisi-tion of large market shares by horizontal mergers, collusion or abuse of market power, some form of direct regulation in the cement industry could be preferable to no regulation. However, to be beneficial, the regulation needs to be directed at preventing abuse of market power, and not the control of new entrants or specific market shares per se. One way to achieve this type of regulation is through the use of production licensing. Production licenses could be used to limit the number of production sites that could be controlled by any one group, both regionally and nationally. They also could be used to require producers to post ex-factory prices for cement and allow them to offer a uniform delivery price that they can vary at will. The administration of this type of regulation is not complex.

CONCLUDING COMMENTS

Cement is a strategic commodity because of its importance as an input to the construction industry and the centrality of that industry to the growth of the Indonesian economy. Regulatory control of the cement industry has continued long after other industries have been deregulated to improve economic efficiency. The existing regulatory control of the industry involves regular negotiations between government agencies and producers on the allocation of cement to domestic market areas, approval of exports and the posting of retail market guiding prices. The objective of this regulation is to ensure that all areas of Indonesia are supplied with cement at reasonable prices. Nonetheless, the recent history of the industry has been one of seasonal shortages with high prices and a lack of sufficient investment in new capacity to alleviate them. It also involves wasteful freight haulage and forgone export opportunities.

Because of the geographic dispersion of markets, relative importance of transport costs, marked economies of scale and high costs of entry and exit, the cement industry is one of the few industries that has a "natural" tendency to produce through a geographically-concentrated oligopoly in an unregulated environment. The experience of the development of the industry in other countries, especially the United States, indicates that the complete deregulation of the industry would not necessarily lead to more competitive behavior among producers. In the absence of legislation to ensure competition, some direct regulation of the Indonesian industry may be preferable to no regulation. The challenge of this type of regulation is to provide the benefits of competitive markets without encouraging collusion.

NOTES

1.   At the time of writing of this chapter Herb Plunkett was a consultant with the USAID-funded Trade Implementation and Policy (TIP) Project at the Ministry of Trade, Indonesia and Anwar Pasinringi was a staff member of the Directorate for Export of Mining and Industrial Products at the same Ministry. In developing this chapter, the authors have drawn on earlier work on the cement industry

undertaken for the TIP Project under the guidance of Professor William Morgan of the University of Wyoming.

2. For a more rigorous proof of this proposition see Willig (1978).

3. For a discussion of "base-point" pricing see Wilcox (1971).

4. For results of an empirical investigation of the changes that occurred in the United States during the 1970s and 1980s see Rosenbaum (1994).

5. For a discussion of predatory pricing and rules to prevent it see Baumol (1979).

REFERENCES

Baumol, W. (1979) "Quasi-Permanence of Price Reductions: A Policy for Prevention of Predatory Pricing," *Yale Law Journal,* 89, (November), pp. 1–26.

Haddock, D. (1982) "Basing-Point Pricing: Competitive vs. Collusive Theories," *American Economic Review,* (June), pp. 289–306.

Karlson, S. (1990) "Competition and Cement Basing Points: F.O.B. Destination, Delivered from Where?" *Journal of Regional Science,* 30, pp. 75–88.

Koller, R. and L. Weiss (1989) "Price Levels and Seller Concentration: The Case of Portland Cement," in L. Weiss, (eds.) *Concentration and Price,* (Cambridge, Massachusetts: MIT Press), pp. 17–40.

Rosenbaum, David I. (1994) "Efficiency vs. Collusion: Evidence Cast in Cement," *Review of Industrial Organization,* 9, pp. 379–392.

Weiss, L. (1989) "Why Study Concentration and Price?" in L. Weiss (ed.) *Concentration and Price,* (Cambridge, Massachusetts: MIT Press), pp. 1–14.

Wilcox, C. (1971) *Public Policies Towards Business,* (Homewood, Illinois: Richard D. Irwin, Inc.).

Willig, Robert D. (1978) "Pareto-Superior Nonlinear Outlay Schedules," *The Bell Journal of Economics,* v. 9,(1), (Spring), pp. 56–69.

CHAPTER 11

Distributional Impact of Government Policies in the Sugar Sector

Martin P.H. Panggabean[1]

INTRODUCTION

In the interest of attaining self-reliance in sugar production, Indonesia, like many other countries, intervenes heavily in the sugar sector. In the regulatory environment prevailing in the 1990s, three interventions were of particular interest. One was an "area quota" policy under which farmers residing in certain areas (e.g., West Java) were required to plant a specified quota of sugarcane. Another was a trade restriction policy under which sugar could only be imported by a government agency, BULOG, and private importers were not allowed to engage in this business. A third was a marketing restriction under which BULOG was the sole designated buyer of sugar from processing mills and, in turn, appointed a small number of licensed agents to distribute the sugar to wholesale outlets. Not all policies affecting the production, marketing and consumption of sugar were in the nature of implicit taxes or restrictions, however. Sugar farmers, for example, were provided input subsidies (on fertilizer, pesticides, and credit) to offset some of the potential profit lost by having the "area quota" imposed on them. Similarly, sugar millers (many of which are state-owned enterprises to begin with) were given a price for their output by BULOG which was sufficient to cover their costs and provide a reasonable profit as well.

As can be imagined, this welter of interventions produces multiple transfers of resources across the different agents that are involved in sugar production, distribution and consumption. Furthermore, changes in one or more forms or levels of intervention can have complex distribution effects which, in turn, can set up complex political economic dynamics. The objective of this chapter is to conduct an empirical analysis of the distributional consequences of the overall sugar policy regime as well as of selected potential policy reforms. This is done by estimating the numerical values of the principal transfers that take place among the key agents involved in the sugar sector, namely, farmers, millers, traders, BULOG, other government agencies, and consumers. The estimates are calculated using data pertaining to input costs, output prices and government policies prevailing in 1991. The choice of year is immaterial to the extent that the empirical methodology used here can be applied on data for any other year also. Our interest is mainly in showing that government regulations have complex distributional consequences and to provide reasonable estimates of these for one important economic sector.

The analysis conducted in this chapter supports two main conclusions:

(a) the main losers from the modeled set of interventions in the sugar sector are Indonesian consumers; as a group, consumers lose a total of 478 billion rupiahs (1991 nominal prices);

(b) partial reforms, that is, reforms which operate on one regulation at a time, are not enough to achieve significant efficiency gains although they may achieve designated distributional objectives by transferring rents or implicit taxes from set of agents to another; by implication, substantial efficiency gains can only be achieved through comprehensive reforms, that is, reforms which relax several important regulations simultaneously.

METHODOLOGY

The basic framework for this analysis is a *Policy Analysis Matrix*, PAM. The fundamental concept of the PAM is the recognition that ideally the economic value of a commodity would reflect the value of the scarce resources which went into its production. A price that reflects true scarcity is called an "efficiency price," and if efficiency price determines the use of a broad spectrum of commodities, the economy would move toward the highest level of national income. The actual price faced by economic agents (producers and consumers) is the "private price" (also known as "market price"). In a competitive economy, the private price of a given commodity is equal to its "social price." Government policies can cause the social prices (which reflect efficiency) to diverge from the private prices.

Governments intervene in the market for various reasons: to increase efficiency (especially in public goods), to correct market failures (i.e., eradicate inefficient monopolies), and to reduce negative externalities. Governments can also intervene to serve non-economic social goals. Equitable income distribution, self-sufficiency in food and price stabilization (especially for agricultural products) are among the common non-economic social goals pursued by public intervention. Though most government interventions in the market are benevolent and are meant to be temporary, sometimes interventions are made without a complete understanding of the problems or the effects of the policies that are instituted to correct them. This lack of a complete grasp on the reality of intervention often leaves in place policies that are no longer appropriate.

The PAM is constructed to capture the effects of government policies toward the system under consideration. At the heart of the PAM is a matrix (Table 1) which consists of two accounting identities. The first identity states that profit is equal to revenue minus costs, measured in either private or social terms, while the second identity measures the differences between the observed parameters and the levels that would exist if the policy-induced distortions were removed.

The sugar sector can be represented by four activities. Each activity has its own PAM. The first activity is "farm production" and it consists of cane production and transportation to the mills. The second activity is "processing" with cane as the input and sugar as the output. BULOG "handling" is the third activity, where all sugar (from farmers and mills) are bought by BULOG at the "provenue price." Taxes and fees for various government and private agencies are then added to the provenue price to calculate the ex-factory price. "Transportation and marketing" of sugar to the wholesale market is the fourth activity.

TABLE 1
TRANSFER SCHEMATIC IN FARM PRODUCTION

| | Revenues | ------Costs------ | | Profits |
		Tradable Inputs	Domestic Factors	
Private Prices	A	B	C	D^a
Social Prices	E	F	G	H^b
Divergences	I^c	J^d	K^e	L^f

(a) Private Profit, D = (A-B-C).
(b) Social Profit, H = (E-F-G).
(c) Output Transfers, I = (A-E).
(d) Input Transfers, J = (B-F).
(e) Factor Transfers, K = (C-G).
(f) Net Policy Transfers, L = (D-H) = (I-J-K).

TRANSFER ESTIMATES UNDER
1991 POLICY REGIME

PAM results for the four activities are presented in Tables 2 through 6. Unless otherwise noted, all calculations are in billions of rupiahs in 1991 prices. The first line is "private" calculations (private profits and losses) and the second line is "social" calculations (social profits and losses). In a competitive and efficient sector, private gains (losses) would equal social gains (losses).

Total transfers from the economy to farm production amounted to Rp. 56 billion. Components of this transfer are: credit subsidies (Rp. 25 billion, this is obviated by a savings of the same amount from undistributed subsidies for alternative crops) and tradable input subsidies (Rp. 55 billion, most of which is fertilizer subsidies). In addition, the market value of the sugar cane is estimated to be Rp. 134 billion, and this represents a subsidy to the cane producers. Therefore, total transfers to farm production is Rp. 190 billion (see Table 2). Note that this large transfer does not necessarily imply that sugar farmers are better off than in alternative situations. It is still possible that some farmers would have had higher private incomes had they been permitted to plant other crops of their choice.

TABLE 2
TOTAL TRANSFERS IN FARM PRODUCTION, 1990–1991
(BILLIONS OF RUPIAHS)

	Labor	Land	Capital	Tradable	Total Costs	Revenue	Profit
Private	173	496	72	146	886	680	-206
Social	173	472	97	200	942	546	-395
Divergences	0	24	-25	-55	-56	134	190

Source: Author's estimates.

Transfers in sugar processing can be divided into three categories. First, a transfer of Rp. 20 billion to the mills which is largely due to the gap between the domestic and the international price of the key input, sugarcane. Second, capital transfers in the amount of Rp. 81 billion from the decision to process cane produced by farmers. Third, subsidy of Rp. 40 billion for the mills' revenues from sugar and molasses. Total transfer in the processing sector given to mills in Java, therefore, amount to Rp. 142 billion (see Table 3).

TABLE 3
TOTAL TRANSFERS IN CANE PROCESSING, 1991
(BILLIONS OF RUPIAHS)

	Labor	Land	Capital	Tradable Costs	Total	Revenue	Profit
Private	160	0	122	220	501	456	-45
Social	160	0	203	240	602	416	-186
Divergences	0	0	-81	-20	-101	40	142

Source: Author's estimates.

BULOG purchases all the sugar from farmers and mills (except for the 2 percent of the farmers' share) at the provenue price. BULOG then adds various taxes and fees to the provenue price. Of these added components, only BULOG and KUD fees (and insurance) seem to reflect some productive activities.Tables 4 and 5 show that BULOG's handling of sugar produced by mills creates a transfer of Rp. 232 billion from consumers to the government. Most of this transfer is caused by various taxes and fees.

TABLE 4
TOTAL TRANSFERS IN BULOG HANDLING, 1991
(BILLIONS OF RUPIAHS)

	Labor	Land	Capital	Tradable Costs	Total	Revenue	Profit
Private	-	-	52	-	52	284	232
Social	-	-	49	-	49	49	0
Divergences	-	-	3	-3	235	232	-

Source: Author's estimates.

The final category of costs of production is the transportation cost from factories to the wholesale level (Table 6). Assuming that transporting each kilogram of sugar cost Rp. 50, the total private cost of transportation from mills to the wholesale market is Rp. 72 billion. Usually, 24 percent of this total cost is counted as labor cost, 51 percent is considered "tradable," while 25 percent is considered "return to capital and management."

TABLE 5
REVENUES COLLECTED FROM BULOG, 1991 (BILLIONS OF RUPIAHS)

	Agency	Source	Amount
1.	BULOG	BULOG fee	7.23
2.	BULOG	Bank Interest	91.81
3.	BULOG	Bag's cost	23.13
4.	BULOG	Insurance	0.22
5.	State Secretariat	Special Project	1.45
6.	Min. of Finance	Taxes	152.84
7.	KUD	KUD fee	7.23
		TOTAL	283.91

Source: Author's estimates.

Private revenue for transportation and marketing comes from the sale of sugar at the wholesale market. This revenue is calculated by multiplying total sugar production by the margin (Rp. 142/kg) between the mill's gate price (Rp. 919/kg) and the wholesale price (Rp. 1,061/kg). The mill's gate-wholesale marketing margin is divided into three components (ADB 1991): wholesaler's margin, interest on sugar stock and wholesaler's cost. Therefore, both the wholesale margin and interest on sugar stock are Rp. 91/kg respectively.

Profit to wholesalers in 1991 were Rp. 132 billion (Table 6). This is based on the non-crucial assumption that wholesalers buy sugar directly from BULOG and bring it to the wholesale market. If there is a transfer of purchasing right from BULOG appointed wholesalers to other wholesalers, then rents obtained by these licensed wholesalers would enter as part of the profit.

TABLE 6
TOTAL TRANSFERS IN TRANSPORTATION, 1990–1991 (BILLIONS OF RUPIAHS)

	Labor	Land	Capital	Tradable Costs	Total	Revenue	Profit
Private	17	0	18	37	.72	20.4	132
Social	17	0	18	39	74	145	70
Divergences	0	0	0	-2	-2	60	62

Source: Author's estimates.

Total Transfers in All Activities

Aggregation of the entire system is accomplished by summing over all activities, and excluding commodity-in-process (Table 7). The private (and social) cost of labor for all the activities is Rp. 350 billion, of which Rp. 173 billion comes from the farm activity, Rp. 160 billion comes from the processing activity and Rp. 17 billion comes from the transportation activity. Similarly, private return to capital in the system is Rp. 263 billion, and consists of Rp. 72 billion from farmers' credit, Rp. 122 billion from mills, Rp. 52 billion from usage by BULOG, and Rp. 18 billion from the transportation sector.

TABLE 7
TOTAL TRANSFERS, 1990–1991 (BILLIONS OF RUPIAHS)

	Labor	Land	Capital	Tradable	Total Costs	Revenue	Profit
Private	350	496	263	403	1,511	1,624	113
Social	350	472	366	480	1,667	1,155	-512
Divergences	0	24	-103	-77	-156	469	625

Source: Tables 2, 3, 4, 6.

With the private cost of tradable inputs amounting to Rp. 403 billion, and private opportunity cost of land and management amounting to Rp. 496 billion, the total cost in the system comes to Rp. 1,511 billion. The total revenue in the system is Rp. 1,624 billion, which is obtained from the sale of the mills' output (Rp. 1,136 billion) *plus* transportation and marketing cost (Rp. 204 billion) necessary to bring the output to the wholesale market *plus* BULOG handling cost (Rp. 284 billion).[2] The system, therefore, made a *private profit* of Rp. 113 billion in 1990–1991.

Social cost for the entire system is obtained by the same method. The total social cost for the system is Rp. 1,667 billion which consists of Rp. 350 billion in labor costs, Rp. 366 billion in returns to capital, Rp. 472 billion in social opportunity costs of land and management, and Rp. 480 billion in costs of tradable inputs. Social revenue is obtained by multiplying outputs produced by the system with the corresponding world prices. In 1990–1991, social revenue for the system was Rp. 1,155 billion. The net result is a *negative social profit* of Rp. 512 billion for 1990–1991.

For the entire sugar production, processing and marketing chain, government policies transferred Rp. 156 billion to the system because market cost of inputs was lower than their social cost. Of this Rp. 156 billion subsidy, tradable inputs users received Rp. 77 billion, while capital users (including credit receiver) received Rp. 103 billion. The government saved Rp. 24 billion of input subsidies by not allowing farmers to plant alternative crops. Revenue was also subsidized by Rp. 469 billion, generating a total transfer (from cost and revenue) to the system of Rp. 625 billion.

Calculation of the transfer from consumers to the government and to the producers proceeds in a straightforward fashion. The method employed is multiplication of "quantity consumed" (which is equal to the sugar produced domestically) with the price differential between the domestic and world prices. The government taxes caused the domestic price of sugar (Rp. 1,061/kg at the wholesale level) to be higher than the world price (Rp. 719/kg). Given quantity consumed of 1,446,000 tons, consumers' loss is equal to Rp. 494 billion. Therefore, total consumer loss in 1990–1991 was Rp. 131 billion (Rp 494 billion minus Rp. 625 billion).

Winners and Losers

The results in the preceding sections demonstrate that sugar production under the modeled set of policies is not socially profitable. Much of the loss can be attributed to the government policy of "self-sufficiency" achieved through high prices to both producers and consumers. The government instruments used to increase national sugar production is the "area quota," especially in *sawah* areas. This has reduced farmers' private return to land and management. Input and output subsidies offset to some extent the negative effect of the area quota.

In the processing sector, losses arise mainly through the implicit subsidy on capital cost. The same capital stock owned by the mills in 1991 could be better employed elsewhere, earning more income and contributing to public revenue. In the consumption sector, the government has increased the domestic price above the world price to reduce demand, while generating revenue (through tax) and saving foreign exchange in the process. This policy also has an income transfer effect: sugar consumers are mainly in the urban areas (which consumed one and a half to two times as much sugar than the rural population), and in the higher income brackets. In general, a complex web of transfers emerges. This is summarized in Table 8.

TABLE 8
SUMMARY OF TRANSFERS AMONG VARIOUS ECONOMIC
AGENTS, 1991 (BILLIONS OF RUPIAHS)

Agents	Receive	Disburse	Net
Farmers	223.0	33	190.0
Millers	166.0	16	150.0
Traders	62.0	0	62.0
State Secretariat	1.5	0	1.5
BULOG'	80.7	3	77.7
Ministry of Finance	179.8	183	- 3.2
Consumers	16.0	494	-478.0

Source: Table 2, 3, 4, 5, 6, 7.

(a) This figure does not include import proceeds calculated at Rp. 55 billion in the base year (1990–1991). In 1990–1991, BULOG imported 274,000 tons of sugar at the world price and sold it at the ex-factory price.

CONSEQUENCES OF SELECTED POLICY REFORMS

What would be the consequences of changing one or more of the interventions described above? We estimate the effects of introducing three possible changes: (a) allowing unrestricted private import of sugar (trade deregulation) while retaining the area quota; (b) lifting the area quota while maintaining marketing restrictions, and (c) restructuring the sugar distribution and marketing system. Each change is assessed from the point of view of efficiency and distributional consequences.

Policy Alternative I: Trade Deregulation with Area Quota

Trade deregulation here is used to indicate a "free" international trading regime. This policy alternative would mean a bigger implicit subsidy to the mills to keep them operational and an even smaller return to farmers' land and management involved in cane production. Under this policy regime, consumers (households and industrial users) gain through lower sugar prices, while the mills' position remains unchanged relative to the benchmark (1991) situation due to subsidies from the Ministry of Finance. Farmers suffer through an even lower return to land and management, while various government agencies lose revenues. The biggest loser is the Ministry of Finance which loses taxes and fees (from ex-factory price components), yet must also subsidize the mills.

Policy Alternative II: Lifting of Area Quota with Restrictive Import Policy

Under this policy alternative, the relative price structure is assumed to stay the same (because there is no trade deregulation.) Therefore, non-credit farmers (27,898 hectares) will still plant cane. It is also highly probable that *TRI* farmers (55,872 ha) in the dry-land areas will still produce cane. However, many farmers in Java will switch to other crops. We estimate that approximately 120,000 ha of land will switch to other crops. The results of lifting the area quota are presented in Table 9.

TABLE 9
TRANSFER OUTCOMES AFTER LIFTING OF AREA QUOTA
(BILLIONS OF RUPIAHS)

	Labor	Land	Capital	Tradable	Total Costs	Revenue	Profit
Private	147	157	112	176	591	756	165
Social	147	149	149	207	651	519	-132
Divergence	0	8	-37	- 32	-62	239	301

Source: Author's Estimates.

Since the area planted with cane is reduced, cane production relative to the benchmark value of 19.4 million tons will be reduced to 7.2 million tons, a reduction of 63%. Therefore, sugar produced by the mills (and hence handled by BULOG) will also decrease by 0.883 million tons (from 1.446 million tons to 0.563 million tons, a reduction of 61 percent). Assuming further that the sugar not produced in Java (883,000 tons) must be replaced by sugar imports to keep prices constant, BULOG will sell imported sugar to the distributors at the same price commanded by domestic sugar.

Since the amount of sugar produced by mills is already diminished, money collected by BULOG is also reduced. Therefore, the net policy effect is a transfer toward BULOG (and *KUD,* Ministry of Finance, etc.) to the amount of Rp. 90 billion, reduced from Rp. 232 billion with the benchmark policy. At first glance, this seems to be a move toward efficiency. Unfortunately, this provides another way for rent-seeking activities.

TABLE 10
REVENUES COLLECTED THROUGH BULOG, 1991
(BILLIONS OF RUPIAHS)

	Agency	Source	------Amount-----		Change
			Benchmark	Simulation	
1.	*BULOG*	*BULOG* fee	7.23	2.81	4.42
2.	*BULOG*	Bank Interest	91.81	35.73	56.08
3.	*BULOG*	Bag's cost	23.13	9.00	14.13
4.	*BULOG*	Insurance	0.22	0.08	0.14
5.	State Secretariat	Special Project	1.45	0.56	0.89
6.	Ministry of Finance	Taxes	152.84	59.49	93.35
7.	*KUD*	*KUD* fee	7.23	2.81	4.42
		TOTAL	283.91	110.48	173.43

Source: Author's estimates.

Table 10 compares the transfers that arise when the area quota is lifted with the benchmark situation. The lifting of the area quota reduces taxes, fees, and charges collected through BULOG by Rp. 173.43 billion. Concurrently, however, a new set of transfers are made to BULOG, its import agents, and the Ministry of Finance. To understand the new set of transfers, two things must be kept in mind. First, sugar that is not produced domestically must be replaced by imports, and BULOG (through its agents) would act as sole importer. Second, wholesalers would buy domestic and imported sugar at the same ex-factory price. Therefore, the change in revenue collected through BULOG (Rp. 173.43 billion) is fully accounted for by the import.It is calculated that the Ministry of Finance receives an additional Rp. 15.87 billion through taxes from sugar imports (from 2.5 percent tariff), while BULOG and its import agents receive an *additional* Rp. 157.56 billion through additional sugar imports. Therefore, the lifting of area quotas works to benefit BULOG and its import agents at the expense of other agencies (*KUD,* State Secretariat, etc.).

From the perspective of the Ministry of Finance, the lifting of area quotas reduces its monetary obligation to farming and processing activities by Rp. 185

billion. On the other hand, The Ministry receives less taxes from domestically processed sugar (decreased by Rp. 93.35 billion), yet receives compensation through the sugar tariff of Rp. 15.87 billion.

The conclusion seems clear. The lifting of the area quota helps farmers (who can plant other crops) and BULOG (which receives substantial import proceeds). Processing activity suffers from the closures of mills. The Ministry of Finance's position is less clear. It stops subsidizing mills, but loses tax and fees from domestically-produced sugar. Consumers' and wholesalers' positions do not change. Consumers still suffer from high sugar prices, while wholesalers still receive an abnormal profit.

Policy Alternative III: Allowing Unrestricted Private Distribution

An option that might contribute to increase efficiency in the sugar sector is more private sector involvement in distribution. Proponents of such an initiative argue that if marketing and distribution cost can be reduced, then provenue price, and thereby mills' and farmers' private profits, can be increased. The key implicit assumptions behind this policy are constant wholesale prices taxes and fees, which implies higher provenue. This argument points to the limited degree of competition provided by a system in which a small number of buyers are licensed by BULOG and prices are fixed by a BULOG formula.[3] Essentially the argument is that the marketing costs can be reduced by increased competition in the sector. Some simulation results are provided in Table 11.

TABLE 11
TRANSFER OUTCOMES FROM CHANGE IN SUGAR DISTRIBUTION ARRANGEMENTS (BILLIONS OF RUPIAHS)

	Labor	Land	Capital	Tradable	Total Costs	Revenue	Profit
Private	357	496	-163	413	1529	1624	95
Social	357	472	366	491	1635	1158	-527
Divergence	0	4	-103	-78	157	466	622

Source: Author's estimates.

As expected, the direct result of increasing provenue price (while squeezing distribution margin and keeping the wholesale price level constant) is to increase farmers' and mills' revenues. Relative to the benchmark (Table 7), farmers' revenue increase by Rp. 31 billion, while mills' revenue increase by Rp. 19 billion.[4] The implied provenue price is approximately Rp. 821/kg (an increase of almost Rp. 100/kg over the benchmark policy). Note that total revenues in Table 11 are the same as in Table 7. This is an effect of having constant wholesale prices. Any increase in revenues accruing to farmers, "mills" or the Ministry of Finance must come, necessarily, from the marketing sector (wholesalers).[5] This policy alternative is a pure wealth transfer scheme: "zero sum game" under the PAM assumptions. Therefore, it reduces inefficiencies in one activity (marketing and transportation) but adds distortions to other activities. The net policy effects are also similar: Rp. 622 billion in Table 11 compared to Rp. 625 billion in Table 7.

To the extent that there are gainers relative to the benchmark in this policy scheme, the size of the gains is small. Farmers are compensated some for their opportunity cost of land. Mills still experience private losses. Consumers do not gain anything (because the wholesale price level stays the same). The biggest losers (Rp. 60 billion), therefore, are the traders who purchase sugar from BULOG and bring it to the wholesale market. The biggest impact of this policy emerges when the retail marketing margin is also considered, with the retail price, instead of wholesale price, constant. The transfer from wholesalers and retailers toward farmers and millers becomes big enough to compensate farmers for their land.

Policy Alternative IV: A Direct Marketing System

Mills outside Java are able to market a certain percentage of their output directly to the market. This is a privilege not enjoyed by mills located in Java who must sell their entire share to BULOG. Selling parts of their 35 percent share directly to the wholesale market would increase mills' private profitability. This argument is supported by a simple calculation: as the share sold directly to the market goes up, so does private revenue. In fact, given the same cost structure, processing industries are breaking even (making zero private profits) when 44 percent of their 35 percent share are sold at the ex-factory price.

Direct losers from this policy scenario are various government agencies who collected revenue through BULOG. Farmers' position is unchanged because under this policy regime farmers are not able to sell directly to the market. Given that social cost and social revenue are unchanged, the size of policy effects (cost and revenue transfer) toward the processing activity goes up, while policy effects on the BULOG handling activity decreases. Again, this policy alternative shows no tendency for increase in efficiency, only transfer of rent from one activity to another, and from one economic agent to another.

CONCLUSIONS

The policy simulations discussed above suggest some lessons for policy reform. A partial reform (either in marketing or production) is not enough to meet both efficiency and self-reliance objectives. These can only be met via *comprehensive* policy reforms which would include trade deregulation, the opening up of the sugar distribution system, and the lifting of the area quota. Of course, while such a total reform approach is attractive, it also carries the risk of significant discontinuity in the sugar production and consumption system. This possibility has to be factored into the analysis since it may impose a large cost to the economy. Therefore, for practical purposes, some sort of policy *sequencing* might be desirable. While each stage of the sequence would constitute a partial reform, the commitment to implementing the whole package over a predetermined time period would ensure that any inefficiencies or inequities that occur in the process will be transitory.

NOTES

1. At the time of the writing of this chapter, Martin P.H. Panggabean was a Research Associate at the Institute for Economic and Social Research, Faculty of Economics, University of Indonesia.

2. Note that the value of private revenue in the system (Rp. 1,461 billion) is higher than the private value of sugar sold at the wholesale market (Rp. 1,375 billion). The difference is accounted for by molasses and other by-products sold by the mills.

3. Instead of relying on market forces to determine the marketing margin, the BULOG formula directly calculates the allowed (2 percent) margin and includes various cost incurred by the traders into the wholesale price level deemed appropriate.

4. An unintended consequence of the provenue price change is the increase in the Ministry of Finance's revenue collected through BULOG.

5. As a check, note that the reduction of wholesalers revenue (Rp. 59 billion) relative to the benchmark in Table 6 is equal to the total increases in farmers' revenue (Rp. 31 billion), mills' revenue (Rp. 19 billion), and the Ministry of Finance's revenue (Rp. 9 billion).

CHAPTER 12

The Impact of Regional Trade Deregulation on Selected APEC Countries and Indonesia

Jeffrey D. Lewis *and* Sherman Robinson

INTRODUCTION

After two decades of relatively modest progress in the area of multilateral trade deregulation and regional trading arrangements, the 1990s witnessed a near stampede. In addition to the much-heralded conclusion of the Uruguay Round Agreement in late 1994, nearly every region of the world has established a bewildering and in some respects conflicting range of preferential trade or integration initiatives. Latin American economies responded to implementation of NAFTA with a combination of lobbying efforts to gain similar access through NAFTA accession as well as a range of new or revitalized competing regional agreements, from the Pacto Andino in the North to Mercosur in the South. Eastern European economies scramble to affiliate with the EU, which in turn worries about whether it is preferable to "deepen" before it "broadens." Australia and New Zealand pursue implementation of their Close Economic Relation, and economies in southern Africa contemplate regional initiatives that revolve around the central role played by South Africa, emerging from isolation after almost two decades of confrontation with its neighbors.

Within East Asia, competing forces are also apparent. The commitment made in Bogor in November 1994 by the APEC countries to create an APEC free trade area by the year 2020 represented a major regional integration initiative. Reconsideration of the potential role for the ASEAN group has been underway for some years as it is felt that this club needs to broaden its scope from traditional concerns with politics and security to economic issues. The original plans for an ASEAN Free Trade Area (AFTA) called for a schedule to reduce tariffs on most products to a maximum of 5 percent among members by 2008. The pressure of events resulted in an ASEAN decision to broaden the scope and accelerate the timetable, with major reforms due to be completed by 2003.

This trend towards regional integration and deregulation represents an important shift in international policy. Only a decade ago, the conventional wisdom was that the scope for successful regional free trade initiatives was relatively limited, a conclusion supported by an international landscape littered with attempts that had fallen short of their original lofty goals. But any conclusion that this trend represents the final triumph of free trade doctrines over insularity and protectionism must be viewed with suspicion. Many recent initiatives seem motivated more by fear of being left behind by one's competitors than by any conviction that the benefits of deregulation or greater integration outweigh the costs. The proliferation of regional agreements has also raised concerns that the world trading system will separate into exclusive blocks. NAFTA has set off a scramble in the Western Hemisphere among those not yet included, and has given rise to fears in Asia over its potential trade diversion (although most empirical estimates suggest that the losses would be small). There is also disagreement within APEC over whether future deregulation should apply to non-members (such as the EU).

There is some basis for the concerns voiced by those who view the process as one of "join or be left behind." The increasing globalization and integration of world markets has generated powerful pressures for change, particularly as more and more regions abandon inward-looking policies and look outward for growth and markets. While a development strategy hinging on import substitution and investment controls once provided insulation (albeit costly) from international economic pressures, the environment has changed. Today, amid increasing competitive pressures in export markets, it is not enough for countries simply to make progress towards a more open trade and investment regime—exporting economies must devote equal attention to what their competitors are doing.

For East Asia, the region that, until the crisis of 1997, had benefited the most from the rapid expansion in world trade over the last quarter century, this means that those economies must run faster just to stay in place. The orderly passing of the mantle of export-led growth from Japan to the Asian "tigers" and then to the next tier has been supplanted by a more chaotic scramble for advantage in an increasingly competitive world. The response to domestic and trade policy deregulation for one country in Asia depends not only on its own actions, but also on what other countries do as well. The impact on the region of China's resurgence, potential competition from Vietnam, and increased private foreign investment flows affect regional policies (such as the ASEAN decision to accelerate its free trade area timetable) as well as national policies.

The political economy of the reform process generates further pressures on reform-oriented policy-makers. Whether unilateral, regional, or multilateral in origin, structural change associated with trade deregulation creates losers among a vocal and often quite powerful group of domestic interest groups. Failure to identify the winners and quantify the gains frequently means that reform efforts fail, and policy-makers are well aware that there is only a limited public tolerance before reform "fatigue" sets in. In this context, it is important to distinguish initiatives that promise large gains to the economy from those that offer relatively little. For example, will Indonesia gain more from implementation of a preferential ASEAN free trade area, or from future extension of the multilateral tariff cuts undertaken in the Uruguay Round?

This chapter offers a preliminary empirical assessment of the impact on Indonesia of alternative regional integration and deregulation opportunities and tries to respond to the following questions:

1. What is the impact of the Uruguay Round on trade, welfare, and economic structure in Indonesia and the other Pacific Rim economies?

2. What are the likely gains from future initiatives, such as implementation of an ASEAN free trade area or further multilateral deregulation along the lines of the Uruguay Round?

We approach these questions using a multi-country, computable general equilibrium (CGE) model to analyze the impact of trade deregulation on countries, sectors, and factors.[1] Our extended APEC-CGE model consists of nine linked country models: Indonesia, Thailand, Philippines, Malaysia, and Singapore (together), China (including Hong Kong), Asian NIEs (Korea and Taiwan), the United States, Japan, and the EU.[2] The structure of the model, the key assumptions and the data on which it is run are discussed in the Appendix.

TOWARDS ASIAN FREE TRADE: APEC MODEL RESULTS

Design of Alternative Scenarios

The scenarios analyzed here involve a sequence of deregulation possibilities for APEC economies, beginning with implementation of Uruguay Round Agreement commitments, followed by possible future multilateral deregulation (i.e., the successor to the URA), adoption of an ASEAN FTA, a possible APEC FTA, and finally, the impact of global trade deregulation involving areas outside of Asia. We contrast the static gains from free trade arrangements with the more substantial improvements that might occur as a result of dynamic linkages between trade expansion and productivity by incorporating the effects on aggregate and sectoral productivity of increased exports and the productivity-enhancing importation of new technologies via imports of capital and intermediate goods.

For each alternative scenario, the model generates results concerning the impact on real GDP, output, trade, value added, real wages, as well as the rental rate of capital and land. Our scenarios should be interpreted as controlled experiments rather than as forecasts of performance that might occur with each option. The actual growth pattern will be the result of many more factors than just trade policy, especially macroeconomic policies. Both the comparative static and dynamic-externality experiments are meant to describe the impact of different patterns of trade deregulation in the medium to long run. Use of the term "dynamic" here does not imply the actual path of the transition, but rather the net cumulative effect over time of positive productivity externalities that could potentially result from regional integration.

The Uruguay Round and Beyond

The Uruguay Round commitments require action on a number of different policy fronts: (1) conversion of many existing NTBs into tariffs and a commitment to real tariff reductions (for some countries) or a promise to "bind" tariffs below certain levels; (2) reduction in export and production subsidies (primarily in the OECD economies); and (3) dismantling the Multifibre Agreement over the coming decade, thereby eliminating the massive distortions that have characterized these industries.

The importance of the tariff and NTB reductions varies substantially by country. Using data obtained from the GATT, we can calculate the change in tariff rates to which each country is committed. Table A.6 (in the appendix) shows the average sectoral tariffs for each region before and after the Uruguay Round, along with figures on the percent reduction in tariffs that occurs from the UR commitments. Tariff reductions for developing countries range from a low of 4 percent in Indonesia (where modest sectoral tariff cuts are concentrated in sectors with few imports), to 8 percent for the Philippines, and 22–23 percent for Thailand and Singapore and Malaysia. The cuts for the OECD countries range from 26 percent in the EU to 40 percent in Japan.

As part of this experiment, we also assume that the non-agricultural NTBs in the OECD economies decline by half as part of the Uruguay Round, resulting in a drop in the average NTB to 7.9 percent in Japan, 2.3 percent in the United States, and 0.9 percent in the EU. Agricultural production subsidies are reduced by 20 percent in OECD economies and 13 percent in developing economies, while agricultural export subsidies are reduced by 36 percent in the United States and EU. And finally, the dismantling of the MFA is reflected in the elimination of export taxes on textiles and apparel in the major developing country exporters—Indonesia, Thailand, Philippines, Singapore and Malaysia, China, and Korea and Taiwan.

Table 1 summarizes the impact of the Uruguay Round on real GDP and exports for the APEC economies. The experiment is carried out in stages: first, the tariff and NTB cuts, and second the (additional) impact of subsidy reduction and MFA removal. Looking first at the tariff effects (columns 1–2), all economies gain from the Uruguay Round, with GDP increments ranging from .01 percent in the United States to 1.33 percent for Korea and Taiwan. The pattern and magnitude of tariff cuts has a substantial impact on how much each country can expect to benefit from post-URA trading opportunities. Economies that have liberalized more are in a position to reap greater efficiency gains from reallocation of domestic resources than those that have acted less boldly. Among the developing economies, Indonesia, China, and the Philippines committed to relatively modest tariff reductions (4–8 percent) and correspondingly gain little in real GDP from the elimination of distortions. Total world exports grow by 2.1 percent, or around $48 billion. The biggest winners are again those economies that have offered up the largest tariff reductions, as the real exchange rate depreciation that results from substantial tariff cuts in Japan and Korea and Taiwan stimulates exports from these economies.

TABLE 1
GDP AND EXPORT GROWTH FROM THE URUGUAY ROUND
(PERCENT CHANGE FROM BASE)

	URA Tariffs Only		Full URA Commitments		Full URA and Externalities	
	Real GDP	Exports	Real GDP	Exports	Real GDP	Exports
Indonesia	0.08	0.07	1.60	3.14	3.40	5.92
Thailand	0.54	3.10	0.81	3.58	3.43	7.15
Philippines	0.21	0.98	1.74	3.37	2.47	2.54
Singapore and Malaysia	0.10	0.64	2.10	1.54	2.79	0.76
China	0.04	0.05	0.61	1.81	0.97	1.61
Korea and Taiwan	1.33	2.43	1.45	2.97	1.78	3.42
Japan	0.66	5.32	0.68	5.49	1.03	5.91
United States	0.02	1.81	0.03	1.99	0.16	2.17
European Union	0.01	1.26	0.02	1.45	0.13	1.59
Total	-	2.14	-	2.56	-	2.82

Notes: Real GDP provides a production-based measure of economic activity.

When we include the subsidy reductions and MFA removal into the experiment (columns 3–4), the outcome is quite similar for the OECD economies, but much more favorable for the developing APEC economies, due to the stimulus provided to exports from elimination of MFA-related export taxes. GDP growth rises sharply in Indonesia and the Philippines to 1.6–1.7 percent, and global export expansion reaches 2.6 percent ($58 billion).

The results in columns 1–4 include no linkages or externalities from the greater openness and trade expansion that occurs as a result of the Uruguay Round implementation. This comparative static experiment does miss some potentially important dynamic feedbacks between trade and productivity which, if captured correctly, will likely increase the benefits accruing to economies committed to greater deregulation through the Uruguay Round. Columns 5–6 summarize the GDP and export implications of the Uruguay Round when the three productivity linkages incorporated in the model are included. Inclusion of these possible dynamic effects further increases GDP growth in the developing ASEAN economies. The biggest relative gainers are Indonesia, Philippines, and Thailand, where GDP growth exceeds 3 percent, and exports expand by over $15 billion. Incremental Indonesian exports occur primarily in the apparel and light manufacturing sectors (which includes products such as footwear).

There are divergent perspectives within Asia on how the trading system should evolve following implementation of the Uruguay Round commitments. Some argue for an ASEAN focus, others expand their sights to include the broader APEC grouping, while another group stresses the need to follow up the successful conclusion of the Uruguay Round with similar initiatives to negotiate further multi-lateral deregulation in world trade. To illuminate the tradeoffs (if any) among these different perspectives, we have run a series of experiments with the APEC-CGE model that quantify the contribution of each to growth and structural change in the APEC economies.

Table 2 reports the impact on real GDP of various regional or multilateral trading initiatives. The numbers reflect the *incremental* impact on GDP of each experiment: in other words, the effect of adding one new feature to those included in the previous experiment. The starting point is the implemented Uruguay Round in the model *without* trade-productivity externalities: in other words, the results reported in columns 3-4 of Table 1. The first experiment considers the impact of another multilateral reform along the lines of the Uruguay Round: tariffs and export subsidies are cut by 36 percent in all countries, non-agricultural NTBs in the OECD economies are eliminated, and agricultural production subsidies are cut by 36 percent as well. In the second experiment, we add to this the creation of an ASEAN FTA, represented by the complete elimination of all tariffs *among* the four ASEAN regions in the model (Indonesia, Thailand, Philippines, and Singapore and Malaysia). Next, we simulate the eventual creation of an APEC FTA, which eliminates tariffs among all the APEC members, leaving protective barriers only against the EU and rest of world. Finally, we consider the case of global deregulation with the removal of all remaining import barriers among the regions in our model.

The results in Table 2 suggest that the different regional deregulation alter-natives would have very different effects on the individual economies. The biggest gains come from completion of a subsequent round of multilateral tariff and sub-sidy reductions along the lines of the Uruguay Round. This URA-II would yield $62 billion of additional exports, and increase real GDP by around $50 billion, more than the estimated gains from actual Uruguay Round. The largest benefit from URA-II accrues to Japan, in part because it achieves further efficiency gains from elimination of the remaining non-agricultural NTBs. But ASEAN economies gain as well: exports grow by $3.6 billion and real GDP expands by $1.7 billion.

Creation of an ASEAN FTA based on free trade among ASEAN economies alone offers only very modest gains. Incremental GDP growth is positive, but small (around $350 million), as is the $1.0 billion increase in total ASEAN exports. Indonesia gains the least in terms of GDP growth (only 0.03 percent), and expands its exports by only around $140 million. While these figures may understate the potential gains from an ASEAN FTA due to factors such as economies of scale due to rationalization of production facilities, or other deliberate policies to encourage intra-ASEAN trade, our empirical results confirm what has been a consistent lesson of the East Asian growth experience: maximum gains are achieved by focusing on international markets, not regional ones.

TABLE 2
GDP AND EXPORT GROWTH FROM FUTURE DEREGULATION
ALTERNATIVES

	URA-II	ASEAN FTA	APEC FTA	Free Trade	Total effect
			Incremental Effect of:		
Change in GDP from Base (Percent)					
Indonesia	0.40	0.03	0.66	0.25	1.34
Thailand	0.59	0.18	0.82	0.37	1.96
Philippines	0.67	0.14	1.17	0.32	2.30
Singapore and Malaysia	0.23	0.04	0.29	0.09	0.65
China	0.12	-0.01	0.15	0.09	0.35
Korea and Taiwan	0.85	0.00	2.00	0.41	3.26
Japan	0.86	0.00	0.77	0.39	2.02
United States	0.05	0.00	0.01	0.02	0.08
European Union	0.13	0.00	-0.02	0.09	0.20
Change in Exports from Base (Billion $)					
Indonesia	0.74	0.14	1.22	0.40	2.50
Thailand	1.51	0.59	2.20	0.99	5.29
Philippines	1.07	0.29	2.01	0.80	4.17
Singapore and Malaysia	0.34	0.06	1.16	0.05	1.61
China	2.11	0.01	3.62	1.29	7.01
Korea and Taiwan	3.08	0.01	6.49	1.52	11.08
Japan	30.60	0.02	12.27	5.25	48.10
United States	9.83	0.00	4.25	1.32	15.40
European Union	13.39	0.02	0.01	12.50	25.92
Total	62.68	1.05	33.23	24.13	121.09

Creation of an APEC FTA, on the other hand, would generate substantial additional benefits beyond a more narrow ASEAN FTA. GDP expands for all APEC economies, while the European Union would experience a small decline. Total GDP expansion reaches $42 billion, and exports rise by $33 billion. Finally, global trade deregulation would generate further gains of $25 billion in GDP across all regions, although the ASEAN economies gain a smaller share of this total, as the benefits are spread around more evenly.

CONCLUSIONS

The last decade has seen major changes in the world trading system. The Uruguay Round of GATT negotiations was successfully completed, yielding less deregulation than was originally hoped, but more than was expected by many. In addition, there has been a proliferation of regional trading arrangements, including NAFTA, Mercosur, and the Pacto Andino in the Americas; APEC and ASEAN in the Pacific; and expansion of the EU in Europe. While the post-war trend toward increased trade deregulation was maintained and deepened in the 1980s, the decade also saw wide swings in bilateral trade balances and real exchange rates, with resulting "structural adjustment" programs in a number of developing and developed countries. These swings also had significant effects on real trade flows.

We have developed a multi-country trading model that focuses on the APEC region to analyze the impact on the Asian economies of trade deregulation under both the Uruguay Round and regional free trade initiatives. The model is used as a simulation laboratory to sort out the relative empirical importance of the various trends in deregulation and macro adjustment. The empirical results lead to a number of conclusions:

1. The lower income APEC countries have committed themselves to only very modest reductions in protection under the new GATT agreement. The gains from deregulation, however, are greater for countries that eliminate protection and domestic distortions in an environment where their trading partners also open their markets. Increasing international market access while maintaining a distorted and protected domestic economy does not yield significant benefits, because the economy cannot adjust to take advantage of the new opportunities.

2. Elimination of tariff and non-tariff barriers in developed countries, especially the phasing out of the Multifibre Agreement (MFA), provides a significant opportunity for Asian developing countries to expand their exports and achieve significant productivity gains. The potential gains are quite large.

3. Creation of an APEC free trade area (APEC FTA) provides significant benefits to the participants, with little effect on non-members. Establishing an APEC FTA leads to some trade diversion away from non-members, but total trade creation is much larger, leading to significant efficiency gains.

4. Creation of an ASEAN regional free trade area provides little benefit to its members. The ASEAN countries would be far better advised to work toward more deregulation under GATT or hasten the creation of the APEC FTA rather than create an ASEAN FTA alone.

5. While establishing regional free trade areas such as the APEC FTA yields significant efficiency gains, even greater gains are achieved by further multilateral deregulation. From an economic perspective, creating a regional FTA is consistent with pursuing continued global deregulation as well. Member countries gain both from the FTA and from further multilateral deregulation.

APPENDIX: THE APEC-CGE MODEL

MODEL STRUCTURE AND ASSUMPTIONS

The APEC-CGE model we have developed is in the tradition of recent multi-country CGE models developed to analyze the impact of the Uruguay Round of GATT negotiations and the impact of the North American Free Trade Agreement.[3]

The model consists of a multi-regional CGE framework containing a twelve-sector, nine-region, general equilibrium model, where the regional CGE models are inter-connected through trade flows.[4] For the purpose of describing the model, it is useful to distinguish between the individual "country" models and the multi-region model system as whole, which determines how the individual country models interact. When the model is actually used, the *within* country and *between* country relationships are solved for simultaneously.

The APEC-CGE model includes several features that are not ordinarily incorporated into other multi-country CGE trade models. First, when modeling import demands, the Almost Ideal Demand System (AIDS) specification is adopted. This specification allows import expenditure elasticity's to be different from one and also allows cross-country substitution elasticity's to vary for different pairs of countries. Second, to capture the potential dynamic effects of trade deregulation, the APEC model can include equations for generating positive externalities through both export expansion and the importation of new capital goods. These new features are described below.

The model data base consists of social accounting matrices (SAMs) for each country, including data on their trade flows.[5] The development of a consistent multi-country data base is itself a major task; for our model, we relied primarily on the GTAP database (Hertel 1996), supplemented by some additional data on factor endowments (particularly labor) and tariff and non-tariff barriers. The SAM starts from multisectoral input-output data, which are expanded to provide information on the circular flow of income from producers to factors to "institutions," which include households, enterprises, government, a capital account, and trade accounts for each partner country, and for the rest of the world. These institutions represent the economic actors whose behavior and interactions are described in the CGE models. The parameter estimates for the sectoral production functions, consumer expenditure functions, import aggregation functions, and export transformation functions were estimated from base-year data and from a variety of econometric sources. The various parameters used in the model represent point estimates for the base year (1992) and the model was benchmarked so that its base solution replicates the base data.

Each sub-regional or "country" CGE model follows closely what has become a standard theoretical specification for trade-focused CGE models.[6] In addition to twelve sectors for each country model, the model has four factors of production (two labor types, land, and capital). For each sector, the model specifies output-supply and input-demand equations. Output supply is given by translog value added cost functions, while intermediate inputs are demanded in fixed proportions. Producers are assumed to maximize profits, implying that each factor is demanded so that marginal revenue product equals marginal cost. However, factors need not receive a uniform wage or "rental" (in the case of capital) across sectors; it is possible to impose sectoral factor market distortions that fix the ratio of the sectoral return to a factor relative to the economy-wide average return for that factor.

In common with other CGE models, the model only determines relative prices and the absolute price level must be set exogenously. In our model, the aggregate consumer price index in each sub-region is set exogenously, defining the *numeraire*. The advantage of this choice is that solution wages and incomes are in real terms. The solution exchange rates in the sub-regions are also in real terms, and can be seen as equilibrium price-level-deflated (PLD) exchange rates, using the country consumer price indices as deflators.[7] World prices are converted into domestic currency using the exchange rate, including any tax or tariff components. Cross-trade price consistency is imposed, so that the world price of country A's exports to country B are the same as the world price of country B's imports from country A. Composite demand is for a translog aggregation of sectoral imports and domestic goods supplied to the domestic market. Sectoral output is a CET (constant elasticity of transformation) aggregation of total supply to all export markets and supply to the domestic market.

Each "country" model traces the circular flow of income from producers, through factor payments, to households, government, and investors, and finally back to demand for goods in product markets. The country models incorporate tariffs that flow to the government, and non-tariff revenues that go to the private sector. Each economy is also modeled as having a number of domestic market distortions. There are sectorally differentiated indirect, consumption, and export taxes, as well as household and corporate income taxes. The single aggregate household in each economy has a Cobb-Douglas expenditure function, consistent with optimization of a Cobb-Douglas utility function. Real investment and government consumption are fixed as shares of GDP in the model simulations.

One implication of including these varied existing distortions, which capture in a stylized way institutional constraints characteristic of the economies, is that policy choices must be made in a second-best environment. In our simulations involving the establishment of FTAs, we are not considering scenarios that remove all existing distortions. Existing taxes and factor-market distortions are assumed to remain in place, along with existing import barriers against the rest of the world.

In this second-best environment, economic theory gives little guidance as to the welfare implications of forming a FTA.

Sectoral export-supply and import-demand functions are specified for each country. In common with other CGE models (both single and multi-country), the APEC-CGE model specifies that goods produced in different countries are imperfect substitutes. At the sectoral level, in each country, demanders differentiate goods by country of origin and exporters differentiate goods by destination market. Exports are supplied according to a CET function between domestic sales and total exports, and allocation between export and domestic markets occurs in order to maximize revenue from total sales. The rest of the world is modeled simply as a supplier of imports to and demander of exports from the nine model regions as a group. Production activities in the rest of the world are not explicitly modeled; instead, this region is assumed to have flat export-supply curves and downward-sloping aggregate import-demand curves.

The model incorporates three different kinds of trade-productivity links. The first relates sectoral productivity to sectoral imports of intermediate and capital goods—the extent of productivity increase depends on the share of intermediates in production. Second is an externality associated with sectoral export performance—higher export growth translates into increased domestic productivity. Finally, there is an externality associated with aggregate exports—increased exports make physical capital more productive, an effect which is embodied in the capital stock input to the production process.[8]

While there is fairly widespread agreement that these externalities exist, there is less consensus on the channels through which they operate, and how large they are. For our purpose, we are more interested in showing how such linkages might affect analysis of the FTA; thus, we have included three different linkages that operate through different channels. With little empirical estimation to draw on, the choice of externality parameters to use in the model is based largely on guesswork. We have chosen fairly modest parameters, to avoid overstating the case; for example, our sectoral export-productivity linkage effects for the developing Asian regions are given an elasticity parameter around one-half that used by de Melo and Robinson (1992) in their analysis of the Korean growth performance.

For many single-country and multi-country models, a lack of detailed econometric work forced modelers to use simple functional forms, with few parameters, for the import-aggregation and export-transformation functions. The common practice is to use a constant elasticity of substitution (CES) function for the import aggregation equation, which is a very restrictive functional form and has led to empirical problems.[9] As a result of these limitations, modelers have begun to explore other formulations, while maintaining the fundamental assumption of product differentiation. In this model, we have used a flexible specification of the demand system called the almost ideal demand system (or AIDS).[10] The AIDS specification allows non-unitary income elasticity's of demand for imports and also pair-wise substitution elasticity's that vary across countries. The specification generates more realistic trade-volume and terms-of-trade effects when analyzing the impact of expanded North American regional trade under an FTA.

The APEC-CGE model, like other multi-country CGE models, has a medium to long-run focus. We assume, for example, that factor markets clear. While sectoral employment changes, aggregate employment is assumed to remain unchanged. We report the results of comparative static experiments in which we "shock" the model by changing some exogenous variables and then compute the changed equilibrium solution. We do not explicitly consider how long it might take the economy to reach the new equilibrium. The model's time horizon has to be viewed as "long enough" for full adjustment to occur, given the shock. While useful to understand the pushes and pulls the economies will face under the creation of an FTA, this approach has obvious shortcomings. In particular, it does not consider the costs of adjustment, such as transitional unemployment, that might occur while moving to the final equilibrium.

ECONOMIC STRUCTURE AND TRADE PATTERNS IN APEC ECONOMIES

Our APEC model is constructed around a nine-region, twelve-sector, four-factor, Social Accounting Matrix estimated for the year 1992.[11] This section outlines the structure of production, demand, income, taxation and trade patterns in the base year for each economic region included in the model, and briefly describes the patterns of protection among the relevant regions.[12]

Table A.1 presents data on factor endowments, intensities, and costs for the regions included in the model, and indicates the enormous differences in size, role of trade, factor endowments and factor cost among these regions. Low-income APEC economies (Indonesia, Thailand, Philippines, and China) as well as Korea and Taiwan exhibit broad similarities: exports and imports represent around 25–35 percent of GDP, Singapore and Malaysia have trade shares over 100 percent, and the much larger OECD economies (Japan, United States, and EU) depend on trade for only around 10 percent of GDP. The low-income developing countries are more poorly endowed with capital relative to labor: capital-labor ratios are lower, the share of agriculture labor in the total labor force remains around one half, and the rental-wage ratio is much higher. The pattern is reversed for Japan, the European Union, and the United States, while Korea and Taiwan and Singapore and Malaysia fall between the advanced industrial countries and the poorer Asian developing countries. Their agricultural labor share is larger than that of the industrial economies, but is much smaller than that in China and ASEAN4. Compared to Japan, the European Community, and the United States, they have a lower capital intensity and a higher relative capital-labor price.

International trade theory generally identifies two different types of international trade. Trade among developed industrial countries with similar endowments and technology is largely "intra-industry," with high exports and imports within sectors, whereas trade between high and low-income economies (with very different factor endowments and technological processes) is largely inter-industry, with more sectoral specialization.[13] With a tremendous range in factor endowments and income levels among the APEC economies, there is ample scope for Heckscher-Ohlin forces (based on different factor endowments) to influence trade.

Table A.2 presents the share of each region's exports and imports in total world trade from the base data used in the model. The OECD economies dominate the machinery and equipment sector, while China and Korea and Taiwan are major participants in the textiles and apparel sectors (along with the EU). The export market shares for manufactured goods in developing ASEAN economies indicate that Indonesia has significant shares only for textiles and apparel (around 4 percent) and wood and paper (5 percent), while Thailand is best represented in the food processing, apparel, and other light manufactured sectors.

Aggregation of individual economies into regions for use in the model involved netting out trade among the combined economies, so that these data will not match data from other statistical sources on world trade volumes.[14] Overall, trade among the APEC regions in the model accounts for 70 percent of total trade, with the rest of the world representing the rest.

Data presented in Table A.3 also reveal sizable differences in structure and international comparative advantage among ASEAN, China, the Asian NIEs, and industrial countries such as Japan, the United States, and the European Union. ASEAN developing economies and China are more primary-intensive than the industrial countries, and their manufacturing sectors, especially the labor-intensive textile and apparel products, are relatively larger than in the advanced countries (with a smaller service sector). Japan, the European Union, and the United States are dominated by a large service sector and sizable intermediate and capital goods sectors. These three sectors account for 85–90 percent of output and value added in these economies, as compared to only around 60 percent in the ASEAN economies (and even less in China).

Trade shares are consistent with intuition about international comparative advantage. For example, labor-intensive textiles and apparel constitute 24 percent of China's total exports, 15 percent for Indonesia, and 12 percent for Thailand and Philippines. Capital and skill-intensive machinery and equipment in turn make up 37–43 percent of total imports for these same economies. The pattern is reversed for Japan and the United States; more than 90 percent of Japanese exports occur in the intermediate, capital good, and service sectors. Korea and Taiwan are in between, with a lower textile export share but a much higher machinery export share than China and ASEAN, but a higher textile export share and a lower machinery and equipment export share than Japan and the United States.

Singapore and Malaysia have the highest trade dependence, importing and exporting nearly 40 percent of total output. The exports/output and imports/absorption ratios for this amalgamated economy provide a striking illustration of the empirical importance of two-way trade: in nine of twelve sectors, Singapore and Malaysia export more than one-third of sectoral output; in six of these nine export sectors, they also import more than one-third of total demand. Fifteen years of market-oriented economic reform have also led China to become more strongly linked with the conczlusion of the Uruguay Round negotiations. The primary source for our tariff data is information obtained by the World Bank following the Uruguay Round from the GATT on the specific tariff commitments made by each participant. After reconciliation of this information to the sector and regional aggregation available in our model data, the result for each region is a set of sectoral tariff rates by origin (although only the average from all sources is shown in Table A.5).[15]

Included in the protection estimates are the tariff equivalent of non-tariff barriers for agriculture, and NTB equivalents for industrial products only for the major OECD economies (United States, Japan, and EU). While some NTBs for the US and EU related to textile quotas and anti-dumping could be obtained from the GTAP data, only statutory tariff rates were available for Japan. Because no Japanese NTBs were included, this protection structure indicated that the United States and EU protect themselves much more heavily against Japanese products than Japan does against United States and EU products. To compensate for the absence of NTB information for Japan, we have incorporated additional information on the *ad valorem* equivalent of Japanese NTBs, drawn from estimates provided in Sazanami, Urata, and Kawai (1995).[16]

The import protection rates show substantial variations by sector and region. The high protection rates for agriculture and food products in the EU, Japan, and Korea and Taiwan reflect the high non-tariff barriers. The pre-URA average tariff rate across all goods averages 10–13 percent for Indonesia and China, 20 percent for the Philippines, and 32 percent for Thailand, although there is a great deal of sectoral variation in the rates.

The domestic tax rates presented in the second section of Table A.5 indicate that most regions subsidize agriculture, with a particularly large subsidy in the United States on grain production while in the EU, Japan, and Korea and Taiwan the subsidy is directed towards other agricultural products as well. The enormous export subsidy provided by the EU to grain exports (and to a lesser extent, to other agriculture as well) is quite noticeable. The prevalence of export taxes in the textiles and apparel in the developing economies are due to the Multi-fiber Agreement (MFA). In our model, we represent the MFA through export taxes levied in the *exporting* economy, thereby implicitly assuming that the rents associated with the MFA accrue to the exporting nations, rather than being shared with the importers. The export-tax equivalent of the MFA ranges from 4–6 percent for textiles to 16–30 percent for wearing apparel in the Asian developing economies.

APPENDIX A.1
FACTOR ENDOWMENT, INCOME SHARES, FACTOR INTENSITY AND TRADE DEPENDENCE IN APEC MODEL REGIONS

	Indonesia	Thailand	Philippines	Singapore and Malaysia	China	Korea and Taiwan	Japan	USA	EU
GDP and Trade Flows (billion US$)									
Exports	39.5	37.6	17.2	105.9	141.2	195.1	411.5	576.5	732
Imports	32.7	43.9	17.1	104.6	157.2	164.2	322.5	618.6	770.2
GDP	129.5	108.3	54.4	102.3	519.9	517.9	3694.2	5898.4	6680.4
Trade Dependence (percent)									
Export/GDP	30.5	34.7	31.6	103.6	27.2	37.7	11.1	9.8	11.0
Import/GDP	25.3	40.5	31.5	102.3	30.2	31.7	8.7	10.5	11.5
Factor Share in APEC Region Value Added (percent)									
Land	13.6	4.9	7.5	6.5	9.8	4.6	1.2	1.6	0.8
Labor	28.9	21.5	41.6	39.1	53.2	53.1	58.8	64.7	65.6
Capital	57.5	73.6	50.9	54.4	37.0	42.3	40.0	33.7	33.7
Labor Cost (thousand $)									
Average wage	0.5	0.6	0.8	3.8	0.3	8.5	31.3	27.9	26.8
Average agri. wage	0.2	0.1	0.5	0.8	0.2	3.9	18.4	14.5	19.9
Average non-agri. wage	0.7	1.5	1.1	4.9	0.6	9.6	32.1	28.2	27.2
Factor Proportions									
Agri. labor/total labor (percent)	46.7	63.0	45.9	25.9	65.7	19.4	5.8	2.1	5.5
Capital/labor ratio ($000/worker)	3.0	8.1	6.1	33.8	1.9	37.0	190.1	123.5	130.0
Rental/wage ratio (percent/$000)	65.6	42.3	20.0	4.1	36.9	2.2	0.4	0.4	0.4

Source: APEC model database derived from GTAP data (Hertel 1996).

APPENDIX A.2
SECTORAL EXPORT AND IMPORT SHARES IN WORLD TRADE (PERCENT)

	Indonesia	Thailand	Philippines	Singapore and Malaysia	China	Korea and Taiwan	Japan	United States	EU	Rest of world	Total
Shares in World Exports:											
Grains	0.1	6.4	0.0	0.0	7.4	0.2	0.0	54.0	10.6	21.1	100.0
Other Agriculture	3.5	3.5	1.0	1.9	6.1	3.7	0.5	21.6	9.7	48.4	100.0
Forestry and Fishery	3.6	5.9	1.2	7.9	4.7	7.5	1.8	17.1	5.4	45.0	100.0
Energy and Minerals	5.0	0.5	0.3	1.9	2.4	0.2	0.4	3.9	6.1	79.3	100.0
Food Processing	1.4	3.6	1.1	4.7	4.1	2.8	1.3	19.8	29.5	31.6	100.0
Textiles	3.6	1.7	0.2	1.5	10.2	20.6	10.3	9.3	22.4	20.2	100.0
Apparel	3.5	3.8	2.1	3.1	28.5	10.1	0.8	4.4	13.4	30.4	100.0
Other Light Manufact.	1.7	2.8	0.6	3.3	17.7	16.2	16.4	10.1	17.7	13.5	100.0
Wood and Paper	4.5	0.7	0.5	3.5	2.4	3.9	3.0	18.9	17.4	45.2	100.0
Basic Intermediates	1.0	0.5	0.3	3.8	2.6	5.4	10.3	17.3	27.9	31.0	100.0
Machinery and Equipment	0.2	0.8	0.3	4.1	2.6	7.0	23.8	22.7	23.4	15.1	100.0
Services	0.4	0.8	0.7	2.4	2.8	4.4	8.7	17.9	27.5	34.5	100.0
Total	1.2	1.2	0.5	3.3	4.4	6.0	12.8	17.9	22.7	30.1	100.0
Shares in World Imports:											
Grains	2.9	0.7	1.3	3.3	9.9	9.3	20.0	2.5	5.9	44.1	100.0
Other Agriculture	1.5	1.4	0.3	2.5	4.8	7.7	14.0	14.0	37.5	16.3	100.0
Forestry and Fishery	0.1	3.7	0.3	1.7	4.0	5.2	41.6	14.8	21.9	6.8	100.0
Energy and Minerals	0.6	1.4	0.9	2.8	2.2	6.3	21.3	22.0	36.0	6.4	100.0
Food Processing	0.7	0.9	0.9	3.0	5.2	4.0	15.8	15.2	22.5	31.9	100.0
Textiles	1.8	1.7	1.3	4.9	16.1	5.1	5.8	10.6	19.4	33.4	100.0
Apparel	0.0	0.0	0.0	0.9	1.3	0.7	10.2	32.4	33.4	20.9	100.0
Other Light Manufact.	0.5	0.8	0.2	3.0	5.8	2.6	8.1	31.6	25.4	21.9	100.0
Wood and Paper	0.6	1.1	0.3	1.7	4.2	3.8	9.6	20.6	33.2	25.0	100.0
Basic Intermediates	1.7	2.6	0.8	4.1	6.9	7.3	8.9	17.0	20.6	30.0	100.0
Machinery and Equipment	1.3	1.8	0.6	4.4	5.5	5.5	4.3	23.6	19.8	33.3	100.0
Services	0.6	0.5	0.3	2.0	3.0	4.1	12.8	12.5	24.8	39.5	100.0
Total	1.0	1.4	0.5	3.2	4.9	5.1	10.0	19.2	23.9	30.9	100.0

Source: Calculated from APEC model database derived from GTAP data (Hertel 1996).

APPENDIX A.3
STRUCTURE OF PRODUCTION, FACTOR INCOME, DEMAND AND TRADE PATTERNS FOR APEC REGIONS, 1992

| | Sectoral Composition (percent) | | | | | Ratios (percent) | | Factor Composition of Value Added (percent) | | | |
	Output (1)	Value added (2)	Final demand (3)	Imports (4)	Exports (5)	Exports/Output (6)	Imports/Absorption (7)	Land (8)	Labor (9)	Capital (10)	Total (11)
Indonesia											
Grains	7.8	7.2	8.0	1.9	0.0	0.1	3.4	31.7	22.2	46.1	100.0
Other Agriculture	7.8	11.8	6.7	2.8	5.7	12.8	5.5	38.7	19.4	41.9	100.0
Forestry and Fishery	2.9	4.4	1.7	0.1	2.9	17.6	0.7		16.6	83.4	100.0
Energy and Minerals	7.8	12.3	0.0	4.3	29.5	65.8	19.0	54.1	9.9	36.0	100.0
Food Processing	5.1	2.1	7.3	2.5	4.1	13.7	7.3		25.2	74.8	100.0
Textiles	4.7	1.5	0.7	4.2	7.0	24.7	13.7		32.6	67.4	100.0
Apparel	1.1	0.3	0.2	0.0	8.1	90.4	9.9		50.2	49.8	100.0
Other Light Manufacturing	1.3	0.8	0.6	2.3	6.2	80.6	50.9		27.5	72.5	100.0
Wood and Paper	3.8	2.7	0.7	2.1	12.9	58.4	15.8		25.0	75.0	100.0
Basic Intermediates	8.8	7.0	2.8	21.	10.5	20.8	30.2		13.8	86.2	100.0
Machinery and Equipment	3.8	2.1	10.8	41.3	5.0	23.0	60.4		29.9	70.1	100.0
Services	45.0	47.6	60.4	16.8	8.2	3.1	5.3		40.8	59.2	100.0
Total	100.0	100.0	100.0	100.0	100.0	16.9	14.5	13.6	28.9	57.5	100.0
Thailand											
Grains	4.0	4.3	1.4	0.4	3.7	17.1	2.2	26.8	11.7	61.5	100.0
Other Agriculture	5.3	6.8	3.3	2.1	5.9	20.7	9.3	28.6	14.7	56.7	100.0
Forestry and Fishery	2.4	3.5	1.9	2.7	5.1	38.9	25.8		13.2	86.8	100.0
Energy and Minerals	2.2	3.4	0.0	7.5	3.1	25.7	45.3	53.0	11.7	35.3	100.0
Food Processing	9.2	6.2	9.0	2.3	10.5	21.2	6.2		15.1	84.9	100.0
Textiles	4.4	2.6	1.0	2.9	3.4	13.6	13.2		20.3	79.7	100.0
Apparel	4.0	2.3	4.0	0.0	9.2	35.4	0.7		34.8	65.2	100.0
Other Light Manufacturing	2.9	3.0	1.6	2.5	10.4	65.5	29.9		14.2	85.8	100.0
Wood and Paper	2.4	1.8	1.0	2.7	2.2	17.0	21.4		20.7	79.3	100.0
Basic Intermediates	7.9	4.7	3.1	24.1	5.4	12.6	38.5		13.4	86.6	100.0
Machinery and Equipment	7.2	4.9	20.6	43.1	22.9	59.0	58.4		24.6	75.4	100.0
Services	47.8	56.5	53.1	9.6	18.2	7.1	4.5		25.3	74.7	100.0
Total	100.0	100.0	100.0	100.0	100.0	18.3	19.7	4.9	21.5	73.6	100.0

STRUCTURE OF PRODUCTION, FACTOR INCOME, DEMAND AND TRADE PATTERNS FOR APEC REGIONS, 1992 (*Continued*)

	Output (1)	Value added (2)	Sectoral Composition (percent) Final demand (3)	Imports (4)	Exports (5)	Ratios (percent) Exports/Output (6)	Imports/Absorption (7)	Land (8)	Factor Composition of Value Added (percent) Labor (9)	Capital (10)	Total (11)
The Philippines											
Grains	6.7	6.5	4.1	1.6	0.0	0.2	4.0	35.6	52.2	12.2	100.0
Other Agriculture	8.1	11.2	5.3	1.1	3.7	8.1	2.4	41.0	55.0	4.0	100.0
Forestry and Fishery	4.9	7.1	5.1	0.6	2.2	8.0	2.2		33.0	67.0	100.0
Energy and Minerals	1.3	1.3	0.3	12.7	3.5	45.5	69.6	39.9	33.3	26.7	100.0
Food Processing	13.5	9.4	17.6	5.6	7.4	9.6	7.3		32.4	67.6	100.0
Textiles	1.2	0.7	0.7	6.0	0.9	12.2	41.2		41.6	58.4	100.0
Apparel	2.0	1.1	1.2	0.5	11.1	70.8	11.7		61.0	39.0	100.0
Other Light Manufacturing	1.1	0.8	0.6	2.0	4.9	80.3	50.8		48.0	52.0	100.0
Wood and Paper	2.3	1.4	1.0	2.0	3.2	23.6	15.8		42.5	57.5	100.0
Basic Intermediates	8.5	3.4	3.5	18.2	6.1	12.7	28.4		27.5	72.5	100.0
Machinery and Equipment	5.0	2.1	8.7	37.2	21.7	75.5	70.8		44.4	55.6	100.0
Services	45.3	55.0	51.8	12.6	35.2	13.6	5.3		40.7	59.3	100.0
Total	100.0	100.0	100.0	100.0	100.0	17.0	16.8	7.5	41.6	50.0	100.0
Singapore and Malaysia											
Grains	1.7	2.7	1.6	0.7	0.0	0.0	13.5	35.5	21.7	42.8	100.0
Other Agriculture	2.3	4.2	2.8	1.6	1.1	16.6	24.3	36.5	22.4	41.1	100.0
Forestry and Fishery	2.0	4.6	1.3	0.5	2.4	44.3	15.3		15.3	84.7	100.0
Energy and Minerals	3.3	7.2	0.2	6.4	4.3	47.6	59.5	55.2	8.0	36.8	100.0
Food Processing	4.9	2.0	5.9	3.2	4.9	37.7	29.0		27.8	72.2	100.0
Textiles	0.9	0.3	2.1	3.6	1.1	47.7	72.2		63.2	36.8	100.0
Apparel	1.2	0.6	1.1	0.8	2.7	61.9	39.8		53.2	46.8	100.0
Other Light Manufacturing	2.6	1.2	2.2	4.0	4.4	66.3	62.4		33.2	66.8	100.0
Wood and Paper	3.3	3.0	1.4	1.8	3.7	42.8	27.3		51.6	48.4	100.0
Basic Intermediates	11.3	8.6	4.7	15.8	14.5	50.3	51.5		21.2	78.8	100.0
Machinery and Equipment	26.2	12.8	20.5	45.7	41.9	63.6	64.1		42.6	57.4	100.0
Services	40.2	52.8	56.1	16.0	19.0	18.6	16.2		49.3	50.7	100.0
Total	100.0	100.0	100.0	100.0	100.0	38.9	38.9	6.5	39.1	54.4	100.0

APPENDIX A.3

STRUCTURE OF PRODUCTION, FACTOR INCOME, DEMAND AND TRADE PATTERNS FOR APEC REGIONS, 1992 (*Continued*)

	Output (1)	Value added (2)	Sectoral Composition (percent)			Ratios (percent)		Factor Composition of Value Added (percent)			
			Final demand (3)	Imports (4)	Exports (5)	Exports/Output (6)	Imports/Absorption (7)	Land (8)	Labor (9)	Capital (10)	Total (11)
China											
Grains	7.6	12.1	7.7	1.4	1.1	1.8	2.4	27.9	58.2	14.0	100.0
Other Agriculture	9.3	17.0	11.2	1.9	2.8	3.7	2.9	29.0	59.0	12.0	100.0
Forestry and Fishery	1.9	3.4	1.8	0.8	1.1	7.1	6.0		80.7	19.3	100.0
Energy and Minerals	2.6	3.9	0.4	3.4	3.9	18.1	17.3	39.4	34.4	26.2	100.0
Food Processing	5.6	2.6	8.5	3.7	3.2	7.0	8.8		24.4	75.6	100.0
Textiles	5.8	2.7	4.0	7.9	5.6	11.0	16.6		42.5	57.5	100.0
Apparel	3.5	1.9	2.8	0.8	18.5	53.7	6.0		54.6	45.4	100.0
Other Light Manufacturing	4.0	2.3	2.6	5.2	17.5	53.6	26.7		46.8	53.2	100.0
Wood and Paper	2.7	1.8	1.3	3.0	1.9	8.7	14.0		45.9	54.1	100.0
Basic Intermediates	13.0	8.2	2.7	17.9	7.4	7.0	16.6		32.5	67.5	100.0
Machinery and Equipment	12.4	7.2	15.8	37.6	19.9	19.7	32.6		43.0	57.0	100.0
Services	31.6	36.9	41.2	16.4	17.0	6.6	7.1		58.3	41.7	100.0
Total	100.0	100.0	100.0	100.0	100.0	11.8	13.3	9.8	53.2	37.0	100.0
Korea and Taiwan											
Grains	2.3	3.5	1.8	1.2	0.0	0.1	5.6	47.2	42.3	10.5	100.0
Other Agriculture	3.5	5.5	2.9	3.0	1.2	5.8	10.4	46.0	45.3	8.8	100.0
Forestry and Fishery	1.2	2.0	1.2	1.0	1.2	17.7	12.9		46.4	53.6	100.0
Energy and Minerals	1.5	2.0	0.5	9.0	0.2	2.5	46.1	28.0	53.3	18.7	100.0
Food Processing	6.7	2.1	11.0	2.7	1.6	4.0	5.5		51.7	48.3	100.0
Textiles	3.6	1.8	0.5	2.4	8.1	36.7	12.4		51.9	48.1	100.0
Apparel	1.4	0.8	1.6	0.4	4.7	48.2	6.7		73.6	26.4	100.0
Other Light Manufacturing	2.7	1.9	0.8	2.3	11.7	70.6	27.2		66.5	33.5	100.0
Wood and Paper	3.0	2.2	1.0	2.7	2.3	12.5	12.2		58.5	41.5	100.0
Basic Intermediates	17.2	10.6	2.2	18.2	11.3	10.9	14.0		37.5	62.5	100.0
Machinery and Equipment	15.2	9.8	15.0	36.1	38.5	42.1	34.7		58.3	41.7	100.0
Services	41.6	57.8	61.3	21.1	19.1	7.6	7.1		55.8	44.2	100.0
Total	100.0	100.0	100.0	100.0	100.0	16.5	14.1	4.6	53.1	42.3	100.0

STRUCTURE OF PRODUCTION, FACTOR INCOME, DEMAND AND TRADE PATTERNS FOR APEC REGIONS, 1992 *(Continued)*

	Output (1)	Value added (2)	Sectoral Composition (percent) Final demand (3)	Imports (4)	Exports (5)	Ratios (percent) Exports/Output (6)	Imports/Absorption (7)	Land (8)	Factor Composition of Value Added (percent) Labor (9)	Capital (10)	Total (11)
Japan											
Grains	1.3	1.4	0.7	1.3	0.0	0.0	4.0	29.5	50.0	20.5	100.0
Other Agriculture	1.3	1.8	0.8	2.8	0.0	0.4	8.6	29.9	49.8	20.3	100.0
Forestry and Fishery	0.7	0.8	0.3	4.2	0.1	1.1	20.6		54.7	45.3	100.0
Energy and Minerals	0.8	0.8	0.0	15.5	0.2	1.8	48.0	32.2	46.5	21.3	100.0
Food Processing	5.6	2.4	7.8	5.5	0.4	0.4	4.2		56.6	43.4	100.0
Textiles	1.0	0.6	0.4	1.4	1.9	11.2	6.6		73.5	26.5	100.0
Apparel	0.9	0.5	1.8	2.9	0.2	1.2	12.5		76.9	23.1	100.0
Other Light Manufacturing	1.1	0.8	1.2	3.5	5.6	30.3	17.5		61.8	38.2	100.0
Wood and Paper	3.7	2.7	1.2	3.4	0.8	1.3	4.1		67.0	33.0	100.0
Basic Intermediates	10.5	6.5	2.2	11.3	10.2	5.7	4.8		47.1	52.9	100.0
Machinery and Equipment	15.7	12.3	14.9	14.4	62.3	23.2	5.1		59.1	40.9	100.0
Services	57.3	69.3	68.7	33.9	18.1	1.9	2.7		59.9	40.1	100.0
Total	100.0	100.0	100.0	100.0	100.0	5.9	4.6	1.2	58.8	40.0	100.0
The United States											
Grains	0.5	0.5	0.0	0.0	2.0	22.9	1.3	19.6	38.3	42.1	100.0
Other Agriculture	1.6	1.1	0.5	1.4	2.4	8.6	5.6	20.0	38.0	41.9	100.0
Forestry and Fishery	0.4	0.3	0.0	0.8	1.0	15.4	13.6		42.1	57.9	100.0
Energy and Minerals	2.4	2.8	0.0	8.4	1.6	3.9	18.4	44.8	25.3	29.9	100.0
Food Processing	4.4	2.3	5.2	2.7	3.8	5.0	3.8		51.0	49.0	100.0
Textiles	0.8	0.5	0.4	1.3	1.2	9.2	10.3		78.6	21.4	100.0
Apparel	0.7	0.5	1.5	4.8	0.7	6.0	30.0		82.4	17.6	100.0
Other Light Manufacturing	0.5	0.4	1.1	7.2	2.4	27.6	52.3		63.8	36.2	100.0
Wood and Paper	3.9	3.1	1.9	3.8	3.7	5.5	5.9		69.8	30.2	100.0
Basic Intermediates	8.8	5.1	4.4	11.2	12.2	7.9	7.8		69.5	30.5	100.0
Machinery and Equipment	11.0	9.0	11.2	41.0	42.4	22.1	22.2		78.4	21.6	100.0
Services	65.1	74.4	73.6	17.3	26.5	2.3	1.6		64.9	35.1	100.0
Total	100.0	100.0	100.0	100.0	100.0	5.7	6.1	1.6	64.7	33.7	100.0

APPENDIX A.3
STRUCTURE OF PRODUCTION, FACTOR INCOME, DEMAND AND TRADE PATTERNS FOR APEC REGIONS, 1992 (*Continued*)

| | Sectoral Composition (percent) | | | | | Ratios (percent) | | Factor Composition of Value Added (percent) | | | |
	Output (1)	Value added (2)	Final demand (3)	Imports (4)	Exports (5)	Exports/Output (6)	Imports/Absorption (7)	Land (8)	Labor (9)	Capital (10)	Total (11)
The European Union											
Grains	0.7	0.6	0.2	0.2	0.3	9.3	1.8	10.6	67.7	21.7	100.0
Other Agriculture	2.7	3.2	0.9	3.1	0.8	2.5	7.2	11.0	68.0	21.0	100.0
Forestry and Fishery	0.4	0.4	0.2	0.9	0.2	3.7	13.6		26.9	73.1	100.0
Energy and Minerals	3.4	1.9	0.2	11.0	2.0	3.6	18.5	18.5	69.2	12.3	100.0
Food Processing	6.9	4.1	8.1	3.3	4.5	4.8	3.2		58.8	41.2	100.0
Textiles	1.7	1.2	1.7	1.9	2.4	8.8	7.7		76.2	23.8	100.0
Apparel	0.7	0.5	0.9	4.0	1.7	15.4	30.0		76.2	23.8	100.0
Other Light Manufacturing	0.8	0.6	1.2	4.6	3.4	26.6	33.6		74.2	25.8	100.0
Wood and Paper	3.6	2.4	1.9	4.9	2.7	4.9	8.9		70.7	29.3	100.0
Basic Intermediates	10.2	7.7	4.0	10.9	15.5	9.4	7.4		47.5	52.5	100.0
Machinery and Equipment	11.1	8.7	9.8	27.7	34.4	20.0	17.3		79.6	20.4	100.0
Services	57.7	68.8	70.9	27.5	32.1	3.6	3.3		65.7	34.3	100.0
Total	100.0	100.0	100.0	100.0	100.0	6.6	6.8	0.8	65.6	33.7	100.0

APPENDIX A.4
SECTORAL EXPORTS, IMPORTS, NET TRADE FLOWS AND TRADE DEPENDENCE FOR APEC REGIONS (BILLIONS OF US$)

	Indonesia	Thailand	Philippines	Singapore and Malaysia	China	Korea and Taiwan	Japan	USA	EU
Exports:									
Grains	0.03	1.39	0.01	0.0	1.61	0.04	0.0	11.70	2.30
Other Agriculture	2.25	2.23	0.64	1.19	3.90	2.39	0.34	13.81	6.18
Forestry and Fishery	1.17	1.90	0.38	2.56	1.52	2.42	0.58	5.51	1.73
Energy and Minerals	11.64	1.17	0.60	4.57	5.53	0.43	0.96	9.27	14.37
Food Processing	1.60	3.97	1.27	5.21	4.52	3.17	1.47	22.17	32.99
Textiles	2.75	1.28	0.15	1.18	7.83	15.98	7.98	7.08	17.24
Apparel	3.14	3.48	1.93	2.91	26.12	9.36	0.74	4.03	12.27
Other Light Manufacturing	2.45	3.91	0.84	4.63	24.78	22.78	22.97	14.12	24.89
Wood and Paper	5.09	0.83	0.54	3.96	2.73	4.47	3.46	21.54	19.80
Basic Intermediates	4.17	2.02	1.05	15.39	10.52	22.01	41.96	70.29	113.49
Machinery and Equipment	1.99	8.63	3.72	44.29	28.14	75.07	256.43	244.44	251.92
Services	3.19	6.86	6.04	20.09	24.08	37.22	74.67	152.56	234.83
Total	39.46	37.67	17.19	105.97	141.27	195.34	411.58	576.51	732.01
Imports:									
Grains	0.62	0.15	0.28	0.71	2.15	2.02	4.34	0.55	1.28
Other Agriculture	0.93	0.92	0.18	1.63	3.05	4.92	8.92	8.96	23.94
Forestry and Fishery	0.04	1.20	0.10	0.54	1.27	1.68	13.42	4.76	7.06
Energy and Minerals	1.42	3.29	2.18	6.66	5.28	14.71	49.97	51.68	84.70
Food Processing	0.81	1.01	0.96	3.34	5.84	4.44	17.64	16.92	25.12
Textiles	1.35	1.29	1.03	3.81	12.40	3.91	4.44	8.16	14.93
Apparel	0.03	0.04	0.08	0.83	1.18	0.61	9.34	29.66	30.53
Other Light Manufacturing	0.76	1.08	0.33	4.14	8.19	3.70	11.39	44.27	35.63
Wood and Paper	0.69	1.20	0.35	1.92	4.73	4.37	10.89	23.50	37.81
Basic Intermediates	7.05	10.58	3.12	16.58	28.10	29.93	36.39	69.36	83.97
Machinery and Equipment	13.50	18.92	6.37	47.78	59.16	59.28	46.33	253.90	213.55
Services	5.49	4.22	2.15	16.70	25.85	34.66	109.40	106.86	211.69
Total	32.69	43.91	17.13	104.63	157.22	164.24	322.47	618.60	770.18

APPENDIX A.4

SECTORAL EXPORTS, IMPORTS, NET TRADE FLOWS AND TRADE DEPENDENCE FOR APEC REGIONS (BILLIONS OF US$) (*Continued*)

	Indonesia	Thailand	Philippines	Singapore and Malaysia	China	Korea and Taiwan	Japan	USA	EU
Net Trade (Exports – Imports)									
Grains	0.59	1.23	0.27	0.71	0.54	1.99	4.33	11.15	1.03
Other Agriculture	1.32	1.31	0.46	0.44	0.85	2.54	8.57	4.85	17.76
Forestry and Fishery	1.13	0.70	0.28	2.02	0.24	0.74	12.84	0.74	5.33
Energy and Minerals	10.23	2.12	1.58	2.08	0.25	14.27	49.01	42.41	70.33
Food Processing	0.80	2.96	0.31	1.87	1.32	1.27	16.17	5.24	7.87
Textiles	1.40	0.02	0.87	2.63	4.57	12.07	3.54	1.09	2.32
Apparel	3.11	3.45	1.84	2.08	24.94	8.75	8.60	25.64	18.26
Other Light Manufacturing	1.69	2.82	0.51	0.49	16.58	19.08	11.58	30.15	10.73
Wood and Paper	4.39	0.37	0.19	2.04	2.00	0.10	7.43	1.96	18.01
Basic Intermediates	2.89	8.57	2.06	1.18	17.59	7.92	5.57	0.94	29.52
Machinery and Equipment	11.52	10.29	2.65	3.49	31.02	15.79	210.10	9.46	38.38
Services	2.30	2.64	3.89	3.39	1.78	2.56	34.73	45.70	23.14
Total	6.77	6.24	0.05	1.34	15.94	31.10	89.12	42.09	38.17

APPENDIX A.5
SECTORAL TARIFFS, EXPORTS TAXES AND PRODUCTION TAXES (PERCENT *AD VALOREM*)

	Indonesia	Thailand	Philippines	Singapore and Malaysia	China	Korea and Taiwan	Japan	USA	EU
Import Tariffs and NTBs:									
Grains	0.5	8.5	10.0	0.3	0.6	309.8	327.3	4.8	69.3
Other Agriculture	62.8	47.9	34.4	0.7	11.4	68.0	31.8	33.2	40.8
Forestry and Fishery	18.9	38.1	12.1	1.9	8.9	6.9	3.4	0.2	8.1
Energy and Minerals	0.6	17.6	10.7	0.2	5.0	4.1	0.7	0.4	0.2
Food Processing	21.8	46.4	24.7	3.3	10.6	29.1	113.7	11.3	23.9
Textiles	33.9	61.4	39.2	7.0	20.2	10.5	10.4	9.8	11.7
Apparel	43.2	79.4	49.4	5.8	8.5	15.4	61.6	20.8	13.2
Other Light Manufacturing	19.0	44.7	35.4	3.5	13.0	11.3	8.2	7.5	5.6
Wood and Paper	10.3	26.6	30.8	3.7	10.3	7.4	4.1	2.1	4.8
Basic Intermediates	6.8	27.6	19.8	4.9	9.9	9.0	87.0	8.6	9.7
Machinery and Equipment	16.2	39.6	22.2	3.5	13.0	13.5	35.2	12.1	9.0
Total	12.7	31.9	19.1	3.0	10.2	14.4	29.0	8.5	7.1
Production Taxes (+) and Subsidies (-):									
Grains	1.8	0.3	1.5	N.A.	2.2	16.1	6.5	40.4	4.8
Other Agriculture	1.7	0.3	2.4	0.2	2.7	14.8	24.8	4.7	28.7
Forestry and Fishery	0.7	1.9	4.2	0.0	7.6	0.2	2.5	2.5	0.5
Energy and Minerals	0.6	8.0	16.3	0.0	8.4	0.2	2.7	7.5	0.1
Food Processing	7.2	14.6	4.9	0.3	11.8	14.5	10.6	4.2	0.5
Textiles	1.6	2.2	2.4	0.8	7.7	1.2	2.3	1.0	0.9
Apparel	20.7	5.5	4.8	0.6	12.3	2.8	1.9	0.6	1.0
Other Light Manufacturing	8.7	5.0	10.5	0.3	14.5	4.2	5.2	1.7	1.0
Wood and Paper	2.6	3.2	2.7	0.8	9.6	1.6	1.7	1.3	1.1
Basic Intermediates	5.5	7.8	11.8	1.1	12.7	1.7	6.3	3.6	1.3
Machinery and Equipment	2.3	9.5	9.9	0.7	10.4	3.7	3.9	1.6	1.4
Services	2.3	2.6	3.5	1.4	6.7	3.6	3.2	6.0	1.3
Total	1.1	4.3	4.4	1.0	7.9	2.6	3.5	4.7	0.3

SECTORAL TARIFFS, EXPORTS TAXES AND PRODUCTION TAXES (PERCENT *AD VALOREM*) (*Continued*)

Export Taxes (+) and Subsidies (-):

	Indonesia	Thailand	Philippines	Singapore and Malaysia	China	Korea and Taiwan	Japan	USA	EU
Grains				0.8				8.2	200.9
Other Agriculture				15.3				-0.0	22.2
Forestry and Fishery				7.4					0.1
Energy and Minerals				10.2	0.1				2.0
Food Processing				6.5				1.3	14.6
Textiles	4.2	4.6	4.7	6.1	6.3	1.4			0.2
Apparel	30.4	16.6	27.2	30.8	18.2	14.4			0.1
Other Light Manufacturing		0.0		0.3					0.0
Wood and Paper				4.5	0.2	0.0	0.0		0.1
Basic Intermediates	0.1	0.2		2.6	0.9	0.2	0.6		4.9
Machinery and Equipment				0.9	0.0	0.1	1.4		0.9
Services				1.8					0.3
Total	2.7	1.7	3.1	3.3	3.8	0.9	0.9	0.2	0.4

APPENDIX A.6
POST URUGUAY ROUND AVERAGE TARIFFS BY SECTOR AND REGION

Pre-Uruguay Round Import Tariff Rates (percent)

	Indonesia	Thailand	Philippines	Singapore and Malaysia	China	Korea and Taiwan	Japan	USA	EU
Grains	0.5	8.5	10.0	0.3	0.6	309.8	327.3	4.8	69.3
Other Agriculture	62.8	47.9	34.4	0.7	11.4	68.0	31.8	33.2	40.8
Forestry and Fishery	18.9	38.1	12.1	1.9	8.9	6.9	3.4	0.2	8.1
Energy and Minerals	0.6	17.6	10.7	0.2	5.0	4.1	0.7	0.4	0.2
Food Processing	21.8	46.4	24.7	3.3	10.6	29.1	108.5	4.8	12.8
Textiles	33.9	61.4	39.2	7.0	20.2	10.5	7.6	9.4	8.6
Apparel	43.2	79.4	49.4	5.8	8.5	15.4	13.8	18.6	13.2
Other Light Manufacturing	19.0	44.7	35.4	3.5	13.0	11.3	8.2	7.5	5.6
Wood and Paper	10.3	26.6	30.8	3.7	10.3	7.4	3.6	1.3	4.6
Basic Intermediates	6.8	27.6	19.8	4.9	9.9	9.0	4.0	3.5	5.9
Machinery and Equipment	16.2	39.6	22.2	3.5	13.0	13.5	3.2	2.9	6.1
Average	12.7	31.9	19.1	3.0	10.2	14.4	13.3	3.9	5.4

Post-Uruguay Round Import Tariff Rates (percent):

	Indonesia	Thailand	Philippines	Singapore and Malaysia	China	Korea and Taiwan	Japan	USA	EU
Grains	0.5	8.5	10.0	0.3	0.6	151.7	183.4	1.7	69.3
Other Agriculture	62.8	47.9	34.4	0.7	11.4	57.0	29.3	33.1	40.8
Forestry and Fishery	18.9	16.2	10.3	1.0	8.2	5.1	2.3	0.1	7.0
Energy and Minerals	0.6	13.3	10.7	0.2	4.9	3.7	0.0	0.4	0.0
Food Processing	21.8	46.4	24.7	3.3	10.6	19.0	70.4	3.3	12.0
Textiles	26.3	28.5	28.3	4.9	15.1	8.0	5.2	6.7	6.4
Apparel	36.3	30.3	31.9	4.7	6.3	13.8	9.2	16.7	11.5
Other Light Manufacturing	17.2	30.1	35.4	2.7	12.3	6.4	6.4	5.0	3.3
Wood and Paper	9.9	17.6	27.6	2.7	9.6	4.1	1.3	0.4	0.6
Basic Intermediates	6.8	24.6	18.8	4.6	9.6	4.4	1.4	1.9	3.5
Machinery and Equipment	15.9	29.7	20.7	2.4	12.5	9.1	0.1	1.7	3.6
Average	12.1	24.4	17.5	2.3	9.4	9.1	8.0	2.8	4.0

APPENDIX A.6
POST URUGUAY ROUND AVERAGE TARIFFS BY SECTOR AND REGION (Continued)

Percentage Reduction in Tariff Rates from Uruguay Round Commitments:

	Indonesia	Thailand	Philippines	Singapore and Malaysia	China	Korea and Taiwan	Japan	USA	EU
Grains						51.0	44.0	63.9	
Other Agriculture						16.1	7.9	0.2	
Forestry and Fishery		57.4	14.8	46.2	7.4	26.2	32.4	28.4	14.2
Energy and Minerals		24.4	0.1	1.2		9.6	99.8	5.0	59.7
Food Processing		53.6	27.8	30.5		34.7	35.1	31.4	6.3
Textiles	22.5	61.8	35.5	17.6	25.1	23.6	31.3	28.5	25.5
Apparel	16.0	32.7		23.9	25.8	9.8	33.2	10.0	13.0
Other Light Manufacturing	9.7	34.0		27.8	4.8	43.4	22.0	32.9	42.0
Wood and Paper	3.5	10.9	10.5	6.4	7.0	45.2	64.4	73.2	87.0
Basic Intermediates	1.1		5.4		3.2	51.2	65.0	46.6	41.0
Machinery and Equipment	1.9	25.0	6.6	29.8	4.2	32.6	96.2	42.8	41.3
Average	4.1	23.6	8.1	22.1	7.3	36.9	39.8	28.2	26.4

NOTES

1.   An earlier version of this model (with six regions and ten sectors) was used to analyze the impact of an APEC FTA on regional economies, and assess the costs of excluding individual APEC members from the FTA. See Lewis, Robinson, and Wang (1995).

2.   Our APEC model does not include all current members of APEC. Excluded from our model are the industrial economies of Australia, New Zealand, and Canada, the small Pacific economies of Brunei and Papua New Guinea, and Mexico and Chile in Latin America.

3.   These models, in turn, have built on multi-country models developed to analyze the impact of the Tokyo Round of GATT negotiations—in particular, the multi-country CGE model developed by Whalley (1985). Our model starts from the WALRAS model developed at the OECD to analyze the impact of the current GATT negotiations on the major OECD countries (OECD, 1990) and the RUNS model described in Goldin, Knudsen, and van der Mensbrugghe (1993). See Hinojosa-Ojeda and Robinson (1992) and Brown (1992) for a review of NAFTA CGE models.

4.   The model also permits regional interactions through endogenous migration of capital and labor, but for all experiments presented in this chapter, this feature is not used. See Hinojosa-Ojeda, Lewis, and Robinson (1994) for analysis of a Greater North America Free Trade Area (GNAFTA) using a similar model that includes labor migration.

5.   Social Accounting Matrices are described in Pyatt and Round (1985).

6.   Robinson (1989) surveys CGE models applied to developing countries. Shoven and Whalley (1984) survey models of developed countries. The theoretical properties of this family of trade-focused CGE models are discussed in Devarajan, Lewis, and Robinson (1990). A full presentation of the APEC-CGE model appears in the appendix of this chapter.

7.   De Melo and Robinson (1989) and Devarajan, Lewis, and Robinson (1991) discuss the role of the real exchange rate in this class of model. We fix the exchange rate for rest of world, thereby defining the international *numeraire*.

8.   The various export and import externality features can be turned on or off as desired in carrying out model simulations.

9.   Armington (1969) used the specification in deriving import-demand functions, and the import aggregation functions are sometimes called Armington functions. Devarajan, Lewis, and Robinson (1990) discuss in detail the properties of single-country models which incorporate imperfect substitution. Brown (1987) analyzes the implications of using CES import aggregation functions in multi-country trade models. Others have criticized the use of the CES function on econometric grounds. See, for example, Alston et al. (1989).

10.   Hanson, Robinson, and Tokarick (1990) use the AIDS function in their 30-sector single-country CGE model of the United States. They estimate the sectoral import demand functions using time-series data and find that sectoral ex-

penditure elasticities of import demand are generally much greater than one in the United States, results consistent with estimates from macro-econometric models.

11.   The data set is drawn primarily from the GTAP 1992 dataset, version 2, which is described in Hertel (1996).

12.   For model regions that are made up of more than one national economy (Korea and Taiwan, Singapore and Malaysia, China, and EU), all figures on exports and imports reported in these tables (and used in the model) refer to trade with economies *outside* that region, and thus exclude trade that occurs among members of the same region. In constructing the regional data sets, this "within region" trade is netted out and treated as another source of domestic demand. Thus care must be taken in comparing trade shares and structure with other published sources on regional trade flows that do not adjust for intra-regional trade.

13.   "Intra-industry" in this context refers to the two-way trade between industries that produce commodities that are similar in input requirements and highly substitutable in use, such as similar televisions manufactured by different producers.

14.   For example, the figures for China exclude the enormous trade flows between China and Hong Kong; similarly, the rest of world figures include only trade between the rest of world and other regions in our model, not among the many countries lumped together in our rest of world aggregate.

15.   Because information on tariffs for Taiwan and China was not available from the GATT, the earlier GTAP rates were used for these economics.

16.   Their estimates, based on unit value index comparisons, suggest sizeable non-tariff protection across a wide range of industrial products. For our purposes, we have chosen to increase reported tariff and NTB rates by one-half of the NTB equivalent calculated by these authors, resulting in the higher average protection rates for Japan reported in Table 5.

REFERENCES

Alston, Julian M., Colin A. Carter, Richard Green, and Daniel Pick (1989) "Whither Armington Trade Models?" *American Journal of Agricultural Economics,* 72, 2 (May), pp. 455–467.

Armington, Paul (1969) "A Theory of Demand for Products Distinguished by Place of Production," *IMF Staff Papers,* 16, 1 (July), pp. 159–178.

Brooke, Anthony, David Kendrick, and Alexander Meeraus (1988) *GAMS: A User's Guide,* (Redwood City, CA: The Scientific Press).

Brown, Drusilla (1992) "The Impact of a North American Free Trade Area: Applied General Equilibrium Models," in N. Lustig, B. Bosworth, and R. Lawrence (eds.) *North American Free Trade: Assessing the Impact,* (Washington, DC: The Brookings Institution).

Brown, Drusilla (1987) "Tariffs, the Terms of Trade, and Natural Product Differentiation," *Journal of Policy Modeling,* 9 (Autumn), pp. 503–526.

Cox, D. and Richard Harris (1985) "Trade Deregulation and Industrial Organization: Some Estimates for Canada." *Journal of Political Economy*, 93, (1), pp. 115–145.

Deaton, Angus and John Muelbauer (1980) *Economics and Consumer Behavior*, (Cambridge, England: Cambridge University Press).

Devarajan, Shantayanan, Jeffrey D. Lewis and Sherman Robinson (1990) "Policy Lessons from Trade-Focused, Two-Sector Models," *Journal of Policy Modeling*, 12, pp. 625–657.

Devarajan, Shantayanan, Jeffrey D. Lewis and Sherman Robinson (1991) "From Stylized to Applied Models: Building Multisector CGE Models for Policy Analysis." *Department of Agricultural and Resource Economics Working Paper No. 616*, (Berkeley, CA: University of California at Berkeley).

Devarajan, Shantayanan and Dani Rodrik (1989) "Trade Deregulation in Developing Countries: Do Imperfect Competition and Scale Economies Matter?" *American Economic Review*, 79, 2 (May), pp. 283–287.

Goldin, Ian, Odin Knudsen, and Dominque van der Mensbrugghe (1993) *Trade Liberalisation: Global Economic Implications*, (Paris, France: OECD).

Green, Richard and Julian M. Alston (1990) "Elasticities in AIDS Models," *American Journal of Agricultural Economics*, 72, 2 (May), pp. 442–445.

Hanson, Kenneth, Sherman Robinson, and Stephen Tokarick (1990) "United States Adjustment in the 1990s: A CGE Analysis of Alternative Trade Strategies." Staff Report AGES9031, (Washington, DC: U.S. Department of Agriculture, Economic Research Service).

Harris, Richard (1984) "Applied General Equilibrium Analysis of Small Open Economies with Scale Economies and Imperfect Competition," *American Economic Review*, 74, 5 (December), pp. 1016–1032.

Helpman, Elhanan and Paul R. Krugman (1985). Market Structure and Foreign Trade: Increasing Returns, Imperfect Competition, and the International Economy, (Cambridge, MA: MIT Press).

Hertel, Thomas W. (ed.) (1996). *Global Trade Analysis: Modeling and Applications*, (Cambridge, England: Cambridge University Press).

Hinojosa-Ojeda, Raúl, Jeffrey D. Lewis, and Sherman Robinson (1994) "Regional Integration Options for Central America and the Caribbean After NAFTA," Processed, November 1994.

Hinojosa-Ojeda, Raúl and Sherman Robinson (1992) "Labor Issues in a North American Free Trade Area," in N. Lustig, B. Bosworth, and R. Lawrence (eds.) *North American Free Trade: Assessing the Impact*, (Washington, DC: The Brookings Institution).

Hughes Hallett, Andrew and Carlos A. Primo Braga (1994) "The New Regionalism and the Threat of Protection," *International Economics Department Policy Research Working Paper No. 1349*, (Washington, DC: The World Bank).

Lewis, Jeffrey D., Sherman Robinson, and Zhi Wang (1995) "Beyond the Uruguay Round: The Implications of an Asian Free Trade Area," *China Economic Review*, 6, 1.

de Melo, Jaime and Sherman Robinson (1989) "Product Differentiation and the Treatment of Foreign Trade in Computable General Equilibrium Models of Small Economies," *Journal of International Economics,* 27, 1-2 (August), pp. 47–67.

de Melo, Jaime and Sherman Robinson (1992) "Productivity and externalities: models of export-led growth," *Journal of International Trade and Economic Development,* 1, 1, 1992, pp. 41–68.

de Melo, Jaime and David Tarr (1992) *A General Equilibrium Analysis of U.S. Foreign Trade Policy,* (Cambridge, MA: MIT Press).

OECD (1990) "Special Issue: Modelling the Effects of Agricultural Policies," *OECD Economic Studies,* 13 (Winter, 1989–1990).

Pyatt, Graham and Jeffery I. Round, (eds.) (1985) *Social Accounting Matrices: A Basis for Planning,* (Washington, DC: The World Bank).

Robinson, Sherman (1989) "Multisectoral Models" in H.B. Chenery and T.N. Srinivasan, (eds.) *Handbook of Development Economics* (Amsterdam, The Netherlands: North-Holland).

Robinson, Sherman, Mary Soule, and Silvia Weyerbrock (1991) "Import Demand Functions, Trade Volume, and Terms-of-Trade Effects in Multi-Country Trade Models," Unpublished manuscript, Department of Agricultural and Resource Economics, University of California at Berkeley.

Sazanami, Y., Shujiro Urata, and Hiroki Kawai (1995) *Measuring the Costs of Protection in Japan,* (Washington, DC: Institute for International Economics).

Shoven, John B. and John Whalley (1984) "Applied General—Equilibrium Models of Taxation and International Trade," *Journal of Economic Literature,* 22, 3 (September), pp. 1007–1051.

Venables, A.J. (1985) "Trade and Trade Policy with Imperfect Competition: The Case of Identical Products and Free Entry," *Journal of International Economics,* 19, pp. 1–20.

Whalley, John (1985) *Trade Deregulation Among Major World Trading Areas,* (Cambridge, MA: MIT Press).

CHAPTER 13

Economic Reforms During the Crisis and Beyond

William E. James *and* Anwar Nasution

For a second time since independence Indonesia has recently faced an economic and political crisis. Like the crisis of the final years of the presidency of Sukarno in the mid-1960s, the most recent economic crisis of 1997–1998 marked the end of the presidency of Suharto following a long period of authoritarian rule. Both crises culminated in a steep recession, a substantial devaluation and high interest rates and inflation. In both episodes, capital flight, bank runs, and panic buying took place on a grand scale while ethnic tensions and anti-Chinese violence were widespread. However, the more recent episode took place after three decades of rapid economic growth that lifted the vast majority of the population out of poverty. This impressive growth record was brought about by a combination of sound economic policies, particularly openness of trade and investment, along with improved education and technical advances, especially in agriculture.

The growth process was initiated following the establishment of Suharto's "New Order" government and Indonesia's embrace of outward-oriented trade and investment policies advocated by a group of western-trained economists known as the "technocrats." The hallmark of this openness was the free movement of capital, a policy that was adopted in the early 1970s and that has been maintained ever since. By guaranteeing investors the right to repatriate their capital, Indonesia was able to restore the confidence of investors who had withdrawn their capital during the crisis years. The open capital account provided discipline over macro-economic policies and for the most part the government abided by conservative fiscal and monetary policies and a realistic exchange rate. Despite the ascendancy of the economists in the early years, Indonesia pursued a contradictory mix of liberalizing and protectionist policies in the three decades of the New Order government as many other factors, both internal and external, pushed and pulled in different directions. Details of the evolution of various policies have been provided in earlier chapters (see, in particular, Chapters 2 and 3). The technocrats had their biggest success in the mid-1980s when, using the oil crises of the time as leverage, they were able to persuade President Suharto to over-ride the objections of protectionist and nationalist interest groups to launch significant liberalizing reforms in trade, investment and financial sector policy. This deregulation episode has been the main focus of this book.

By the mid-1990s, however, the balance of political favor had begun to shift against the liberalization camp. This was partly due to the very success of the liberalization episode that relaxed the sense of crisis that had enabled the reforms to be launched in the first place. At the same time, nationalist, protectionist, and crony interests, who had never been too far from the ear of the president, began to reassert themselves. Signs of reform fatigue began to emerge. At the macro-level, there were indications of erosion in fiscal and financial discipline. At the micro-level, there was a slowdown in the progress of deregulation and, more alarmingly, an increase in the brazenness with which cronies began to divert national policies and resources towards their own interests. Every significant case of privatization, for example, began to feature the involvement of the President's own family or cronies. These distortions were not in themselves a threat to overall economic growth as long as investors remained confident in the ability of the government to maintain sound macroeconomic and financial policies.

This ability was tested in the regional crisis of 1997. This crisis, which began in Thailand, quickly put pressure on Indonesia's external account, as capital began to flee to safer havens in the West, leading very soon to a siege of the banking system. The banking system, opened to competition by the financial sector reforms of 1987–1988 but weakened since then by unsound and poorly supervised lending to crony interests, could not withstand the siege. Confidence in the economy eroded rapidly as the perception grew that the cabinet was divided over the response to the crisis and the president was not in control (his health had begun to fail). This loss of confidence was reflected in the large outflows of capital that started in the fourth quarter of 1997 and continued into the first quarter of 2000. The crisis also resulted in a substantial and rapid depreciation of the Rupiah, heightened ethnic rioting and tensions, and the resignation of President Suharto in 1998.

In this concluding chapter we will first consider the reforms that were implemented during the crisis under the tutelage of the IMF and the status of trade and investment policies under the successor governments of B.J. Habibie and Abdurrahman Wahid (popularly known as Gus Dur). In particular, we will examine the issue of institutional reforms and governance that are critical to long-term prospects of the Indonesian economy and comment on these prospects in light of international economic conditions, including key issues relating to market access for Indonesian products and services.

Indonesia's Financial Crisis and the IMF Reforms

As late as October of 1997, Indonesia was regarded as an ideal performer in terms of poverty reduction and macroeconomic management (Hill 1999). The fact that Indonesia approached the IMF that month was regarded as a precautionary move rather than as behavior indicative of an economy on the verge of a financial crisis. Fundamentally, the Indonesian economy was characterized by sound monetary and fiscal policies and, in the opinion of the World Bank and IMF, adoption of a more flexible exchange rate policy would be expected to lead to appreciation of the Rupiah, given the country's attractiveness to foreign investors.

Misjudgment of Indonesia's precarious position was in large part a result of lack of transparency on the part of banks and the corporate sector regarding the size of short-term borrowing and the overall stock of short-term private external debt. Nevertheless, greater caution was in order given Indonesia's high debt-service ratio and known stock of public and private external debt. The former hovered near 30 percent of exports and the latter was known to exceed $100 billion (World Bank 1998).[1]

The reverse order of sequencing of reform Indonesia followed (see Chapter 2 in this volume) may have contributed to the misallocation of capital in the Indonesian economy. In general, both the coverage and speed of deregulation of the financial sector were broader and more rapid than in the real sector of the economy. In contrast to the order of reform suggested by economists who have thought about these issues, Indonesia also adopted a different sequence of reform in its financial sector.[2]

Deregulation in the banking industry was initiated on June 1, 1983, and was followed by major reforms beginning in 1987-88. However, it was not accompanied by needed improvements in bank supervision and corporate governance. The weak supervision of banks and finance companies encouraged excessive investment in the economy as a whole. This was true not just for Indonesia but also for many other countries in East Asia (McKinnon and Pil 1996). Moreover, private banks often were affiliated with business conglomerates and, thus, the banks did not properly screen loans to affiliated companies. This type of improper lending behavior was further encouraged by the expectation that in case of difficulty, the banks would receive assistance from the central bank. This behavior ignored the costly nature of cleaning up non-performing loans, as attaching collateral is a costly and time-consuming process and thereby makes it more difficult to solve the problem of adverse selection (Mishkin 1997).

Despite the fact that markets for many tradable goods were gradually opened by unilateral trade liberalization that began in the mid-1980s, non-tradable products and many services were largely shielded from competition. Consequently, the rapid build-up of short-term private external debt in the immediate period before the crisis erupted (1994–1997) was associated with excessive investment in real estate and buildings, financial services and retail trade. Inflated property values and overly optimistic expectations regarding economic growth prospects fed the property speculation. The open capital account, inefficient domestic banking sector and highly concentrated corporate ownership structure coupled with implicit government guarantees placed the economy in a precarious position once short-term private debt exceeded the international reserves of the government.

Government efforts to monitor private external debt and regulate such borrowing were clearly inadequate. The poor supervision of financial institutions permitted banks to circumvent legal lending limits with impunity. Contagion was clearly a major factor behind the spread of the currency turmoil to Indonesia in late 1997 and early 1998. Following the initial IMF letter of intent, Indonesia shut down 16 private banks that were judged to be insolvent and adopted a standard package of expenditure reduction and switching policies. Despite the apparent willingness of the government to swallow the IMF medicine, the Rupiah continued to depreciate and by January 1998 had lost 80 percent of its value against the dollar. Rather than blaming the IMF for this failure, however poorly conceived the initial program was, one must consider the broader political context.

The new cabinet Suharto announced was dominated by cronies like Mohammed "Bob" Hasan (as Minister of Industry and Trade). Moreover, the elevation of B.J. Habibie to Vice President, jolted the currency to its lowest level ever. The new cabinet was greeted with incredulity as market participants juxtaposed the ministerial line-up of cronies with the necessary reforms they would be expected to carry out. In an effort to shore up the currency and stem the flight of capital, Suharto agreed to sign off on a second letter-of-intent on January 15 that required the government to implement sweeping reforms that would wipe out almost all protection and monopoly in the economy.

The credibility of the government to carry through with the IMF-mandated reforms was undermined even as the new cabinet prepared to assume the reigns in March 1998. A little-known U.S. academic, Steven Hanke, had suddenly appeared on the scene as a top confidential advisor to Suharto in late 1997. Hanke was able to convince Suharto that adoption of a currency board would deliver the economy from the crisis at one fell swoop. However persuasive Hanke's arguments were to Suharto, among the vast majority of economists and technocrats, they fell on deaf ears and, in any case, were looked upon askance by the IMF itself. The lack of international reserves available to back the currency and the fact that adoption of a currency board would not address the loss of confidence in the banking system and the problem of corporate debt were reasons why many economists opposed the currency board. In addition, it was suspected that advance information about the currency board could be used to advantage by well-connected insiders.

Suharto's ouster of Dr. J. Soedradjad Djiwandono as Governor of Bank Indonesia (BI) in March 1998 (J. Soedradjad Djiwandono 2000) was possibly related to his opposition to instituting a currency board system.[3] Soedradjad had also been positive to trade and investment liberalization and had maintained good relations with the international donor community and with the technocrat group of economists. In his position as Governor of BI, Soedradjad was likely to follow the IMF program closely and to resist pressure to deviate from the stabilization and reform policies, which Suharto found increasingly inconvenient. The ouster of Soedradjad can perhaps be understood more clearly in this context as is possible that Suharto wished to signal his opposition to the reforms through this action.

In any case, the deep economic contraction that took hold in early 1998 sealed Suharto's fate. In May, student demonstrations against Suharto were put down with lethal force. Immediately, widespread rioting and violence, much of it directed at the Chinese business community and at Suharto cronies, forced a visibly weakened Suharto to resign.

Political Change and Economic Reform

Following Suharto's resignation in May 1998, Vice President B.J. Habibie took the reigns of power as provided for in the Constitution. As President, Habibie, to his credit committed himself to implement fully the IMF reforms as specified in the second letter of intent and to hold elections as soon as was practicable. Implementation of the reform program by Habibie, who was regarded by the technocrats as their main foe, could not be taken for granted. However, despite some delays and repeated modifications, the reforms were firmly observed even though they were against the financial interest of the Suharto group.

Among the major changes that were agreed to by the government was the ending of government financial support for IPTN, the airplane company that was the crown jewel of the state-owned companies under Habibie's control. Monopolies over domestic agricultural commodities such as cloves were also abolished and the powerful Bureau of Logistics (BULOG) was forced to give up its import monopoly over rice and its control over other key commodities. Local content requirement programs for dairy milk and other industries were ended. The national car program was discontinued. Export cartels such as that of APKINDO over plywood were abolished and prohibitive export taxes on logs and rattan were drastically cut and were to be replaced with resource rents. In general, export taxes were to be limited to a maximum of 10 percent or were to be scrapped altogether on items such as leather. An ambitious trade liberalization program was designed which would result in maximum tariffs of 10 percent by 2003 for almost all products. Quantitative restrictions on imports were to be eliminated along with import surcharges. Investment restrictions were also eased, including permission for foreigners to invest in palm oil estates. Domestic trade restrictions were likewise relaxed and controls over foreign investment in domestic distribution were dropped. A number of institutional changes requiring new laws were also agreed to and are discussed below.

Among the new laws and institutional changes, legislation to make Bank Indonesia (the central bank) independent would soon have consequences that were unforeseen. The sweeping economic reforms were followed by major political changes that culminated in freely contested elections. Habibie's candidacy in the presidential elections of October 1999 was scuttled by a scandal surrounding the bailout of Bank Bali. However, the record of political and economic reform during the interim presidency of Habibie is quite impressive. In the aftermath of both of the crises that ended the Sukarno and Suharto presidencies, successor governments were required to implement wide-ranging reforms.

The difference, however, this time around is that future economic reforms will have to be implemented in a newly democratic polity where various interest groups and individuals are free to express their viewpoints and to protest decisions that they disagree with. In this environment, unlike under the old authoritarian system would-be economic reformers have a tougher job. Instead of having to convince just one man of the virtues of a reform, now those wishing to promote a more open and competitive economy must work to build a constituency for reform amidst a skeptical public and their political representatives so that a majority supports the proposed reforms.

Concerns About Further Reforms

One of the most commonly expressed objections to further deregulation and liberalization of trade and investment is that of alleged adverse distributional consequences. Simply put, it is believed that liberalization will benefit foreign interests and relatively well to do individuals at the expense of domestic enterprises and lower income households, particularly those that are employed in import-competing sectors. Typically, domestic firms of small and medium size, the rural poor and labor employed in farming and domestic-market-oriented enterprises are regarded as vulnerable to foreign competition in this view.

The view that liberal trade policies are associated with concentration of capital and wealth and, therefore, pose a threat to social equity and harmony among various groups in society, has been influential among Indonesians (Dick 2000). During the Sukarno period, this point of view was the justification for the "guided economy" policy. In other words, market forces and the economic agents that carry out market transactions needed "guidance" in order to ensure that economic activity was not harmful to social stability. Though this view was discredited by the disastrous economic consequences of Sukarno's policies, it has re-emerged in the post-Suharto era, particularly among young Indonesians who did not experience the hunger and instability of the "guided economy" period.

Economists have not done a very good job in convincing the public that liberal trade and investment policies have helped to generate high growth in income and employment and have substantially reduced the incidence of poverty in Indonesia. In this context, we note that protection is usually afforded in an inverse relationship to an industry's comparative advantage. In other words, protection is inversely related to an activity's employment of relatively abundant factors of production, particularly of the general labor force. One of the purposes of trade liberalization is to foster growth in sectors that have a comparative advantage and to reduce resource flows into sectors without it. Naturally, this results in a redistribution of income and wealth. It appears obvious that among the main beneficiaries of deregulation have been the millions of new entrants to the labor force who have been employed in labor-intensive sectors. The direct and indirect employment effects of growth have been shown to be quite substantial (see Chapter 7 in this volume).[4] Providers of low cost domestic services and producers of articles of mass consumption have also greatly benefited from having access to lower cost imported inputs. The net effect of liberal policies on income distribution is likely to be quite favorable as a result.[5]

In the wake of the financial crisis, flexibility in labor markets was crucial to cushioning the impact of massive devaluation and the subsequent shift in relative prices on low-income households in Indonesia. Real wages adjusted rapidly so that there was less unemployment and a smaller rise in poverty than would have otherwise taken place (Manning 2000). Export-oriented agriculture and trade-related services helped to absorb workers shed by adversely affected sectors such as construction and banking during the crisis. Hence, continued and deepened liberalization of trade and investment will be vital to providing more remunerative employment opportunities to Indonesia's ever-expanding labor force.[6]

The Recovery and Structural Change

One of the most serious problems that arose as a result of the cabinet shifts in early 1998 was that Bank Indonesia (BI) lost monetary control. BI liquidity credits to domestic banks ballooned as BI sought to bail out the banking system. In January of 1998, Suharto issued a blanket guarantee covering all depositors and creditors, despite opposition to such a guarantee by the Governor of BI and the Minister of Finance (Djiwandono 2000). This policy was chosen in desperation. Public confidence in the banking sector was extremely fragile. The loss of confidence was the result of the previous closure of 16 national banks amid rumors that other banks were in even worse condition than those that were shut down. Data on monetary aggregates and prices soon made it apparent that a bout of high inflation in 1998 was inevitable. The rapid expansion in BI liquidity credits caused the monetary base to double between November 1997 and April 1998. Inflation accelerated during the year and peaked at over 80 percent as measured by the consumer price index (CPI).

If monetary control had not been re-established by the new team at BI during the second semester of the year, hyperinflation would have been a distinct possibility. With a freely floating Rupiah, BI had to sharply raise interest rates in order to reign in inflation and this deepened the recession. In its attempt to prevent the sharp devaluation of the Rupiah and the rapid increase of short-term interest rates, Bank Indonesia intervened heavily in the foreign exchange market and in the process depleted its owned and borrowed external reserves. Without a credible monetary policy and a reduction in inflation and in interest rates following disinflation, economic recovery would have been very unlikely.

A number of policy measures were undertaken to improve the governance system. Efforts to improve disclosure requirements, to strengthen the accounting and legal systems and to improve both market transparency and contract enforcement were made. Indonesia is now committed to adopt the Basle principles covering the prudential rules and regulations that govern the banking system. Legal reform has also been undertaken to improve "exit policy' by modernizing the antiquated bankruptcy code. Finally, preparation of privatization plans has helped to improve the governance system of state-owned enterprises.

Recovery in economic activity became apparent by the fourth quarter of 1999 and growth accelerated in the first half of year 2000. The recovery was led by a sharp rise in net exports and a rebound in fixed investment in the first half of 2000. Real private consumption expenditure is estimated to have contracted by between 5–6 percent between 1997 and the first quarter of 1999 (Ramstetter 2000). A recovery in consumption expenditures in the remainder of 1999 helped to set the economy on a course of recovery.

Overall, there is some evidence that the structure of production and employment had shifted from non-tradable to tradable goods and services between 1996 and 1999 but the change was far less dramatic than one would expect from the massive depreciation of the Rupiah. Agriculture, mining and manufacturing experienced fluctuations in both GDP and employment shares, but by the recovery period the changes in the structure of output and employment were not pronounced outside of the decline in construction.

Within manufacturing, however, there were some significant differences among the sectors in this regard. Wood and metal manufacturing had declining shares of output, as did machinery. However, the machinery sector (including both electrical and non-electrical machinery) appears to have rebounded strongly in 2000 compared with 1999, led by strong export performance that year (Ramstetter 2000).

Inflation Targeting, Floating Exchange Rate, and Open Capital Account

Open economies face a macroeconomic policy "trilemma." They must choose two among the three choices of an open capital account, a fixed exchange rate and an independent monetary policy (Rodrik 2000). Countries that wish to maintain monetary autonomy and an open capital account must adopt a floating exchange rate, as is the case in Indonesia. Indonesia had adroitly managed its international reserves in support of its pegged exchange rate policy prior to the outbreak of the Asian currency crisis in July of 1997. However, there was always tension between targeting the exchange rate and the rate of inflation or of some monetary aggregate. Upon adoption of a more flexible exchange rate, a number of countries have adopted inflation targeting as a means of reigning in inflationary expectations that may arise with a floating exchange rate (Blejer et al. 2000). Chile, Mexico, Israel, and Brazil are among the emerging market economies that have successfully adopted inflation targeting.

The acceptance of a non-discretionary rules-based monetary stance such as a quantitative inflation target requires policy credibility, independence, transparency and accountability of the monetary authority. A rules-based approach in general increases transparency and requires consistency in commitment to contain inflation. Under present conditions of volatility in the demand for money, targeting monetary aggregates is problematic. Hence, an increasing number of countries have found it preferable to accept a freely floating exchange rate, maintain an open capital account and choose to adopt a quantitative inflation target (Blejer et al. 2000).

There are several advantages of adoption of an inflation-targeting approach. Such an approach can help to restore confidence in macroeconomic management through selection of an attainable target range for inflation. It is now recognized that although there may be a short-run trade-off between variability of output (and, hence, employment) and prices, in the long-run economic growth is negatively correlated with inflation. Inflation targeting has the advantage of providing for stable and predictable prices and price trends. Among the key issues to consider in adopting inflation targeting is the choice between a range and a point target, the selection of an appropriate index with which to measure inflation, and the relationship between price expectations and inflation forecasts.

In general, countries that had experienced high rates of inflation and that have subsequently chosen inflation targeting have opted for gradualism in reducing the target rate or range of inflation. In the transition to inflation targeting countries with floating exchange rates must ensure complete independence of the monetary authority so that it is free to adjust the instruments of monetary policy in order to contain inflation at the target rate or within the target range. In this context, the central bank must not be constrained by the need to finance the government budget.

Indonesia passed legislation in 1998 that gave Bank Indonesia independence, although the Wahid government has sought to unseat the present Governor for his alleged role in the Bank Bali scandal. The present atmosphere surrounding BI is still one of crisis. In order to improve its credibility once the crisis subsides, BI must have an effective monetary policy. Announcing a clear-cut objective for monetary policy such as a target range for inflation may help in this regard. An effective monetary policy requires use of indirect instruments with a close relationship to inflation. Indirect instruments such as short-term interest rates are generally preferred to direct instruments such as credit rationing in implementing monetary policy.

Another key requirement for inflation targeting to work is that the central bank must communicate with the public so that it is seen as accountable for its performance and transparent in its operations. Its selection of an appropriate inflation measure and independent monitoring of inflation by an objective statistical institution will help in this regard. BI can also continue to produce its own forecasts of inflation that should be regularly communicated to the public at large. In the case of Indonesia, a target range of inflation should initially be chosen that is within reach and that will not require output contraction in the short-run. Bank Indonesia should also be careful not to adopt other objectives (i.e., a specific level of the Rupiah) that are not consistent with the inflation target. Gradually the target range can be lowered and narrowed one the credibility of BI is re-established.

Restructuring the Corporate and Banking Sector

The banking sector has undergone some significant restructuring and bank re-capitalization is nearly complete (Ramstetter 2000). The number of banks has been reduced through closures and a series of mergers and acquisitions from 237 in June 1997 to 161 in June 2000 (World Bank 2000). A key problem facing the government is that Bank Indonesia was forced to issue a large volume of variable rate bonds to shore-up the banks and to take over the assets of failed banks. Hence, increases in interest rates associated with tight monetary policy will necessarily raise the domestic interest burden of the government budget that is already estimated to rise from 0.02

percent of public expenditures in 1999/2000 to over 4 percent in 2000/2001. The Indonesia Bank Restructuring Agency (IBRA) is charged with disposing of the assets through a privatization program, but progress has been agonizingly slow, as political interference in the process has repeatedly blocked sales of these assets.

Corporate debt restructuring has been very slow despite the formation of a cabinet-level Financial Sector Policy Committee (FSPC). The Jakarta Initiative (JI) aimed at voluntary debt workout programs for Indonesian corporations has also had very limited success. The pace of corporate debt resolution needs to be hastened in the coming years. This will be essential to revive the interest of domestic and foreign investors in Indonesian equities and to increase the efficiency of capital markets in Indonesia. Corporate debt resolution is also required in order for the banks to resume lending on a scale commensurate with their deposit base. This is vital to allow companies to restore production by making use of existing capacity and for new companies to expand through investment.

Real Economy, Competitive Markets, and Trade Liberalization

With signs of economic recovery, including acceleration of economic growth to the 4–6 percent range, it is apparent that fixed capital formation by domestic investors is on the rise. In this context, it is important to recognize that capital formation in Indonesia has always been dominated by domestic investors as FDI has never amounted to as much as 10 percent of gross fixed capital formation, even at its peak in the mid-1990s. However, FDI is likely to follow the upward trend in domestic investment and so contribute to the on-going recovery.

Despite the negative net FDI flows reported in the balance of payments statistics of Indonesia (IMF 2000), there is evidence that foreign multinational corporations did not reduce their presence in Indonesian manufacturing during the crisis, as their shares in manufacturing employment and value-added actually increased between 1996 and 1998 (Ramstetter 2000). In addition, in electrical and non-electrical machinery their shares of employment increased sharply to 65 percent and 36 percent respectively (Takii and Ramstetter 2000). These sectors have experienced an export boom with shares in total exports rising from around 9 percent in the first half of 1996 to over 17 percent in the first half of 2000.

Export growth has picked up considerably with economic activity in 2000. Over the first 11 months of the year total exports had year-on-year growth of over 28 percent and non-oil exports recorded 23 percent growth. Hence, exports for the year are likely to top $60 billion for the first time. Imports have also recovered with growth of nearly 38 percent in January-November 2000 compared with the same period in 1999. Capital goods imports rose by 51 percent in the first ten months of 2000 compared with the same period in 1999, an indication of the revival in domestic investment.[7] The strong foreign trade performance in 2000 is in line with the on-going economic recovery.

Trade liberalization has reduced Indonesia's simple average tariff from over 20 percent at the beginning of the 1990s to around 11 percent in 1997. At present, however, many tariffs on agricultural commodities, textiles and apparel, base metals and metal manufactures, and transportation equipment are quite high (20–30 percent). Tariff peaks of 200 percent remain on automobiles and import licenses are still required for autos, metal waste products, and a number of steel and metal manufactures. Export taxes are still imposed on a number of commodities. Hence, further trade liberalization and the associated gains in competitiveness still remain to be exploited.

Domestic market concentration (as measured by the four-firm concentration ratio) is quite high in Indonesian industry (see Chapter 6 in this volume).[8] Import competition is important in limiting monopoly or oligopoly power in many sectors of the economy. Further reform and deregulation would help spur domestic competition, particularly in sectors where import competition plays a more limited role (e.g., in non-tradable goods and services).

Indonesia introduced a new Law on Banning Monopolistic Practices and Unfair Business Competition in March of 1999 during the term of President Habibie. The Competition Law (see Thee 2000a) was enacted despite some protestations that it was really not necessary since trade and investment liberalization alone would increase competition in the economy by increasing the number of trading partners and would limit the ability of any domestic firms to exercise market power. The Competition Law, however, can be justified in that it addresses the need to curb market power in areas where trade reform is unlikely to have much effect, including in sectors producing non-tradable goods and services, where international export cartels exist, and where high transport costs exist (Thee 2000a).

A number of measures have been introduced in order to promote healthier market competition and to reduce transactions costs. First, the new government has decided to review and dismantle all government contracts that were offered through corruption, collusion, and nepotism. Second, in order to improve domestic competition, various types of explicit and implicit marketing arrangements will be eliminated. This includes the dismantling of the exclusive access of state-owned banks to public sector deposits.

The Competition Law of 1999 has been criticized for failing to make its primary objective clear, for failing to tackle the issue of barriers to competition that have been generated by government policy and regulation over markets, for failing to distinguish between market structure and anti-competitive business practices, and for setting arbitrary market shares as the litmus test for whether or not firms are engaged in anti-competitive practices (Thee 2000a). It remains to be seen if the enforcement of the Competition Law will be effective in promoting free and open competition and protecting consumer interests.

There have been several new laws and institutions of importance to economic performance enacted since the downfall of Suharto, including formation of a Commercial Court under a new Bankruptcy Law, several laws concerning corruption in public life, establishment of a National Law Commission and various efforts at reforming the judiciary, including the Supreme Court. However, as of this writing, none of these legal reforms have produced tangible benefits. The courts have consistently ruled in a fashion that suggests the old "New Order" system still retains lingering power (Lindsey 2000). Even where blatant cases of corruption have been successfully prosecuted the failure to enforce penalties against those responsible raises doubts about the rule of law in Indonesia.

Reducing Barriers to Investment

Regulation of investment, both domestic and foreign, had been quite rigorous and restrictive until the mid-eighties. Deregulation of investment significantly improved Indonesia's investment climate thereafter (see Chapter 3 in this volume). Indeed, during the nineties until the crisis took place, both domestic and foreign investments were booming. The crisis, however, led to a sharp contraction in investment and to net negative foreign direct investment flows. In order to reverse the adverse investment sentiments, both Habibie and Wahid adopted reforms aimed at reducing barriers to investment. In May 1998, the Minister for Investment announced a policy of simplifying investment-licensing procedures.

Under the new policy, foreign investments of up to $100 million could be approved by the Minister of Investment and did not require the President's approval (as was the case for all FDI projects under Suharto). A "single-stop" office was created to ease investor task in gaining the necessary approvals to go ahead with new projects or expansion of existing ones. Finally, the negative list of industries or sectors off-limits to foreign investors was reduced by Habibie from 35 to 9 in January 1999 and was further reduced to 7 by Wahid in July 2000.

Ownership restrictions on FDI have been largely lifted and present no serious obstacle to the operations of foreign MNCs in Indonesia. However, political uncertainty and lawlessness, arbitrary tax and pricing decisions by public authorities, instability of the Rupiah, and increases in minimum wages in excess of labor productivity gains have been cited as problems by foreign investors (Soesastro and Thee 2000). For example, in 1999 of 285 reported overt acts of piracy against foreign vessels conducting trade, 113 incidents took place in Indonesian waters or ports (Dick 2000). There has been a clear upward trend in crime and ethnic violence in Indonesia, including recent bombing of the Jakarta Stock Exchange. Improvement in security and political stability would seem to be priorities in restoring investor confidence.

Summing Up the Case for Open Trade and Investment Policies

Trade and investment reforms enabled Indonesia to make gains in productivity and efficiency that moved the country from low-income to middle-income status in just three decades (Thee 2000b). The resulting increases in real national income stimulated employment in manufacturing and modern service industries bringing about higher real wages and productivity. The ability of Indonesian enterprises to sell their goods abroad was facilitated by on-going multilateral trade liberalization under the auspices of the GATT and, since 1995, the WTO.

Market access improvements associated with the Uruguay Round of 1994 are projected to boost Indonesian real income (1.6 percent over the base case) and exports (3.14 percent over the base) between 1995 and 2004 and unilateral trade liberalization could be expected to lead to similar gains (see Chapter 12 in this volume). The potential gains from new rounds of liberalization, particularly for agriculture and services, could add further to these gains. It is important to recognize that realization of such gains is contingent upon the success of the WTO system in promoting the cause of freer trade in the face of a number of protectionist challenges. In this context, the failure of the November 1999 Seattle Ministerial Meeting of the WTO to launch a new global round and the emergence of a strong lobby against global trade liberalization are causes for concern.

Among the main threats to market access for countries like Indonesia are the possible development of closed regional trading blocks in Europe and the Western Hemisphere, the rising use of antidumping and the emergence of other contingent forms of administered protection by an expanding number of trading partners. The WTO provides a means of redress against these potential threats. Indonesia and other developing countries may wish to influence the WTO agenda to address these problems in future negotiations. More discipline over antidumping, strengthening of article XXIV enforcement, and strengthening GATT/WTO disciplines in the area of rules of origin are examples. Clearly, the implementation of the Uruguay Round Agreement in the area of textiles and apparel will also be a key issue in the coming years.

Weak institutions and limited capacity to implement effective governance in the private corporate sector and in the bureaucracy are still severe limitations in Indonesia. Foreign technical assistance in institution building, including training of staff in various facets of commercial law, competition policy and enforcement, and in understanding and enforcement of multilateral obligations and codes will be necessary in the years ahead. The process of institutional reform and change is underway in Indonesia and although there are numerous difficulties and obstacles, it is clear that democratic change is taking place.

As Soesastro (2000) expresses, much is expected of civil society in Indonesia, which together with the market economy and the government, is one of the three interfaces of democratic society. The rise of civil society in the form of voluntary organizations, political parties and movements, has been gaining momentum after long decades of suppression. This process will create a greater balance between the society and the government and will influence the direction of economic and social policies so that key problems of poverty, environmental degradation and ethnic and religious tensions can be addressed effectively.

The presence of open trade and investment policies will improve economic conditions for the vast majority of Indonesians and provide increased means to address the serious problems confronting Indonesia. As has been seen elsewhere in East Asia, economic and social progress lead to increased demands for democratic governance and an improved quality of life. Such a process of change is now underway in Indonesia though the road ahead is long and difficult.

NOTES

1.   World Bank (2000) reports the actual value of public and private external debt was substantially higher than $100 billion and was really $136 billion. Debt service payments were actually 35 percent of exports in 1997.

2.   McKinnon (1991), for example, suggests the following sequence of deregulation in the banking industry. First, commercial banks should be tightly monitored and regulated. This may include temporary credit rationing. Second, efforts should be made to recapitalize the existing banks and their clientele. Third, during the transition period, the banking industry should be temporarily closed to new entrants, both domestic and foreign, since they are not burdened with low yield loans and can easily out-compete the preexisting banks.

3.   Personal correspondence between one of the authors and Soedradjad confirms his strong opposition to the ideas of Professor Hanke regarding the appropriateness of a currency board system for Indonesia. A leading Japanese expert on Indonesia and its external debt, Professor Shinichi Ichimura, has also expressed reservations to the authors regarding Hanke's views as applied to Indonesia. The reason Suharto chose to dismiss Soedradjad remains unclear, however.

4.   Fujita and James (1997) and James and Fujita (2000) estimate the employment effects of manufactured exports in Indonesia from 1980–1990 and 1985–1995.

5.   Krugman (1993, p. 147) points out: " . . . evidence suggests that protectionist economies have a less equal income distribution than those with freer trade."

6.   Labor markets in Indonesia appear to be quite flexible, so that increases in external demand may manifest themselves more in gains in real wages than in the volume or quantity of employment.

7.   Data are from Badan Pusat Statistik downloaded from www.bps.go.id.

8.   Bird (1999) estimates the four-firm concentration ratio (CR4) in Indonesian domestic industry to have declined from 64 percent in 1975 to 54 percent in 1993. The CR4, when adjusted for foreign trade, falls to 41 percent in the latter year, indicating that import competition is quite important in limiting potential for anti-competitive behavior in Indonesia.

REFERENCES

Bird, Kelly (1999) "Concentration in Indonesian Manufacturing, 1975–93," *Bulletin of Indonesian Economic Studies,* 35 (1) (April), pp. 43–73.

Blejer, Mario, Alain Ize, Alfredo Leone, and Sergio Werlang (eds.). (2000) *Inflation Targeting in Practice,* (International Monetary Fund, Washington, DC).

Dick, Howard (2000) "Representations of Development in 19th and 20th Century Indonesia: A Transport History Perspective," *Bulletin of Indonesian Economic Studies,* 36 (1) (April), pp. 185–207.

Djiwandono, J. Soedradjad (2000) "Bank Indonesia and the Recent Crisis," *Bulletin of Indonesian Economic Studies,* 36 (1) (April), pp. 47–72.

Fujita, Natsuki and William E. James (1997). "Employment Creation and Manufactured Exports in Indonesia, 1980-90," *Bulletin of Indonesian Economic Studies,* 33 (1) (April), pp. 103–115.

Hill, Hal (1999). *The Indonesian Economy in Crisis: Causes, Consequences and Lessons,* Singapore: Institute of Southeast Asian Studies.

International Monetary Fund (2000). *International Financial Statistics,* September, (CD-ROM, Washington, DC).

James, William E. and Natsuki Fujita (2000) "Employment and Manufacturing Exports in Indonesia: An Input-Output Approach," Working Paper Series 2000–06, International Centre for the Study of East Asian Development, Kitakyushu (May).

Krugman, Paul (1993) "Protection in Developing Countries," in Rudiger Dornbusch (ed.), *Policymaking in the Open Economy,* New York: Oxford University Press: 127–148.

Lindsey, Tim (2000). "The Failure of Law Reform," *Bulletin of Indonesian Economic Studies,* 36,(3) (December), p. 9.

Manning, Chris (2000) "Labour Market Adjustment to Indonesia's Economic Crisis: Context, Trends, and Implications," *Bulletin of Indonesian Economic Studies,* 36 (1) (April), pp. 105–136.

McKinnon, Ronald I. (1991) The Order of Economic Liberalization: Financial Control in the Transition to a Market Economy, (Baltimore: The Johns Hopkins University Press).

McKinnon, Ronald I. and H. Pil (1996) "Credible Liberalization and International Capital Flows: The Over-Borrowing Syndrome." In Takatoshi Ito and Anne O. Krueger (eds.) *Financial Deregulation and Integration in East Asia.* (Chicago: University of Chicago Press).

McLeod, Ross H. (2000) "Government-Business Relations in Suharto's Indonesia," in Peter Drysdale (ed.), *Reform and Recovery in East Asia,* London: Routledge: 146–168.

Mishkin, Frederic S. (1997) "Understanding Financial Crises: A Developing Country Perspective." *Annual World Bank Conference on Development Economics 1996.* (Washington, D.C.: the World Bank).

Ramstetter, Eric D. (2000) "Survey of Recent Developments," *Bulletin of Indonesian Economic Studies,* 36 (3) (December), pp. 3–45.

Rodrik, Dani (2000) "How Far Will International Economic Integration Go?" *Journal of Economic Perspectives,* 14 (1) (Winter), pp. 177–186.

Soesastro, Hadi (2000) "Governance and the Crisis in Indonesia," in Peter Drysdale (ed.), *Reform and Recovery in East Asia,* (London: Routledge, pp. 120–145).

Soesastro, Hadi and Thee Kian Wie (2000) "Comprehensive Investment Policies in a Competitive Environment," Paper presented at a Conference on The Indonesian Economic Recovery in a Changing Environment, Jakarta, October 4–5.

Takii, Sadayuki and Eric D. Ramstetter (2000) "Foreign Multinationals in Indonesian Manufacturing, 1985–1998: Shares, Relative Size, and Relative Labor Productivity," Working Paper Series 2000–18, International Centre for the Study of East Asian Development, Kitakyushu (September).

Thee Kian Wie (2000a) "Competition Policy in Indonesia and the New Anti-Monopoly and Fair Competition Law," Paper presented at the International Conference on Competition Policy and Economic Adjustment in Indonesia, World Bank, Asian Development Bank, USAID and AUSAID, Jakarta, August 20.

Thee Kian Wie (2000b) "Reflections on the *New Order Miracle,*" in Grame Lloyd and Shannon Smith (eds.), *Indonesia Update 2000,* Singapore: Institute of Southeast Asian Studies and the Australian National University, forthcoming in 2001 (revised draft October 26, 2000).

World Bank (1998). "Indonesia in Crisis: A Macroeconomic Update," *Indonesia: Country Economic Memorandum,* Washington, D.C.

World Bank (2000). *Indonesia: Accelerating Recovery in Uncertain Times,* Brief for the Consultative Group on Indonesia, Washington, D.C. (October 13).

Index

AFTA (ASEAN Free Trade Area), 158-169; effect on GDP and exports, 163

APEC (Asia Pacific Economic Cooperation), 157-169; CGE model, 165-170; effect on GDP and exports, 163

APKINDO (Indonesian Plywood Association), 193

ASEAN (Association of South East Asian Nations), 158-169

ASKINDO (Indonesian Cocoa Association), 118

Balanced budget policy, 31

Bank Bali, 193

Bank Indonesia, 195-197

Bank of International Settlements, 34

Banking sector restructuring, 197-198

BKPM (Board of Investment), 39, 53

Bogor Agreement, 157

BPS (Bureau of Statistics), 91

Bugis, 116

BULOG (Bureau of Logistics), 32, 120, 125-134, 143-155; post-1997 crisis, 193

Capital account deregulation: Indonesian experience, 30-31; sequencing, 27-28

Cement: distribution quotas, 136; economies of scale in production, 138; ex-factory pricing, 139; guiding prices, 136; production licensing system, 141

Cocoa: causes of rapid output growth, 13, 116; "hands off" policy regime, 13; marketing boards, 117-119; marketing in Indonesia, 117-120; pod-borer disease, 116

Competition: Law of 1999, 199; restrictions in Indonesia, 98-99

Concentration: and deregulation, 102; and export shares, 102; ratios in manufacturing sector, 101

Crisis of 1997, 191-193; role of unorthodox sequencing in, 7, 191-193

Deregulation: effect on exports, 87-88; effect on firms by size, 97; effect on manufacturing sector, 92-97

Devaluation of Rupiah: during 1983-1986, 2; during 1997 crisis, 190

Domestic content requirements, for soymeal, 126

DSP (*Daftar Skala Prioritas* or "Priority List of Investments"), 47

Dutch Disease, 1

Duty drawback system, 2

East Asian Miracle, 8-10

Economic reforms: role of credibility, 30, 38; role of government commitment, 38; role of leadership, 30; role of macroeconomic management, 38; post-1997 crisis, 189-202

Exchange rate management, 29

Exports: bans, 32; changes in composition, 72; determinants of demand and supply, 79-80; growth, 72; income elasticity of demand, 73; labor intensive, 108; price elasticity of demand, 73; resource intensive, 108

Female workers: employment growth, 111-112; earnings, 112

Financial Sector Policy Committee, 198

Financial sector reform, 3

Foreign direct investment: comparison with domestic firms, 58; definition of, 45; and employment in Indonesia, 12-13; and Indonesian exports, 56, 96; and NIEs, 55, 109, 110; priority list, 34, 47; and total factor productivity; and wages, 19

GATT (General Agreement on Trade and Tariffs), 160

Gradualism, 5

About the Editors and Contributors

Nisha Agrawal is a Lead Economist in the World Bank Office in Vietnam.

Takamasa Akiyama was formerly a Lead Economist in the Research Department of the World Bank.

Bejoy Das Gupta is the Deputy Director of the Asia-Pacific Department at the Institute of International Finance, Washington, DC.

Dipak Dasgupta is a Sector Manager in the Middle East & North Africa Department of the World Bank.

James Hanson is Senior Financial Policy Adviser in the Financial Sector Strategy & Policy Department of the World Bank.

Edison Hulu is Senior Researcher in Derivatives at the Jakarta Stock Exchange, Indonesia.

Farrukh Iqbal is the Regional Coordinator of East Asia Programs at the World Bank Institute.

William E. James is a Senior International Economist with Nathan Associates, Inc. currently on assignment at the Ministry of Industry and Trade in Indonesia.

Jeffrey D. Lewis is Economic Adviser in the Economic Policy and Prospects Group of the World Bank.

Anwar Nasution is the Senior Deputy Governor of Bank Indonesia.

Akihiko Nishio is Program Coordinator in the China Department of the World Bank.

Mari Pangestu was formerly the Executive Director of the Center for Strategic and International Studies in Indonesia.

Martin P.H. Panggabean is with a major bank in Indonesia.

Anwar Pasinringi is at the Ministry of Industry & Trade, Indonesia.

Herb Plunkett is an Assistant Commissioner of the Productivity Commission in Canberra, Australia.

Jacqueline L. Pomeroy is Senior Social Scientist in the World Bank Office in Indonesia.

Faham Rashid is with The Monitor Group in Cambridge, Massachusetts, USA.

Sherman Robinson is the Director of the Trade & Macroeconomics Division at the International Food Policy Research Institute, Washington, DC.

Sherry M. Stephenson is the Deputy Director of the Trade Unit at the Organization of American States, Washington, DC.